Performed Ethnography and Communication

Performed Ethnography and Communication explores the relationships between these three key terms, addressing the impact of ethnography and communication on the cutting edge of performance studies. Ranging from digital performance, improvisation and the body, to fieldwork and staged collaboration, this volume is divided into two main sections:

- "Embodied technique and practice," which addresses improvisation, devised theatre-making, and body work to consider what makes bodies move, sound, behave, mean, or appear differently, and the effects of these differences on performance.
- "Oral history and personal narrative performance," which is concerned with the ways personal stories and histories might be transformed into public events, looking at questions of perspective, ownership, and reception.

Including specific historical and theoretical case studies, exercises and activities, and practical applications for improvisation, ethnography, and devised and digital performance, *Performed Ethnography and Communication* represents an invaluable resource for today's student of performance studies, communication studies or cultural studies.

D. Soyini Madison is Professor of Performance Studies at Northwestern University, USA.

Performed Ethnography and Communication

Improvisation and Embodied Experience

D. Soyini Madison

LONDON AND NEW YORK

First published 2018
by Routledge
2 Park Square, Milton Park, Abingdon, Oxon, OX14 4RN

and by Routledge
711 Third Avenue, New York, NY 10017

Routledge is an imprint of the Taylor & Francis Group, an informa business

© 2018 D. Soyini Madison

The right of D. Soyini Madison to be identified as author of this work has been asserted by her in accordance with sections 77 and 78 of the Copyright, Designs and Patents Act 1988.

All rights reserved. No part of this book may be reprinted or reproduced or utilised in any form or by any electronic, mechanical, or other means, now known or hereafter invented, including photocopying and recording, or in any information storage or retrieval system, without permission in writing from the publishers.

Trademark notice: Product or corporate names may be trademarks or registered trademarks, and are used only for identification and explanation without intent to infringe.

British Library Cataloguing-in-Publication Data
A catalogue record for this book is available from the British Library

Library of Congress Cataloging-in-Publication Data
Names: Madison, D. Soyini, author.
Title: Performed ethnography and communication : improvisation
   and embodied experience / D. Soyini Madison.
Description: Milton Park, Abingon, Oxon ; New York, NY:
   Routledge, 2017. | Includes bibliographical references.
Identifiers: LCCN 2017031658| ISBN 9781138789012 (hardback) |
   ISBN 9781138789029 (pbk.) | ISBN 9781315765075 (ebook)
Subjects: LCSH: Theater—Anthropological aspects. |
   Ethnology—Fieldwork. | Theater and society. | Acting.
Classification: LCC PN2041.A57 M33 2017 | DDC 791—dc23
LC record available at https://lccn.loc.gov/2017031658

ISBN: 978-1-138-78901-2 (hbk)
ISBN: 978-1-138-78902-9 (pbk)
ISBN: 978-1-315-76507-5 (ebk)

Typeset in Sabon
by Sunrise Setting Ltd, Brixham, UK

I dedicate this book to every student I have had the opportunity to teach.

Contents

List of figures x
Acknowledgments xiii
Prologue xv
Introduction: performance and what it does to ethnography xvii

PART I
Embodied technique and practice 1

1 Embodied technique and practice 3

   Technique 4
   Practice 5
   Interview with Ben Spatz 6
   Examples of technique and practice 11
   Case study one: Digital Portobelo with Renée Alexander Craft 17

2 Improvisation 25

   The inherited body we bring to performance practice 25
   Key concepts in improvisational acting and performance 28
   Examples 40

3 Devised theatre 43

   Ethnographic data and process 44
   Suggested stages for devised performance 45
   In summary 60
   Interview with Honey Pot Performance 61
   *Case study two: the digital in dialogic performance across
      two continents 73*

4 Movement and scenes of body work 78

Warm-up improvisations for neutral mask 79
Efforts and factors from Laban/Bartenieff 80
Improvisation exercises for efforts and factors 82
Improvisational exercises for BESS 87
The 5Rhythms from Gabrielle Roth 89
Augusto Boal and Newspaper Theatre 92

PART 2
Oral history and personal narrative performance 117

5 The value of oral history and life story 119

Who owns the story? 120
Interview with E. Patrick Johnson 123
Oral history and narrative as permission, public pedagogy,
  and provocation 126
On truth 128

6 The narrative/narrated event and the anatomy of emotion 132

The narrative event 132
The narrated event 135
Case study three: holograms in a live staging of history:
  Triangle Shirtwaist Factory fire 137

7 Anatomy of emotion: the brain, performance, and oral history 140

Proprioception 141
Mirror neurons and simulation theory 142

8 Performing oral history and life stories 144

Solo performance 144
Exercises 148

9 Viewpoints in rehearsal 155

Examples 155
Selected viewpoints for oral history performance 160
Case study four: the storyteller's magnified embodiments
  in real-time telling 161

10 Jerzy Grotowski's plastiques and Viola Spolin's
   speech and sound   166

   The brain of the body and the body of the brain 166
   Interview with Stephen Wangh 167
   Examples 172

   *Epilogue: the intermix of performance, ethnography,
      and communication*   179
   Appendix: illustration of creativity and the brain   183
   Bibliography   185
   Index   196

Figures

1.1 Labor Rites. The performers become the mountain as Sisyphus pushes the "mountain" up the hill. True to the jazz aesthetic, actors are human and non-human figures: fantastical and surreal. Choreographer, Joel Valentin-Martinez. Photograph by Rafi Letzter   6

1.2 Labor Rites. The three narrators—two Wise Clowns and the Recorder/Girl—hold the decorative box containing field journals that record the personal narratives of labor activists. In a symbolic gesture, the narrators enact the weight of these stories and the comedy and tragedies they hold. Photograph by Rafi Letzter   7

1.3 Class improvisation. Anthropology students at the University of Cape Town, South Africa symbolically express how they would hold, move, and value a book of complicated truths. D. S. Madison, photograph   8

1.4 Labor Rites. Techniques of collective reading and listening to field journals. All actors in varied positions as one woman raises her hand in a traditional and solemn "amen" to a labor activist story. Photograph by Rafi Letzter   15

1.5 Labor Rites. Techniques of passing along support and nourishments to fellow factory workers during a window factory strike as the original factory workers rejoice (digital projection) in victory. Photograph by Rafi Letzter   16

1.6 Labor Rites. The practice of collective action in the long history of labor rights and picket lines. Choreographer, Joel Valentin-Martinez. Photograph by Rafi Letzter   16

2.1 Class improvisation. Performance studies students at Northwestern University improvise: "What to do with the tree?" Evolved into the trope of protection. D. S. Madison, photograph   38

2.2 Class improvisation. Anthropology students at the University of Cape Town improvise a tableau of "What to do about the one who knows the truth?" D. S. Madison, photograph   39

2.3	Class improvisation. Anthropology students at the University of Cape Town improvise a tableau on "The response to the song of the free bird." D. S. Madison, photograph	39
3.1	An example of a word cloud reflecting concepts, methods, and sensations related to performed ethnography	48
3.2	A word cloud reflecting intersections of performance, technique, communication, and ethnography	49
3.3	Class improvisation. Devising variations of fear in the woods in formations of lines and levels. D. S. Madison, photograph	62
3.4	Class improvisation. Cape Town. Devising the idea "which history is inside the book?" D. S. Madison, photograph	62
3.5	Class improvisation. Cape Town. Carrying a truth of history. D. S. Madison, photograph	63
3.6	Honey Pot Performance: the mapping sessions	66
3.7	Honey Pot Performance: the mapping sessions	67
3.8	Honey Pot Performance: the mapping sessions	67
4.1	Labor Rites. Efforts and factors in the labor of factory work. Choreography by Joel Valentin-Martinez. Photograph by Rafi Letzter	109
4.2	Labor Rites. Rhythms of chaos as the devil punishes Sisyphus. Choreography by Joel Valentin-Martinez. Photograph by Rafi Letzter	109
4.3	Labor Rites. Newspaper Theatre as Wise Clowns witness the journalist write his story in the present while imagining it unfolding before their eyes. Upstage actors read the article in future time. Photograph by Rafi Letzter	110
8.1	Labor Rites. Two moments in time: Occupy Wall Street and the narrative event reflected in the journal. Photograph by Rafi Letzter	147
8.2	Labor Rites. Two moments in time: Occupy Wall Street and the narrative event reflected in the journal. Photograph by Rafi Letzter	148
8.3	Labor Rites. Life story of Lucy Parsons recounting the execution of Albert Parsons and passing down the story, in her shawl, as a symbolic gesture to the Girl/Recorder. Photograph by Rafi Letzter	153
8.4	Labor Rites. Mother Jones recounts giving her shoes to those striking workers in need as she passes down the stories, symbolized in her shoes, to the Girl/Recorder. Photograph by Rafi Letzter	153
8.5	Labor Rites. Rose Schneiderman recounts the New York Shirtwaist Factory fire where workers jumped from windows and fell to their death. Photograph by Rafi Letzter	154

9.1	Labor Rites. Viewpoints. Spatial relationship, gesture, duration, and shape. Window factory workers contemplating a strike for living wages. Photograph by Rafi Letzter	159
9.2	Labor Rites. Viewpoints. Spatial relations, topography, rhythm, kinesthetic response. The anarchist Lucy Parsons recounts the four labor activists sentenced with her husband, Albert. Each makes an abrupt turn to look up at Lucy when their sentence is called, against the stillness of Albert, looking out to the audience. Photograph by Rafi Letzter	159
10.1	Labor Rites. High jump and body in motion with arms up high to reflect the digital image of multiple arms held high in joy and command for economic justice. Choreography by Joel Valentine-Martinez. Photograph by Rafi Letzter	176
10.2	Labor Rites. The full body reach and stretch of factory work and collective labor. Choreography by Joel Valentine-Martinez. Photograph by Rafi Letzter	177
E.1	The Summer Institute, 2017	181

Acknowledgments

To the dedicated cast of Labor Rites pictured throughout this book: Brittany Blum, Antora DeLong, Ryan J. Duncan, Kelly Engler, Phoebe Gonzalez, Aissa Guerrra, Kenya Hall, Caroline Harris, Caroline Henry, Malia Hu, Shaker Islam, Hannah Kopen, Jacqueline Maize, Isabella Mehiel, Willie Robinson, Augustine Santellan, Andre Sguerra.

To professor Helen MacDonald and her Anthropology students at the University of Cape Town, South Africa for examples of improvising field data: Chloe Cormack, Shannon Cupido, Pieter du Plessis, Laura Irvine, Jodi Le Roux, Nkosinathi Mncwabe, Simone Oosthuizen, Nathan Taylor.

To graduate students who generously perform, protect, care for, and nurture each other: Jose Alvarez, Simran Bal, Robert Biedrzycki, Marcellus Burt, Jian Jun Chen, Joseph Chookaszian, Samuel Davidson, Alexander Johnson, Margaret Kidd, Kun Lei, Gervais Marsh, Gabrielle Randle, Timothy Suh, Benjamin Zender.

Thank you to colleagues in the Performance Studies Department and the School of Communication at Northwestern University for your support and excellence.

To Joel Valentin-Martinez, Omi Osun Joni L. Jones, E. Patrick Johnson, Michael Rohd, Ramon Rivera Servera, and Judith Hamera for being models of praxis and the intelligence of deep skinned, radical, unapologetic empathy.

To Links Hall, Honey Pot Performance, and Kuumba Lynx for your generosity in emboldening so many through live performance and beautiful imaginings.

To Val Gray Ward, Useni Eugene Perkins, Jackie Taylor, Runako Jahi, and the memory of Abena Joan Brown for your commitment to community and the groundwork for Chicago's Black Theatre history.

To Torkwase and Mejai Dyson, who live the sentiment of Thelonius Monk that a genius is the one who is authentically their self.

To Chaunesti Webb, whose hard work, adeptness, and love for performance was a driving force in getting this book done.

To Reighne Madison Dyson, whose keen observation and curiosity asked the question that motivated this book.

To Frank Joseph Costanza, whose sharp wit, abiding intelligence, and fearless ethics reminds me everyday that writing about methods must be grounded in purpose and deep caring.

Prologue

Dear reader

When my granddaughter was about nine years old, I was driving her to school one morning when she suddenly asked: "Why do people cry at movies and when they hear sad stories?" She was not simply asking why people cry when they are sad; she was asking how empathy works. At nine years old, my granddaughter had not yet grown suspicious of empathy nor been exposed to the many critiques and intellectual arguments against it. Empathy has fallen out of favor in much scholarly discourse, perhaps for good reason. We must now attend to empathy with more courage and risk—with greater historical precision and emotional truth. But in this moment, she didn't care about all that; she simply wanted to know why people are sometimes moved to tears when they witness suffering (and, I would add, beauty). Her question was both innocent and ancient. It was universal and deeply intimate. If this book is about anything, it begins with my granddaughter's question: How can human imagination and communication grab our attention, move us to tears or laughter, affect our nervous systems, invoke embodied knowledge, and move us across thresholds of living connections we thought were beyond our reach, interest, or favor?

What I have come to know, in the most persistent ways, is that what is lastingly felt and deeply learned comes interactively and collaboratively through the body and imagination working together. The kind of learning, discovery, and realization where we come to know what is hard to forget happens through an active and intentional mind and body interplay. I hope to show you how to do this, especially for ethnographers and those conducting fieldwork who want to publicly stage their data, or present it before local audiences, while aiming to move them to laughter and tears. I hope to offer alternative approaches to teachers and workshop leaders who are exploring ways to engage flights of the imagination and embodied communication to build critical skills and textual analysis, as well as forms of narration and personal storytelling. All this becomes the groundwork leading to deeper domains of empathy. Now, we enter my affinity for methods and my abiding respect for skills. The question of how to actually DO all this and identifying the skills TO DO IT is also the purpose here.

I offer a collection of ideas and approaches from cross-sections of performance makers and thinkers. I am more of a curator or caravan driver than an author, more of a bricoleur who gathered varying approaches in order to present a span of multi-layered methods I selected a range of conceptual arguments to theorize methodological significance. This book is a caravan, of sorts, a band of acting, movement, and improvisation techniques to help us enter the realm of "Doing" and "Embodiment." I suppose this text can be considered a toolbox or manual for becoming more interactive and empathetic communicators in resolving conflict, making connections, and embodying deep listening. This caravan of approaches and the ruminations that conceptualize them are also intended to provide processes and step-by-step procedures that build toward the collaborative work of devised theatre and solo performances. In sum, there are two main thrusts of the book: first, discussions and methods of interactive, creative communication; second, discussions and methods of staged or public performance. The thread that binds and defines both thrusts is the interest in ethnographic and fieldwork data as well as oral history and personal narratives. In addition to, or even beyond, the ethnographic realms this caravan of "ways of doing" also centers on performances that may or may not necessarily lead to ethnographic projects but remain centered on aesthetic, communicative, and social enactments, such as solo-performance, devised theatre, and communication workshops to resolve conflict as well as classroom or graduate seminars where embodied techniques, that is, theatre games, movement exercises, and improvisation are used to analyze, probe, and excavate field data, oral history, ethnographic research, or a literary text.

As I contemplate my granddaughter's question, I know too often there are insurmountable thresholds to cross before we can feel the feelings of others. The question of *HOW* we feel the feelings of others is one of the most difficult existential questions to contemplate. It is my hope this book will add to critical discussions of empathy through terrains of embodiment and the ubiquity of performance.

Sincerely
D. Soyini Madison
Evanston, Illinois

Introduction
Performance and what it does to ethnography

Ethnography of performance/performance ethnography/performed ethnography
or
The be, been, and being in performed ethnography

Performances of fieldwork data are referred to by many names: documentary theatre, ethno-drama, non-fiction-storytelling, performance ethnography, verbatim theatre, public voice ethnography, reality theatre, ethno-performance, ethnographic performance, and so forth. However, for the purposes of this book, I choose to use the term *performed ethnography*.[1] This choice is not to claim the other terms are wrong, or are less accurate, but to acknowledge a point of emphasis. I choose the term, perform-*ed* ethnography, to emphasize the dramatic scenarios, public staging, crafted theatricality, and improvisational enactments of fieldwork and ethnographic data that will *be*, that have *been*, and that are *being* perform*ed*. Situating performed ethnography in the future perfect tense indicates both an event that is expected or planned to happen in the future or that will have occurred at a future point. In this instance, we deliberately acknowledge performances that occur during fieldwork. These grounded fieldwork performances are then translated and adapted for the stage to be performed. In addition, this vision of future performances, which will move forward from the time and place of the fieldwork, also emphasizes the aesthetics and critical process of adaptation, representation, and embodiment. The translations of past fieldwork performances will enter artistic and rhetorical processes where fieldwork data is framed and where it is adapted, directed, and ultimately communicated to others. Most importantly, we are making a distinction here between perform*ance* and perform*ed* in that perform*ed* ethnography will have enacted, re-presented, and theatricalized those quotidian, symbolic, cultural, and local acts of performance ethnography. In summary: *when performances in the field or performance ethnography is adapted for the stage or communicated through modes of performance it becomes performed ethnography.*

I want to emphasize that performance ethnography is focused more on theories and practices of local performances and its resonances within the domain of fieldwork. The researcher may not necessarily have the intention of transforming local field performances into a staged performance or performance event. I make a distinction between performances in the field, that is, performance ethnography and the transference of those performances to a *theatrically framed re-presentation*, namely, perform*ed* ethnography to acknowledge the shift—from field site to staged adaptation—not only in time, space, intent, technique, ethics, bodies, history, affect, power, audience, access, and so forth, but because too often we collapse *performance* ethnography and *performed* ethnography into one overarching category and thereby ignoring their profoundly different contexts, implications, and ethical responsibilities. Or, if we do note the distinctions between *performance* ethnography and *performed* ethnography, we tend to privilege one over the other. I am not advocating that everyone should do both; instead, I'm concerned that we understand the unique dynamics between the two. In other words, focusing on one and not the other or a commitment to one instead of the other is NOT the same as thinking one is less valuable than the other. Those who choose performance ethnography as fieldwork inquiry sharing their work through publications, public address, or advocacy initiatives yet have no intention of turning it into a public performance or theatrical adaptation are still engaging theories and politics of performance in powerful ways. Therefore, in performance ethnography, we recognize and attend to the ongoing performances inside the field that are always and already occurring before the ethnographer arrives, for example, cultural dance, storytelling, sacred and secular rituals, dress and food customs, oral histories, everyday symbolic acts, the ethnographers' relational gestures and embodied reckonings, and so on.

The perfor*mance* in performance ethnography

Because performance ethnography locates the inherent and generative realms of local performances that constitute a field site, and because not all ethnographic "data" of field performances are re-enacted and presented on a public stage, it follows that studying performances inside the field is also a study of embodied and epistemological moments of social processes and how felt-sensing realities are reciprocally made through local and indigenous performance. I have taught graduate and undergraduate seminars in ethnographic theory and method for many years, and some of the most cherished, influential, and moving texts are performance ethnographies that do not enter the terrain of a performance practice or staged event. Students across the campus from anthropology, English, sociology, education, communication studies, women's studies, comparative literature, and more, become members of the seminar out of a need to understand ontologies of performance inherent in their disciplines and research methods. Most of these students have not and will not stage their performance ethnographies.

In contrast, my students and I have also learned and been inspired from being the audience to many performed ethnographies where the adapter, director, performers, and crew were not necessarily field researchers or involved in the original fieldwork data. Yet, the production was a beautiful and powerful ethnographic representation that expanded our understanding of fieldwork theory, methods, and ethics. I encourage my students to attend performed ethnographies to become better field researchers whether they intend to stage their own research or not.

In summary, by delineating "perform*ed*" and "performance" ethnography, I am resituating the more popularly held notion that performance ethnography is the deliberate staging of field notes and turning instead to an emphasis on local and symbolic enactments of performances within the field and on the ground of social life and processes. This is done to establish and honor the existence of local performances as vibrant and urgent and to mark the significantly different implications that undergird local performances in the field from those that are staged re-enactments of field notes. Arguably, this distinction is there before we enter the field and the stage and cannot necessarily be collapsed under one term.

Now, we will turn to the aim of this book: why and how do we do performed ethnography? What are the theories and debates about it and what are the methods and techniques to create it?

Subjectivity, belonging, and the other: audience as an "echo chamber"

In bringing your ethnographic research and experiences to the stage, you may choose from a range of materials in various forms and combinations: interview transcripts, field notes, email correspondences, personal memories, diaries, blogs, television broadcasts, newspaper articles, court proceedings, historic documents, music, sound, digital imagery, visual archives, dance, symbolic movement, poetic texts, literary fiction and non-fiction, as well the improvisations and devised scenes developed in rehearsals and workshops (Alexander 2006; Denzin 2003; Johnson 2003; Madison 2012; Rohd 1998; Saldaña 2011). Performed ethnography holds endless possibilities for inter-textual performance. Several metaphors are equated with performed ethnography in creating a multi-layered text as an act of bricolage: gathering up a diversity of whatever can be imagined, available, or found. Here it is a nomadic text that deliberately wanders across compilations of field data, memories, and aesthetic forms and processes to weave the life of the mind with being mindful of life, of blending textuality with orality, of critically unraveling both margins and centers, and of opening more paths for possible relations with unfamiliar (sometimes unknown and even undesirable) spaces that are near and far.

Performed ethnography raises several questions: By what describable and material means will the subjects and interlocutors themselves be affected by the performance? Can or should the performance contribute to a more active and involved citizenship? Does performed ethnography have a responsibility to disturb systems and processes that limit freedoms and possibilities on the ground? In what ways, will the performers themselves probe questions of otherness, belonging, and materiality to reflect upon their own subjectivity, cultural politics, and art? Another question we should ask ourselves is: Should we assume the performed ethnography is always a good idea? What are its failures?

In addressing the challenges and pitfalls of staging ethnographic data, we will also shift our focus to the audience: Who is the audience we are performing before and what do we intend for them to experience? Remembering the long history of live performances in the staging of contested identities, Jose Estaban Munoz reminded us of the "burden of liveness" in colonial entertainment intended for the pleasure and gaze of an elite or dominant bloc, the purpose of which sustained hierarchies thereby erasing alternative histories, futures, and yearnings. The "burden of liveness" for Munoz "structures temporality" in that "the minoritarian subject" is constrained and circumscribed with a temporality that only adheres to the present and "to be only in the live means one is denied history and futurity." For Munoz, when the minoritarian subject only exists in the present moment "the privilege or the pleasure of being a historical subject" is denied as well as the "luxury of thinking about a future" (1999).

Fixed time becomes one of the greatest challenges in staging qualitative research data where subjects are not suspended in a present that stagnates and denies their humanity of origins, histories, and contexts, and therefore makes them invisible as living, ongoing agents of change and alternative possibilities. In this instance, as performance makers we are constantly teasing the edges between flat surfaces or mockery of stereotypes on one end and embellished felicitation or romanticizing on the other. We sometimes fall into spectacles of difference to avoid dull didacticism, over-determining the presence of a present moment and setting into motion stick figures void of alterity and possibility.

Charlotte Aull Davies states, "The ethnographer moves on [but] temporally, spatially, and developmentally, the people he or she studied are presented as if suspended in an unchanging and virtually timeless state," she goes on to assert, "as if the ethnographer's description provides all that is important or possible to know about their past and future" (1999: 156).

How do we heed these warnings and how do we avoid the static and unchanging story while performing in present time, where presence is all there is to experience and witness in this live performance? We may begin through the tensive and complicated trinity of subjectivity, belonging, and otherness. I focus upon this trinity because it is quintessentially created and sustained through dialogues about how subjectivity, belongings, and otherness are revealed and sustained within infinitely changing demands across life forces of time and space. This is a move against the burden on liveness and stick figures as forever stagnant to that of enlivening formations and ongoing contestations.

I've encountered several students and members of the academy who have grown weary of discussion that focuses on the other, subjectivity, belonging, and dialogue. The complaint has been that these terms are overused, and moribund in their critical effectiveness and intellectual inventiveness. In sum, these ideas do not hold weight anymore in this "post" era of virtual realities, fluid forms, infinite truths, and an indeterminate world, yet it is because of the virtual, fluid, infinite, and indeterminate that subjectivity, belonging, and Other—especially within ethnographic contexts—are useful now as they always have been, living in these times where difference and dialogue are under siege in such violent and life-threatening ways—in our communities, nation, and the world in the fear and disdain for Otherness. These terms might invoke weary idealism but putting them in action on the ground of fieldwork also invokes new and never before experienced challenges with each instance and coming generation. Ethnography is always a meeting of multiple sides in an encounter with and among others, one which requires presence, listening, and dialogue toward a possible new thing: an insight, knowledge, experience, or a relationship, a different reality, yet there is the expectation of something more and sometimes unknown. It is through the realms of belonging and dialogue when the Other ceases to be suspended in time and whose subjectivity is realized. This is the hope of performed ethnography and where one beginning point is to ask the question: By what means do local people themselves benefit from the performance? We may start with the notion of voice. By voice, I do not simply mean the representation of an utterance, but the embodiment of a material self, a full presence that is in and of a particular world. We are not content with "being heard and included" as its focus, but as its starting point; instead, the notion of voice is an embodied, historical self that constructs and is constructed by a matrix of social, affective, and political processes. The aim is to embody and re-present subjects as made by and makers of lifeworlds and history in their full sensory, social, and political dimensions. The performed Others are embodied subjects constituted in the substance of who they are, where they are, and how they do what they do. We are inspired and compelled to enter, albeit symbolically and temporarily, into their locations. Through performance, we are placed, subject to subject, in that contested space while, as the feminist critic bell hooks (1990) describes, oppressed "people resist by identifying themselves as subjects by defining their reality, shaping new identity, naming their history, telling their story" (43). Performed ethnography is voices wedded to emotions and histories that are unfolding. Local people themselves may benefit from these performance unfoldings through the creation of space that gives evidence not only that "I am here in the world among you," but more importantly that "I am in the world under particular conditions that are constructed and that can be deconstructed and reconstructed through collective will." Human desire implores that we be listened to, apprehended, engaged, and free to imagine in and with worlds of Others and that we are all historical beings where others necessarily constitute the making of a self. This idea of the self through the other reflects Mikhail Bakhtin's (1981) words, "Nothing is more frightening than the absence of an answer" (111). Here, I am substituting what it means to answer for *response* as in "call-and-response." More than a general notion of answer as a rejoinder or resolution that might shut down dialogue, the answer begins the conversation and sets the call on its dialogical path or on a divergent one. The answer as a response is a profound giving back, a form of reciprocity that affirms we are not alone. It is akin to a West African ontology of belonging: "I am because we are, and we are because I am."

Aimee Carrillo Rowe states, "there is no subject prior to infinitely shifting and contingent relations of belonging." Indeed, what we call "subjectivity" may be thought of as an "effect of belonging—of the affective passionate and political ties that bind us to others" (Rowe 2005: 17). Because performed ethnography requires that we delve more deeply into the desires resonating within the locations of others, it becomes the move beyond the acknowledgment of voice within experience to that of embodied engagement. Subjectivity linked to performance becomes a poetic and polemic admixture of competing, comparative, and contingent bodies in time and space.

Turning to enactments of dialogue as both inspiring and enriching belonging, we come to realize that dialogue as constituted by performance emphasizes the living communion of a felt-sensing, embodied interplay and engagement among multiple beings and expressive forms. It is intensely committed to keeping the insights between, and the conversation with, the researcher and others open and ongoing. It is a reciprocal giving and receiving rather than a timeless resolve, without history or futurity. The dialogical stance is situated in multiple expressions that transgress, collide, and embellish realms of encounters. Dialogue is both difference and unity, both agreement and disagreement, both a separation and a coming together. For Conquergood, ethnographic, performative dialogue is more like a hyphen than a period. Dialogue is therefore the quintessential encounter with others and becomes a performed pathway to belonging. Moreover, it is through dialogue and meeting others that I am most fully myself. The wonderful paradox in the ethnographic moment of dialogue and otherness is that communion with another brings the self more fully into being and belonging, and, in doing so, opens you to know others more fully, underscoring Mikhail Bakhtin's famous quote:

> I am conscious of myself and become myself and myself only while revealing myself for another, through another and with the help of another. The most important acts constituting self-consciousness (toward a thou). Separation, dissociation, enclosure within the self is the main reason for the loss of one's self. The very being of man is the deepest communion ... To be means to be for another, through the other, for oneself.
>
> (Bakhtin in Madison 2012: 11)

If we labor toward the deep and abiding enactments of subjectivity that are reciprocally constituted by dialogue to inspire belonging, then we recognize this labor as a responsibility. For Levinas, "Prior to any act, I am concerned with the Other, and I can never be absolved from this responsibility" (Moran 2000: 348). To be face to face with the Other, for Levinas, demands protection and loving justice: "Prior to any act, I am concerned with the Other and I can never be absolved from the responsibility ... to see a face is already to hear 'Thou Shalt Not Kill'" (43–44). Ethics in this sense is to respond, and this response demands that I take responsibility for the freedom, welfare, and equity of Otherness. Levinas states:

> The human face is the epiphany of the nakedness of the Other, a visitation, a meeting, a saying, which comes in the passivity of the face, not threatening, but obligating. My world is ruptured, my contentment interrupted. I am already obligated. Here is an appeal from which there is no escape ... It is looking into the face of the Other that reveals the call to responsibility that is before any beginning, decision or initiative on my part.
>
> (Levinas in Moran 2000: 139)

The face, in this instance, becomes a metaphor for an Other and therefore includes gestures, speech, or any material presence or proximity to a living being (Tom Burvill in Balfour 2013: 202).

Although to Levinas, art represented an absence of another (203) and a dangerous substitution for the presence of the face itself, this concern would fall outside the embodied experience of performance. Art, for Levinas was a "form of sovereign knowing of the other, which does not hold me accountable to the other but, instead, dislodges the face-to-face encounter with that of an image" (203). As Burvill notes "performance, as an embodied and interactive event, as processual practice unfolding within the co-presences" of audiences and embodied actors in "real time" would not comply with Levinas' critique (203). Burvill continues, "Levinas' insistence on the event of the ethical encounter suggests something embodied something that happened, something that is performative" (204), he goes on to include that, "even an angry response is better than the refusal to engage" (206). The point here is that "Levinas' idea of the active, responsive, corporeal encounter with alterity that is so pertinent to ethical responsibility" is captured in and quintessential to performance (210).

The "corporeal encounter" in performance may exceed even Levinas' face-to-face disposition. The meeting of corporeality is not only the connection between the actor who embodies an Other through a performance emanating from their internal and external life, but it is a corporeal encounter encompassing audience, performers, and Others in a circularity of relations that becomes in Alison Jeffers' words an "echo chamber" of responses. These echoes of responses to performance expand the face-to-face while simultaneously augmenting Levinas' notion of Otherness as "anarchic responsibility" (2013: 299–303). The responsible anarchism toward otherness is a commitment not simply to the survival of the Other, but to their flourishing and to the possibilities of loving the Other. Levinas stated: "Anarchistic responsibility has no rules with no limits" (Levinas 1996: 84). For the performance maker, I read this anarchy as claiming the freedom to be boundlessly imaginative and fearlessly creative. Anarchy in this instance is both a reminder and permission to go outside the box and beyond our own expectations to make beautiful and memorable art, not only for ourselves and the Other, but for the audience "echo chambers" that are set loose when the performance ends. Jeffers invokes Levinas' idea of responsibility and anarchy to cast light on the "practice of being an audience" where audience members are within two affective sensations of presence: face to face with performers and shoulder to shoulder with other audience members. This signals, according to Jeffers, a willingness to listen (whether active or participatory) when this listening practice is "also the desire to listen as a group." Truly listening in the theatre is "also listening ethically." This alchemy of listening face to face and shoulder to shoulder is the practice of being an audience, reminds us that the anarchist responsibility is to provide an echo chamber for those "voices that reach us from the stage, to make them reverberate and to amplify what we hear" (308).

What of those fieldworkers who employ their data to contribute to a more enlightened and involved citizenship? Creating performances in which the intent is largely to invoke interrogation of specific political and social processes means that in our art, we turn to our audiences as citizens with the potential for collective and involved action, and change is part of the foundation upon which a performance of possibilities is based.

Performed ethnography assumes responsibility for political effectiveness and communicates the principle that we are all part of a larger whole and are therefore radically responsible to each other for all our individual selves. Linda Alcoff (1991) describes a web in which our social practices are made possible or impossible by agents and events that are spatially far from our own body and that, in turn, can affect distant strangers: "We are collectively caught in an intricate, delicate web in which each action I take, discursive or otherwise, pulls on, breaks off, or maintains the tension in many strands of a web in which others find themselves moving also" (20). Now, pivoting from the emphasis on human unity and relatedness, we will turn to the differences and particulars of singularity, that is, the value of not being the same, the small story—one of a kind—of expression.

Performed ethnography invites the audience to travel empathically to other worlds and to feel and know some of what others feel and know. Two lifeworlds meet, and the domains of outsider and insider are both and simultaneously demarcated and fused. I have an identity separate from the subject, and the performance clearly illuminates our differences. In the performance space, I am outsider in this particular world. While I see that I am an outsider to the subject's experience, the performance does its work to pull me inside. I am now in the midst of a profound meeting. Do I remain here at the margins of the meeting, or is the performance beautiful enough and political enough to compel me to travel more deeply inside the mind, heart, and world of the subject? Or, to create a critical view that is less about empathy and more about critique: Brecht's mirror and hammer. In this ability to travel across worlds, two identities meet, engage, and become something more.

Empathy is not necessarily without critique or action. Maria Lugones describes this process of intersubjectivity:

> The reason why I think that traveling to someone's "world" is a way of identifying with them is because by traveling to their "world" we can understand what it is to be them and what it is to be ourselves in their eyes. Only when we have traveled to each other's "worlds" are we fully subjects to each other.
>
> (Lugones in Madison 1994: 637)

Performance becomes the vehicle by which we travel to the worlds of subjects and enter domains of intersubjectivity that problematize how we categorize who is us and who is them and how we see ourselves with other and different eyes. As I argue that action beyond the performance space is of essential benefit to the subjects, so it is to audience members as well. Ideally, as an audience member consciously re-enters the web of human connectedness and then travels into the lifeworld of the subject, where rigid categories of insider and outsider transfigure into an intersubjective experience, a path for action is set. Action, particularly new action, requires new energy and new insight. In performed ethnography, when audience members begin to feel the affective tension and incongruity between the subject's yearnings and those macro processes and systems that challenge and undermine their lives and futures there is the potential for something more and new to be learned about alterity and what might come next under the workings of power. We understand that audiences, as involved citizens, can be both disturbed and inspired to act upon or contemplate this alterity long after the final curtain. Whether one likes the performance or not, one can hardly undo (or unknow) the image and imprint of performative voices upon one's own consciousness. Performing subversive and subaltern voices proclaims existence, within locales and discourses that are being witnessed, and this witnessing has implications and possibilities.

When we stage oral histories and ethnographic data that unsettle representations of subjects as fixed in time but inspire an echo chamber of impression, disturbances, inspiration, and action, we are continually inventing something new. In this merging of data and performance this new creation is not just a merging of two grand entities—performance and data—but a merging of constellations, of circulations and economies, of bodies in motion and in world making. It is reminiscent of Lefebvre's grey area of third space as an other-than space that is always hovering beyond what is being offered or presented. It is where two phenomena will always necessitate a third where "a critical 'other-than' choice" becomes an embodied performative that speaks and critiques through its otherness (Lefebvre 1980). This alterity, which constitutes the "other-than," does not imply or derive "from an additive combination of [its] binary antecedents but rather from a disordering, deconstruction, and tentative reconstruction of their presumed tantalization producing an open alternative" (Bhabha in Soja 1996). This open alternative is not an "everything" and "anything goes" for "tantalizing" meanderings. It is a tactical intervention that recognizes political economies of geography and space as both fixed and fluid, deepened and contested, by historical subjects and their emboldened actions made more known, public, and contested through the social justice agenda of performed ethnography. Edward W. Soja invites us to think about "third space as an-Other way of understanding and acting to change the very spatiality of human life" (Soja 1996: 82–83).

Reflections on oral history and performed ethnography

When private matters are made public through the performance of oral history, we are aligned with each other as a human species (Rowe 2007). We realize that in this great human paradox we are both the same and different. The fact that all living organisms came from the stars and our biochemical relationship with one another is manifest in our universal need and quest for clean air, water, food, shelter, sleep, security, motion, love, symbols, and purpose is our unifying inheritance. These, and more, are our shared requirements across our natural worlds and environmental landscapes, yet, our access to, and experience with, these human universals form a range from inspiring to tragic across our collective and individual lives. These very particular and different encounters are where countless original stories abound. Our planetary and atomic, cellular inheritance not withstanding, there will always be a new, fresh story to tell that is identical to no other. These stories lie on the borders of our shared species on one side and our different geographies, materialities, and histories on the other. The vast substance of time and space in the evolution of human belongings and power conjoin to make narrative intelligible and pleasurably awe-inspiring as well as complicated and abundantly risky. As long as humans exist, we will never run out of new and different life stories to tell and witness, both different and similar, passed down and censored, emanating from the ones that came before. The capacity for narrative is infinite and beyond measure, as every idea and feeling is the seed for storytelling, both real and imagined. Our stories might be the only element in life that will always be abundant and plentiful—more than enough for everyone—if there is life, the planet, and the will and freedom of expression.

Stories take countless forms from those that unfold in photographs, graffiti, sculptures, paintings, the dressed body, and there is an implosion of visual forms and embodiments. Stories unfold in science experiments, in our natural and built environments, for example, the story of a cell, a river, a house, the Milky Way, and so forth. However, when stories are adapted and performed on stage, as our own and others, we ask ourselves: What constitutes this life that I must now embody and performatively communicate?

In thinking about oral history in the act of performance, one of the initial challenges for the performer is entering the selfhood to be embodied. How is selfhood performed, and what constitutes it? How can performance adhere to the ways in which identity changes, transforms itself, and multiplies? Because the performer is transported slowly, deliberately, and incrementally at each rehearsal or each encounter crossing a threshold to the knowledge and lifeworlds of the subject, and because they encounter partial maps of consciousness, affect, and contexts, the performers must enter a realm of receptiveness. As a performer, this receptiveness that is required will change you. You are not the same person you were before you experienced this encounter or after the performance demand to be receptive. We understand that this receptiveness is never devoid of the generative filter of the performer's own knowledge, body, and history. It is this merging when the magic happens in a transference and a reciprocity of selves in the performance of oral history. Narrative evokes performance choices and performance choices evoke narrative. The subject's story and lifeworld guides me, what I do and who I become. My story and life are enfleshed in this narrative unfolding—both constitute the other. I have argued, for the performer, this is an endeavor to encounter an individual consciousness shaped by a social world, that also affects what our bodies do and become. The performer may research all the crucial elements that encompass a cognitive map of the social, economic, cultural, and political practices that constitute the subject's world. Moreover, the performer may be committed—doing what must be done or going where one must go—to experience the felt-sensing dynamic of that world: its tone-color—the sights, sounds, smells, tastes, textures, rhythms—the visceral ethos of that world. I have argued that in personal narrative performances, particularly for performed ethnography, performers are not only performing the words of subjects, they are performing the subjects' political, social, and economic landscapes. Cultural studies scholar Lawrence Grossberg calls this "spatial territorialization"; he writes:

> it involves an organization of places and spaces, of people, practices, and commodities. It is in this sense that discourse is always placed, because people are always anchored or invested in specific sites. Hence, it matters how and where practices and people are placed, since the place determines from and to where one can speak.
>
> (Grossberg 1994: 20)

Selfhood particularly in performed ethnography is then constituted by identification with specific cultural and social practices, forms of empowerment, and modes of belonging. At the same time, this zeitgeist is also contingent upon how these practices within locales change over time. Identity can be definable but because it is also multiple, contested and constructed performed ethnography represents how subjectivity and identity are both a matter of difference and a matter of identification.

As the performer enters domains of spatial territorialization and narrative consciousness, performance becomes the vehicle by which a representation is manifest and through which living moments are embodied. As representation and embodiment conjoin in performed ethnography and oral history, there has been much criticism regarding the value and practice of representation as compared with embodiment and activism. The criticism demands more focus on embodiment and the efficacy of affect that discourses of representation lack. The view is that, rather than representation, it is the embodied and affective act that invoked activism. For example, I was invited by a university to give a talk about local activism in Ghana, West Africa. After the talk, a male graduate student in the audience expressed his discontent with my common reference to Stuart Hall's words, "How a people are represented is how they are treated," and he felt I was placing too much emphasis on representation, particularly from the "British School of Cultural Studies" (Hall 1997: 27). I was confused, not only by his indictment of British cultural studies and what it might imply, but his critique of representation that was unspecified. When I asked him what should replace representation, he said: "Activism." I was taken aback by the response after citing example upon example of Ghanaian activists putting their bodies on the line to defend human rights and the fight for economic justice in their homeland. Many critiques of representation are necessary and insightful as I will take up in the next section. But none of them can completely negate the effects and consequences that representation has upon those identities and lives being projected to audiences, listeners, and observers.

Representation is mediated through the performer's body—what it does in the performance space. Therefore, in performed ethnography and documentary performances, we understand representation as first and foremost an act of responsibility. We are responsible for the creation of what and who is being represented; our representations carry with them political material, ideological and political ramifications far beyond the reach of the performance. Again, because "how a people are represented is how they are treated," the act of representation is consequential. The body politic responds to individuals and communities by the way they come to know and encounter them, which is itself based upon a complex configuration of discourses, embodiments, and experiences—meanings and feelings—all of which is no less profound than how these lives enter their consciousness through representations in cultural performances.

The concern is that representation becomes a distraction from the materiality of presence. In Tony Perucci's important essay, "Dog Sniff Dog" (2015), on Mary Overlie's philosophy and practice of Viewpoints, he describes the importance of what Overlie calls "presence work" as displacing representation. Presence work is non-representational in its focus on the body as it is, not as it can be metaphysically or metaphorically represented. The body as non-representational opens pathways to a materialist action of the unmitigated now, without the distraction of artifice, imaginative transcendence, or the "emotion-manufacturing" that aligns with representation (110). He cites Barbara Rose:

> There is no wish to transcend the physical for either the metaphysical or the metaphoric. The thing, thus, is presumably not supposed to "mean" other than what it is; that is, it is not supposed to by suggestive of anything other than itself.
> (Rose in Perucci 2015: 108–109)

Perucci states: "Global acts of occupation realize an embodied presencing over representing, where the physical holding of space is a materialist claim to power" (110). So, the disgruntled male student who disparaged my mention of representation, despite a talk about Ghanaian activists who put their bodies on the line to defend the rights of women and girls against neo-liberal policies that threaten safe, local access to water, left me dumbfounded. However, I learned from that experience, because I have come to realize the difference and to make a distinction between discussions of non-representational performance that expand the repertoire of activist aesthetics and those other anti-representational critiques like that of the male graduate student that are so fixed against any mention of representation they do not hear anything else. The student closed the conversation and was thereby blinded by the form, content, and tactics for art making that in Perucci's words does the labor of creating change and "material connectedness" (110). The hybrid of representational and non-representational forms in performed ethnography is what I am interested in in this book.

Defense of representation

> Peter [Brook] showed us photos of the Ik at particular moments in their daily lives—people eating , laughing, or just sitting. We looked at the image in the photo, and then we imitated the body position and the facial expression. We started from the outside, but little by little we tried to feel what the person in the photo had felt at the particular moment. If you don't attempt to get "inside" the image, you can't really construct a good imitation. Equally, if you really imitate the outside image in detail, your body position will start to generate feelings inside.
> (Yoshi Oida, "An Actor Adrift" in Wangh 2000: 243)

In the examples of virtuosic performances like those of Anna Devere Smith and E. Patrick Johnson, it was "transformation through imitation" (Kemp 2012: 138) that enabled the actors to represent or embody each of their characters. In rehearsal and character preparation, it was a matter of "mirroring" their characters' words and actions that created the felt-sensing embodiment required to enact them and represent them authentically and persuasively. In other words, Johnson and Smith engaged in processes of *imitation* to build their performances. As cognitive evidence supports imitation as a "tool in extending an actor's range in the creation of characters" (139), it is a method of creating and representing a character. Moreover, this process of imitation is now passed from the actor's body to the spectator. A double mirror is formed: As the actor mirrors a character, the spectator mirrors the actor mirroring the character. This means the spectator mirrors the character through the actor's representation. What the body *witnesses* through *representations* also creates sensations, emotion, and thought in the witness. "We experience the action and emotion of others as we watch them" (141). Kemp further elaborates:

> Mirror neurons (MNs) are neurons that fire in the premotor cortex when one executes a goal-directed action and also when one observes a similar action executed by someone else. MNs were originally discovered in macaque monkeys by a team of scientists including Vittorio Gallese who, with Alvin Goldman, built on this discovery to identify a mental mechanism in primates by which an observer mimics, resonates with, or re-creates the mental life of others based on direct observation of their movements. In a paper published in 2004, Gallese and others lay out the evidence that mirror neurons are also active in humans, both for action and emotions.
>
> (Kemp 2012: 141)

As we witness an action, just as when we imagine it, our brains respond similarly as if we executed the action. We feel deeply by a representation whether we believe it to be true or not, because "our emotions and feelings can arise through the mirror neuron mechanism when observing another's emotion or when imaginatively responding to fiction" (158).

Obviously, we can never abandon representation. It is part of what makes us human and sentient beings, nor do we truly desire to do so. What we can and must do is continue to examine the best and worst of it and embrace both representational and non-representational work and discover new ways to configure and disfigure them. In performed ethnography and documentary performance, we understand the burden of representation centers on factors of responsibility, ethics, and artistic labor and how these factors culminate in a conscious effort to break through unfair closures of identity and unsettle caricatures of subjectivity toward alternative identities as well as more and different representations—more and different ways of re-presenting subjects and their ways of speaking. In addition, the claim is not that performed ethnography is exclusively giving voice to the voiceless, it is understood that local subjects and interlocutors can speak and have been speaking in spaces and places often foreign to us, long before we arrive in the field. Nor do we assume that performed ethnography is the ultimate or final opportunity to enable people to name themselves, act upon their histories, or imagine their futures. We understand in performing the life histories of others that their history of speaking before, during, and after our arrival requires research. This is another layer of ethics informed by researching the history and contexts of interlocutors' personal narratives and tellings. It is a dramaturgy of voices from the field.

How we come to embody other territories of subjectivity and discourse, how we invent and inherit techniques of performance, how we conjoin the meetings of history and imagination—the performer's and the subject's—is the continuing work of oral history performance.

Note

1 I prefer not to use the term ethnodrama because the word ethnography is shortened and now enters the classic definition of ethno. From www.merriam-webster.com/: "indicating race, people, or culture: ethnology. via French from Greek ethnos race. 'race, culture,' from Greek ethnos 'people, nation, class, caste, tribe; a number of people accustomed to live together.' Relating to or denoting a particular ethnic group." While ethno implies a shortened version of ethnography and a provocative, definitional realm of race and ethnicity, it eclipses the act of engaged and systematic knowledge that is embedded in the term ethnography: www.merriam-webster.com/ "The study and systematic recording of human cultures; the systematic, rigorous investigation of a situation or problem in order to generate new knowledge or validate existing knowledge." Ethnography, as a full term, captures both ontology and epistemology where knowledge production and the nature of life lived together are both included in the term. The word "drama" in ethnodrama eclipses the offerings in the field of performance studies that opened new intellectual pathways in our theoretical and critical understanding of culture, performance formations, and Otherness as well as breaking new ground in the geographies of space relative to subaltern locations and indigenous embodiments. This *performance turn* was a significant intervention that carried with it particular ways in which we experimented with different methods of incorporating spaces of belonging through performance and performed ethnographies and a critical ethics in enactments of knowledge. It is for these reasons that I choose to conjoin performance and the performed with ethnography. It is not my intention to create or deepen a divide between disciplinary notions of drama (or theatre) and performance studies, because we know they are inseparable or interchangeable in a variety of techniques and purposes. In this instance, I illuminate performance to recognize the particular conjoining of ethnographic methods with performance theory, and to recognize performance studies in uniquely articulating ethnography as co-performative witnessing in the felt-sensing encounters of field research. Sometimes I will use documentary performance interchangeably with performed ethnography because documentary is certainly in keeping with the non-fiction world of enlivened action or the documentation of "real stories." However, not all documentary work is necessarily ethnographic. I recognize that a performance paradigm privileges particular, participatory, dynamic, intimate, precarious, embodied experience grounded in historical process, contingency, and ideology. Another way of saying it is that performance-centered research takes as both subject matter and method the *experiencing body* situated in time, place, and history. A performance paradigm honors face-to-face encounters that often displace abstraction and reductions. Performance studies situates ethnographers within the delicately negotiated and fragile "'face-work' that is part of the intricate and nuanced dramaturgy of everyday life" (see Alexander 2005; Conquergood 2003; Hamera 2007; Johnson 2003; Saldaña 2011; Spry 2011).

Part I

Embodied technique and practice

Chapter 1

Embodied technique and practice

> The tendency in practice theory is to characterize a practice like swimming or cooking as an "amalgam of elements," as "complexes" or "bundles" of meanings, competences, and material objects ... In contrast, I propose to do away with "practice-as-entity"—a phrase with no comprehensible meaning since it is neither abstract nor specific—and recognize instead that concrete moments of practice are structured by knowledge in the form of technique. The immediately allows us to distinguish between a given *practice* of swimming, bounded in time and space, and the *technique* of swimming which is not merely a repeated pattern or set of rules but an area of practical and technical knowledge. Conceiving of the relationship between technique and practice in this way solves several problems in practice theory. It also opens the door to an epistemological understanding of practice that can inform our thinking about power, agency, society, and material reality.
>
> (Spatz 2015: 40–44)

Beyond biology and sociality, what makes some bodies move, look, sound, behave, or mean something different from other bodies or, more importantly, the same as other bodies? Why should it matter that race, gender, sex, class, sexuality, and geography variously influence what our bodies do from the smallest unconscious gesture to the largest spectacular event? And how does all this body talk specifically and profoundly affect the very foundation of those everyday improvisational moments of our lives as well as those intensely crafted collaborations of staged performances? These questions invoke an important insight offered in the resonating question, most recently illuminated in the work of Ben Spatz: "What can a body do?" Those things our bodies *can* do, that is, walking, talking, eating, swimming, reading, dancing, telling jokes, making love, playing the piano, public protest, family dinners, brain surgery, meditation, acting, building rockets, sweeping the floor, Yoga, praying, and so on, and the *way* we do all these things—including how we *learn* to do them through repetition and inheritance as well as social and environmental relations—are all *doable* through trans-historical techniques that ultimately give form, content, and context to examples of specific practice (Hamera 2007; Jones 2015; Martin 1998;

Mauss 1973, 2006; Spatz 2015). What our bodies can do, through the infinite manifestations of practice that are constituted by unwavering technique, is made possible through the "transmission of embodied knowledge" (Hamera 2007; Martin 1998; Spatz 2015). It is the passing on and circulation of embodied knowledge that produce the techniques that lead to the practices inherent in the ordinary and extraordinary realities of life.

This section is organized in two parts. The first part begins with brief working definitions of technique and practice followed by three vignettes to serve as examples of how technique and practice are manifest in social life. The second part is a discussion of how conceptualizations of technique and practice affect performance and communication.

Technique

> In practical terms, technique provides social bedrock for imagining new ways of being together and being oneself (13) ... In his moving essay "Worn Worlds: Clothing and Mourning," Peter Stallybrass reflects on wearing the jacket of his late collaborator Allon White. "Bodies come and go," he observes. "The clothes that receive those bodies survive" (Stallybrass 1999: 29). So, it is with technique, which likewise survives the bodies which enact it, even if the enactments themselves are always and inevitably disappearing. Sometimes technique is an unwanted and burdensome legacy to be resisted; at others, it is a generative inheritance.
> (Hamera 2007: 8)

Technique is material. It is a doing. It is embodied knowledge. It is transmitted and it is always already relational. Technique is not possible without others. Technique is more than representation, signification, and symbol because it encompasses a corporeal effort (conscious or unconscious) of things repeatedly learned and done over time and space. As bodies negotiate, circulate, and interact with other bodies they simultaneously learn what Kenneth Burke calls "equipment for living" in the form of transmitted techniques that are then reproduced and recirculated. Because technique is learned and layered by histories and inheritances, if we turn to the embodiments of the oppressed and marginalized, we move beyond discourses of disempowerment and enter the epistemological depth of subaltern knowledge. There is a "common curriculum" across social lives that sustain and (re)produce themselves (Spatz 2015). Spatz provides a "working definition" of technique:

> Here, I have traced a selective genealogy that conceives of technique as vital, dynamic, and complex. In this conception, technique is a kind of knowledge (Aristotle) that moves across time and space (Mauss) in ways deeply influenced but not entirely determined by social power relations (Foucault). It structures every aspect of human embodiment and works by indirect as well as direct means (Crossley). Furthermore,

> embodied technique of all kinds, from the mundane to the highly specialized, interacts in and through specific bodies and moments of practice (Martin).
>
> (Spatz 2015: 38)

Embodied techniques exceed the narrow notion of being a mindless procedure, automated action, or skilled method. Judith Hamera describes technique as "relational infrastructure" as it "offers templates for sociality" (2007: 19). Hamera goes on to explain, "Technique translates individual bodies into a common 'mother tongue' to be shared and redeployed by its participants: a discursive matrix, a vocabulary and a grammar, to hold sociality together across difference and perpetuate it over time." She further adds, "At its most basic level, technique births new templates for sociality by rendering bodies readable, and by organizing the relationships in which these can occur" (19). The conceptualization of technique as "relational infrastructure" and as "transmitted knowledge" is particularly useful as we explore the intersections of performance, ethnography, and communication (Hamera 2007).

Practice

> If we look at chunks of human life bounded in time and space, we are looking at practices. If we look instead at the transmissible knowledge that links such chunks together across time and space, we are looking at technique (45) … Practice is never reducible to technique. As the image of fractally branching pathways suggests, technique is only ever a network of filaments that gives structure to practice. There is no such thing as a pure enactment of technique. Therefore, practice is always larger (as a sum of all its filaments and pathways) than the techniques that give it form … All the countless layers of sedimented technique that structure an in instance of practice nevertheless fail to determine it. Every chunk of practice exceeds the technique that structures it.
>
> (Spatz 2015: 57)

Practice is a unique moment of action structured by knowledge in the forms of technique. The distinctions between technique and practice are illustrated here in a jump rope game. The jump rope game of double Dutch is centuries old and spans the world. It requires two long ropes turning rhythmically in opposite directions where one or more players jump simultaneously in the center of the two ropes while the rope-turners keep the rope moving, sometimes at higher and higher speeds. Knowing how to turn two ropes in opposite, synchronized, speed and directions while counting, keeping score, and chanting a double Dutch tune to beats and steps of the jumpers is a learned *technique*.[1] How to jump and turn is not unique to one moment in time; there are world-wide double Dutch competitions. Double Dutch is a *practice* when we move beyond the social transmitted knowledge of the jumping,

6 Embodied technique and practice

Figure 1.1 Labor Rites. The performers become the mountain as Sisyphus pushes the "mountain" up the hill. True to the jazz aesthetic, actors are human and non-human figures: fantastical and surreal. Choreographer, Joel Valentin-Martinez. Photograph by Rafi Letzter.

now turning this learned technique into a concrete action, example, or a "moment of doing" double Dutch.

The practice of double Dutch is more than the content of its technique; it is the context of who, what, and where. To be more precise, in terms of communication, practice is an act, agent, agency scene, and purpose that is structured by technique. While technique is "precisely repeatable" and "bound to a particular moment, place, or person" it is "not ahistorical but transhistorical: it travels across time and space, 'spreading' from one society to another," while it links "diverse practices to one another, whether or not its practitioners are aware of this connection" (Spatz 2015: 41).

Interview with Ben Spatz[2]

DSM: *It seems embodied research is inseparable from history and relations as well as the time and labor required to make it generative or consequential. I'm thinking about politics and the material resonances of embodied research. How would you describe your method of embodied research and its unfolding? Is there a memorable example of rupture or realization that set your process in a different or added direction ... a moment that emerged, something newly done or deeply felt?*

Embodied technique and practice 7

Figure 1.2 Labor Rites. The three narrators—two Wise Clowns and the Recorder/Girl—hold the decorative box containing field journals that record the personal narratives of labor activists. In a symbolic gesture, the narrators enact the weight of these stories and the comedy and tragedies they hold. Photograph by Rafi Letzter.

BS: *I am always thinking these days about the institutionality of the laboratory. Much has been written about the violence of the laboratory space, from Linda Tuhiwai Smith noting that research is a "dirty word" in Australian indigenous communities to Karen Barad choosing the strikingly violent metaphor of the "cut" to describe how scientific measurement produces knowledge. Yes, the laboratory is "inseparable from history and relations," it is a place of time and precisely of labor. I constantly return to Bruno Latour's 1983 statements about the power of the laboratory to transform the world: "Give me a laboratory and I will raise the world!" This transformation does not have to be a violent, colonial one. It all depends what kinds of labor take place in the laboratory, what*

8 Embodied technique and practice

Figure 1.3 Class improvisation. Anthropology students at the University of Cape Town, South Africa symbolically express how they would hold, move, and value a book of complicated truths. D. S. Madison, photograph.

kinds of cuts are made. I imagine another kind of laboratory as a leverage point for another kind of world.

This past summer has taken me through moments of enormous discovery. After two months of narrowly focused embodied research in songwork, my team was visited by anthropologist Caroline Gatt, who suggested that we bring our books into the workspace. That proposal set off a chain reaction which has exploded my concept of embodied research and rendered our methodology more genuinely empirical than I could previously have imagined. With this shift it finally seems possible to imagine new forms of institutionality that are more adequate to the sonic and movement dimensions of embodiment and perhaps less wholly inadequate to our present social and environmental crises.

Many people are writing about the new omnipresence of digital media and suggesting parallels with the early print era. I myself have long believed that performance studies as such would not be thinkable outside the history of cinema and audiovisual recording. But only in the past couple of months have I begun to think that the new availability of digital media could open other kinds of institutionalities having to do with embodiment itself. The development of cinema since the early 20th century did not lead in this direction. The artistic power of the director and the economic power of the producer marginalized the power/knowledge of performers in film and pushed those who care about the agency of the body into live performing arts, where at least the performer still retains a degree of freedom. But maybe this trajectory can now be altered.

DSM: *Your distinction and analysis of "technique" and "practice" have been exceedingly helpful to me in my ethnographic work and how I think about the profundity of the small gesture or the taken-for-granted things our bodes can do. Your work has been instrumental in how I now (re)think about enactments of fieldwork and oral history relative to justice. How would you describe justice and how the distinction/comparison of technique and practice might figure into it?*

BS: *First, what you have written here means the world to me. My whole project of theorizing technique (as knowledge and in relation to practice) is inextricably bound to an underlying orientation towards justice and ecology. However, it has not always been clear to me how to articulate this impulse without reducing the emergent qualities of embodiment to existing quantities in social scientific or other critical language. I deeply admire historians and cultural critics and have often regretted my own apparent inability to insert myself directly into public discourse as they do. At the same time, I am looking for a way to speak publicly that does not foreclose the grounding of my perspective in my own embodiment. This again is why the intersections of body, book, and video have been so astonishing to me in the past two months. We have public intellectuals who make discursive arguments and we have public performers who sing and dance but at present we have virtually no place for public orators who combine these modes of enactment.*

I have now started to look in both the critical Jewish tradition and the critical Black tradition at the idea of the prophetic and I am starting to wonder whether the prophetic has to refer to a particular combination of discursive content and embodied technique. It seems to me that in critical fieldwork and oral history there are tremendously profound potentials for prophetic enactments of justice but that these have been barred from the public sphere during the reign of the logos. *If indeed the* logos *is now going to be demoted and begin to function alongside the audiovisual, then there is an opening for a realignment of knowledge communities in the name of justice. Of course, the audiovisual can be coopted and controlled just like the linguistic. It is a question of who controls the media, or rather a question about the structure of the institutionalities of media, which is why all my energy (including* JER*) is currently focused on trying to develop new pathways and relationships between embodied practitioners and the audiovisual field.*

Can there be techniques of justice, or only practices of justice? The ancient Greek philosophers looked for techniques of the good, but in poststructuralist contexts, it seems impossible to pin down anything so reliable. I know that technique is much more than language; that language is only one kind of technique. Perhaps rather than universal techniques of justice what we need are techniques that function at the level of the planetary in this particular moment. In that case maybe these new media will make possible songs and images of justice that allow for its institutionalization in ways we cannot yet imagine. The book I am writing now is based on the question: "What is a song?" When Caroline Gatt asked me why I was working with songs (and not books or computers), I said that in this moment it seems like humanity may have to give up many things in order to survive, but one thing I am certain we do not have to give up is songs. I want to be able to speak—or rather, to practice—about justice publicly, but I do not yet feel able. I hope that by answering a question like "What is a song?" I will then be able to grasp "What is justice?" in a more adequate way.

DSM: *You seem driven. You are abundantly busy. Alice Walker says—and I am paraphrasing her—"We must do the work our soul must have." It seems that you are doing "soul work." Why do you do this work? What moves you to do this work.*

BS: *This question is most difficult to answer because so many layers of myself overlap in my work: the personal, the ethno-cultural, the political, and the spiritual bordering on the mystical—which always risks the messianic. Even before all the recent critical work on whiteness in the US, I constantly interrogate my projects to examine whether they are not falling into the traps of some kind of savior mentality, wanting to prove myself "good" or "innocent" or to earn my way out of guilt rather than purely serving. But I also realize that—as the Walker quote suggests—the only way to serve is to find ways of serving that are also healing to oneself.*

I guess I would say that I am driven by two things: a constant fear about ongoing social and environmental violence and a desire to integrate different aspects of my being. The fear is rational to a degree, in that it responds to actual facts about climate change, the prison–industrial complex, the refugee crisis, etc. But it is also a kind of lived trauma which I would now link to the particular history of European Jews and the extremely vexed position of critically oriented white Jews in the United States: the ingrained sense of worry and impending doom; the commitment to social justice; the struggle with complicity to racism; and even the particular relationship to reading and writing that comes from being the source but not the endpoint of Christian imperial logos.

I would connect this last point, about the Jewish relationship to logos, *to my own youthful experience of feeling trapped within a fluency of reading and writing. From this sense of being trapped within a critical discursive space, I was driven to go on a long journey away from language in order to find my own embodiment. Later I came back to writing and found that I could use my skill with language strategically, to make space for critically informed embodied practice. Today I am driven, on one level, by the idea that the digital audiovisual space of the internet might just be that urgently needed commons in which our species can find a way to pull itself back from the brink of self-destruction; and, on another level, by the ongoing personal need to bring together speech and song, book and video, so that I can finally undertake public (that is, serving) work in a way that does not sever my linguistic self from the physical, vocal, erotic, vulnerable, "grain" of my body.*

I feel that I have been loaded with a great gift of love from a series of teachers. I want to give this love back into the world and it cannot flow (or can only flow partially) through pure song, like a performer; or pure thought, like a critical theorist; or pure care, like a spiritual teacher. To flow fully into the world, it needs all these channels to be open at once. I am looking for that: for a way to reconcile the spiritual force of that love with the kind of critical thought we so badly need.

Examples of technique and practice

I. Speaking with others as transmitted knowledge and technique

Speaking techniques begin at birth. In tracing the lineage of how we learn to speak, particularly through transmitted knowledge, it begins, for the hearing child, with the capacity of the brain to listen.[3] Newly born babies hear voices speaking to them and speaking to other voices, and by two years old, babies have heard many sounds and words; they have attained a large vocabulary, although they understand more words than they can speak. Most babies can put simple words together to express their feelings, ideas, and needs. They begin to play with the sounds and words they have heard around them: "dada," "baba," "mama," and so forth. As the baby continues to grow, they learn techniques of forming sentences, word patterns, intonation, volume, pronunciation, pitch, tone, and pace, as well as an admixture of vocal affect and responses. They have obviously learned all this, over time, through imitation and repetition by listening to those voices around them. Repetition and imitation are powerful teachers of technique, but we also learn language through overlays of experience and guided instruction. I this case I will focus on *familial and community vocal techni*ques, for example, storytelling as grammar patterns, naming things as vocabulary building; vocalizing emotion as expressive phrasing; conversations as vocal turn-taking. Example: A renowned scholar of modern American literature was the guest speaker at an Ivy League university for an annual lecture that features a celebrated scholar in the field of American studies. Only academics of the highest esteem were extended this invitation. The speaker for this year was the first African American woman to be given the honor. Her topic was metaphors of speech and freedom in the American novel. The lecture hall was filled with students, faculty, and administrators awaiting the presentation of this internationally celebrated scholar and intellectual. At the end of her presentation, everyone in the room rose to their feet with an extended standing ovation. Her eloquence was appreciated by the extended applause. After the lecture, she attended an informal dinner and drinks with a small group of dear, old friends and two members of the lecture committee. Everyone was very relaxed and enjoying the evening. Toward the end of the evening, after much conversation and laughter, they began sharing stories and anecdotes about the trials and tribulations of academic life. Then the speaker and her dear friend began to reminisce and share their own stories of the old days as Black graduate students attending Ivy League universities. The two committee members looked on as they witnessed the speaker and their colleague seem to transform before their eyes. It was a though these Black women were now different people. They were interacting with a familiarity and intimacy in the *way* they spoke—intonation, pitch, tone—and *how* they employed language. Their word pronunciations, grammatical arrangements, vocal textures, vernacular phrasings, and gestural expressions had now changed. These Black women were now code switching to another Black identity that was genuine, intrinsic, and deeply held for them, but unfamiliar and foreign for the committee members. The committee members realized and respected they were witnessing a code-switching moment and the multi-lingual technique of the speaker and her friend who was also their colleague. This is an example of fluidity and simultaneity of techniques. It is also an example of how the women demonstrated language techniques learned from a shared tradition and culture embodied through family and community rituals, practices, and knowledges of Black vernacular speech.

II. Cooking as transmitted knowledge and technique

While living in Ghana, West Africa,[4] conducting field research, I observed the preparation of a staple food, known as fufu, being prepared almost everywhere: inside homes, outside in marketplaces and along the roads of cities, towns, and villages. Fufu is common practice in many countries of West Africa and the Caribbean. Fufu is the national and main dish of Ghana. It is a doughy firm substance usually served with soup, such as ground nut, palm nut, goat, or light soups. During fieldwork, I understood the preparation of fufu as a quotidian performance. At the time, what I didn't realize was how this preparation was a carefully learned and inherited technique relative to the depth of agility, patience, timing, measurements, and care required of the "pounder" and the "driver." The pounder stands next to a very large wooden bowl or mortar, and with both hands on a tall, heavy, rounded wooden pole or pestle the pounder with rhythmic force continuously pounds combinations of boiled cassava with yam or plantain. He pounds the pieces until the mixture forms into a soft fluffy dough. The driver sits beside the large wooden bowl or mortar and, in between the heavy pestle thrashing down on the bowl, the driver reaches their hand into the bowl turning the cassava between the thrashing pestle, while also adding water to prevent stickiness. The longer the pounding the smoother the fufu. The fufu is then tossed by hand and formed into several moist, smooth, balls for each family member or guest. The fingers are placed in position to slice a certain portion of fufu from the ball, using the fufu to scoop up the soup. The soup and fufu are eaten together for a delicious meal. This is the basic and universal *technique* of making fufu; this technique is what makes fufu what it is. However, for this technique to be turned into practice the making of fufu requires a time and place, and within each time and place, or practice, certain elements of the technique may change depending on location, resources, capabilities, and environment afforded.[5] One day at the market, I looked on as a group of foreign students were learning how to make fufu from a few local women. I noticed on several occasions that students, expatriates, and tourists were intrigued by the preparation and rhythmic pounding of fufu. On this day, there was a bit of awkwardness and a bit of fear; I recognized it from my own lessons: the fear of being out of rhythm and your pounding pestle breaking the driver's hand; adding the right amount of moisture in the dough; turning the mixture fast enough; forming the balls properly; eating soup with your hands. Making fufu is a learned technique by no small measure. On this day, technique blossomed into an experience that was relational, insightful, and memorable. The students heard stories of learning how to make fufu and braggadocio of who makes the best fufu. They observed the orchestrated sounds of laugher, local vernacular, the accents of expats looking on and passing by and in their marketplaces. They were amused by the jokes in Ghanaian languages about abrunis[6] trying to learn how to pound fufu, fearing a broken hand from the pounder. They were self-reflexive about the wonder of cooking as uniquely human, social, and expressive. They understood the deep layers of this practice, constituted by technique, across continents and traditions of Black diaspora as both different and the same everywhere and how this sameness and difference can reveal so much about the quotidian performance of fufu. This experience and understanding on that day was the practice that exceeded the technique.

III. Social dancing and leisure as transmitted knowledge and technique

Leisure time is your own time; it is freedom of choice and comes from the Latin word *licere*, meaning to "be allowed." Leisure time is "done for its own sake,"[7] not necessarily out of responsibility, requirement, or duty but for the opportunity to feel joy and pleasure—for rest and relaxation. It is time away from time that has psychological, social, and emotional implications, for example, to think different thoughts, to change body rhythms and speed, to create and imagine, to be social and closer to others. Leisure time is where techniques of sociality are profoundly manifest from long naps to sports; hobbies to gossip; reading a book to social dancing, and more. Leisure time "allows" and provides the opportunity for joy and for humans to recognize and reclaim themselves. This brings me to the universality of social dancing, more specifically, urban social dancing, and, more locally, the origins in the late 1950s and 1960s of Chicago bop. Techniques of social and/or urban "partner" dance are the grandchild of Lindy Hop.[8] One partner leads (usually the male) and the other partner follows (female). While dancing, the leader and follower will sometimes merge and at other times change roles. The technique involves a synchronized six-count step; hand-holding with strategic (coming together and releasing apart) force combined with intervals of neutral steadiness as well as hand-holding that is loose with little body contact. These synchronized movements' rhythm variations are inside a frame held within the parameters of the couple. There were certain movements or steps within the basic structure of the bop aligned with a particular city or high school. Most large cities identified with a specific style of bop. Social dancing arises and is sustained by collective participation and collaboration. The steps form a collective belonging and a shared mode of communication, yet discreetly stylized by unique locations. The techniques of social dance are colored by specific geographies of social practice. Underscoring the fluidity of bop techniques across urban cities, the following example takes us to a 1960s Chicago bop practice from a moment in time during the Viet Nam War era.

James, arriving from a tour of duty in Viet Nam, finally comes home to his family and friends. It is an adjustment for him. After being away with all that he experienced during the war, this home that is deeply known, familiar, and remembered now feels strangely unfamiliar and disorienting. His wife is preparing a welcome home party for James, inviting scores of friends and his very large family of brothers, sisters, mom, dad, cousin, and many young nieces and nephews. James is ambivalent about the party. Several family members and friends remain opposed to the war, as there are certain family and friends who are conscientious objectors. He agrees to the party in deference to his wife's wishes and the desire for the family (who also sacrificed during his absence) to come together, share together, and mark that their time of waiting and worrying for him was finally coming to an end. James was nervous about seeing everyone, but understood the party was as much or more for those he left behind at home than it was for him. The day of the party arrived and it was a huge gathering: multi-generational from small children to elders; across Chicagoland from Northside to Southside and Eastside to Westside; and, differing viewpoints from the left, middle, and right of politics and war. The party started and among the welcoming hugs, boisterous greetings, and cheers of joy there was loud talking, honest questions, opinionated debate, and shared stories about all things from Chicago neighborhoods and children growing tall to popular culture, music, and the Viet Nam War. As the Motown sounds blasted from the record player, everyone—new friends, old friends, and strangers—partnered in six-count steps. In a social choreography of Chicago bop techniques: children danced with their grandparents as Northside bop and Southside bop partnered in synchronized combinations. The party could not resolve James's feeling about the War. His future would be committed to making those feelings about war and peace matter to the world. But in this moment, James remembered joy in the familiar and the names, faces, and their stories he had forgotten. He felt the freedom of his body moving in step with a dance partner who knew him and anticipated his steps. He remembered music as a sign of community and belonging and how that belonging is manifest, in a celebration of time out of time, when dancing bodies—among friends, family and strangers—come together through a shared social inheritance of technique.

***

Figure 1.4 Labor Rites. Techniques of collective reading and listening to field journals. All actors in varied positions as one woman raises her hand in a traditional and solemn "amen" to a labor activist story. Photograph by Rafi Letzter.

Figure 1.5 Labor Rites. Techniques of passing along support and nourishments to fellow factory workers during a window factory strike as the original factory workers rejoice (digital projection) in victory. Photograph by Rafi Letzter.

Figure 1.6 Labor Rites. The practice of collective action in the long history of labor rights and picket lines. Choreographer, Joel Valentin-Martinez. Photograph by Rafi Letzter.

Case study one: Digital Portobelo with Renée Alexander Craft

DSM: Please give us a brief description or overview of Digital Portobelo.

RAC: Digital Portobelo: Art + Scholarship + Cultural Preservation is a cultural preservation and collaborative research initiative that focuses on an Afro-Latin community located on the Caribbean coast of Panama who call themselves and their performance tradition "Congo." It represents an extension of an ethnographic project that I began in 2000, which served as the basis for my monograph, *When the Devil Knocks: The Congo Tradition and the Politics of Blackness in 20th Century Panama.*

DSM: How did it all begin?

RAC: It was initiated through an inaugural Digital Innovation Lab/ Institute for the Arts and Humanities Fellowship at UNC in 2013.

DSM: What are its features?

RAC: It features an online, interactive digital repository of written and performed scholarship focused on the Congo tradition of Portobelo. It includes visual art, audio and video interviews with English and Spanish transcripts, and short contextual videos focused on the Congo community of Portobelo.

DSM: What was your purpose or objective in creating Digital Portobelo?

RAC: For years, I shared my photographs and recordings with interviewees on a small scale. But the majority of my audio and video recordings stayed sealed in oversized Tupperware containers in my closet rather than in the possession of Portobelo community members, because I did not know how to effectively contribute to the type of a larger scale cultural preservation initiative that the community desired.

DSM: And then something changed ...

RAC: Yes, by 2012 to 2013, user-friendly, open-source digital tools and greater support—in the form of monetary resources, trained personnel, and expanding digital infrastructures at UNC as well as in Portobelo—allowed me to respond to the community's call through a digital intervention.

DSM: This opened up more ways to include forms of performance as documentation and community collaboration?

RAC: As a critical/performance ethnographer, I have sought to use live performance and performance-installation projects as a means to make my research more accessible, especially to the communities reflected by and invested in its outcomes. In that tradition, Digital Portobelo aspires to serve as a public platform that might allow researchers and community members to address pertinent questions and find answers together.

DSM: How would you describe the specific goals of Digital Portobelo?

RAC: I would say that Digital Portobelo has six goals: first, to establish a dual-language (English/Spanish) digital space for researchers to return the stories, interviews, photographs, and videos we have collected to the populations from which they came; second, to foster a collaborative digital environment in which community members and researchers can share information, correct absences and errors, and create ongoing dialogues related to Congo traditions and culture; third, to create a mechanism for local community members to archive and share their cultural practices and memories; fourth, to develop skills in the local community for recording and studying oral history through a curriculum on media literacy and production; fifth, to contribute to the growing body of work on Afro-Latinidad and on the complexity of Afro-Panamanian history and culture; and sixth, to offer academic communities a new digital resource through which to study Afro-Latin history and culture in our classrooms as well as through our research experiences.

DSM: These are very comprehensive and impressive goals. Please share your process and the stages of developing Digital Portobelo.

RAC: As a performance studies trained scholar, I approached developing Digital Portobelo the way I approach creating other staged performances. I spent a good deal of time engaging with the problem I intended Digital Portobelo to address and what work I wanted it to do. I wondered, in the words of director Joseph Megel, "What journey do you I want to take the audience on?" Then, I began to conceptualize the work and assemble various teams of collaborators including translators, transcribers, documentarians, library scientists, and computer scientists. In the language of theatre, my teams of collaborators included those focused on: script, design, and production. As the primary researcher and director of the project, I worked with each team to share my initial vision, to learn alongside them, and to ensure that their creative and technical contributions amplified the research without creating any sense of distortion.

DSM: You approached the project performatively from the very beginning with a spirit of collaboration.

RAC: Yes. In preparing to stage this work as an interactive digital platform, I needed to translate my audio and video recorded interviews as well as my written research into a digital "script." That meant working with a wonderful and generous digital integration project manager, Pam Lach, and, what I would call, a "digital production team" to digitize, transcribe, translate, and digitally code all of the interviews. Whereas a theatre production's design team might include set, costume, sound, and lighting designers; my digital humanities design team included those focused on gathering, creating, and managing the digital tools and frameworks capable of visually rendering the work in an engaging and intuitive way. My collaborators are a mix of students, colleagues, community-members, and professionals.

DSM: Digital technology opens paths for collaboration across geography and time. The possibilities for performance and communication across distance are rich. You are doing this work.

RAC: We see this because Digital Portobelo blends a traditional WordPress website with a unique and dynamic way of interacting with ethnographic interviews and oral histories. It affords audiences the opportunity to listen to an interview delivered through SoundCloud while Spanish and English transcripts scroll on-screen. This allows audiences to jump to any of section of an interview and immediately start listening. In addition to ten complete interviews, which are available for download as PDFs, audiences can filter and interact with 105 themed sections of the interviews through clickable photo-based topic cards. These cards allow the relationships between the themed sections of interviews to be visualized, or represented spatially, in a variety of configurations. The website is accessible in English (digitalportobelo.org) as well as Spanish (portobelodigital.org). In order to accommodate access across multiple types of devices and multiple speeds of digital access, Digital Portobelo may be experienced intact through its primary URLs, as an audio archive via SoundCloud, as a collection of videos on YouTube, or through its presence on major social media platforms. In addition to the materials mentioned above, the site includes a complete "how to" guide that walks audiences through how to create similar projects using mostly open-source tools.

DSM: What stage of development are you in now?

RAC: Digital Portobelo is currently in its second phase of development, which focuses on community outreach and engagement.

This phase seeks to create a series of workshops, presentations, user guides, and dialogical encounters with scholars focused on Afro-Latin identity and culture in the Americas, cultural practitioners and preservationists interested in the potential of Digital Portobelo for this and allied projects, and educators interested in how the project might serve as a pedagogical tool.

DSM: Are there other community-engagement initiatives?

RAC: One of Digital Portobelo's most recent community-engagement initiatives is the "Portobelo Panama Intergenerational Oral History Project." With the support of a 2016–2017 Whiting Public Engagement Fellowship, my collaborators and I designed the project as a pilot seven-day initiative that taught the basic techniques of oral history interviewing to middle and high school students and paired them with community elders to conduct initial interviews. My primary collaborators in this project included Dr. Laurel Cadwallader Stolte (Program Coordinator, Dual Language Immersion Program, Southwest Elementary School, Durham, NC), Ari Blandon "Mamá Ari" (Founder, "El Grupo Congo Mama Ari," a youth initiative celebrating Congo dance and culture), and Margarita De Loney (Stanford University doctoral candidate whose Portobelo-based research is connected to Mamá Ari). We designed the workshop's process to foster intergenerational listening, conversation, and knowledge-sharing with the belief that we are all witnesses and guardians of important pieces in the histories of our communities.

DMS: Can you describe the day-to-day schedule? What do the days look like?

RAC: In our pilot program, day one was an Introduction and Overview. Margarita, Ari, and I introduced the project to youth participants and gave them a demonstration of Digital Portobelo/Portobelo Digital, which includes interviews with relatives of many of the participants. Following our introduction, overview, and question/answer period, we paired six younger students with six older students to learn techniques of oral history and to put them into practice by interviewing six community leaders, cultural experts, and/or elders. At the conclusion of the session, "Mama Ari" led a workshop to help each pair rehearse talking with their elders about the project and inviting them to be interviewed. We then directed each pair to choose three potential community members to invite into the process. We suggested three potential interviewees, understanding that some might not have the time, availability, or interest. Participants' homework was to visit potential interviewees prior to our next meeting to make the invitation. Each participant received a dedicated notebook for the project. Day two focused on "Open Questions, Closed Questions, and Cultivating Curiosity Digital Portobelo." The session started with participants sharing their experiences of inviting elders into process and their announcement of their chosen interviewee. Next, Laurel led a workshop focused on interview techniques that allowed participants to practice open and closed questions as well as how to actively listen and offer productive follow-up questions. Each pair generated 15 to 20 questions, which they worked with Digital Portobelo workshop leaders to narrow to ten—four to be asked by the younger member of the pair and six to be asked by the older member.

DSM: The days are filled with digital forms of engagements and processes of experimental learning that is all at once performative, communicative, and ethnographic ...

RAC: Yes! Day three is interview "Prep—Tools, Techniques, and Rehearsal." Each of our 2017 student pairs received a digital recorder, which was donated for use in the project by UNC's Southern Oral History Program. Margarita, Laurel, and I demonstrated how to use the recorders and discussed best practice in choosing appropriate recording locations. We dedicated the remainder of the session to: first, reviewing and building upon productive techniques for interviewing, second, "setting the stage" for an interview by settling in, testing equipment, and properly welcoming interviewees into the space, and third, allowing each pair to rehearse introductions and practice recording two-to-three questions. Days four and five focused on inter-generational interviews. Pairs met with their interviewees during our regularly scheduled workshop time while workshop leaders made themselves available for questions/concerns. Having worked closely with "Mama Ari" and the students in the past, Margarita served as their main point of contact. Day six of our schedule focused on "Creativity as a Tool for Critical Reflection." With the help of internationally renowned local artists and Digital Portobelo/Portobelo Digital collaborators Gustavo Esquina and Manuel "Tatu" Golden, Digital Portobelo workshop leaders guided participants to reflect on a meaningful quote or theme from their interviews and create art pieces that uplifted portions of their interviews. With the support of Whiting Fellowship funds, we provided them with a variety of materials with which to create their art objects and invited participants to offer their creations as gifts to their interviewees in appreciation for their time.

DSM: You have provided a model of digital ethnography intersecting with performance as well as the ethics and responsibility of community collaboration and cultural preservation. How does your concern for reflecting on this process fit?

RAC: Day seven was the stage of reflection and celebration. During our final session, we invited interviewees to join participants to reflect on the process, celebrate their shared accomplishments, and discuss a vision for how the project might proceed over the next year. With the support of Whiting Fellowship funds, we provided refreshments for the gathering.

DSM: How would you describe the results or efficacy of Digital Portobelo?

RAC: My team and I have successfully established a dual-language (English/Spanish) digital environment that encourages collaborations between community members and researchers as well as serves as a digital repository for both. Two of the most meaningful and practical outcomes of the site include the ability to document and share sociohistorical changes in Portobelo that far exceed the temporal frame of the book project as well as the ability to engage with a generation of Portobelo-based students who were born into digital technologies and into a more globalized experience of their local community than the generations that preceded them. Portobelo middle and high schools have a tourism and local history tract that plans to integrate Digital Portobelo into its curriculum. Thus far, US-based university professors of Spanish, anthropology, communication, drama, and geography have made me aware of their use Digital Portobelo in their classrooms. The project has also achieved its goal of serving as a platform that community-based documentarians may use to preserve local history. We are working with digital humanists in the US and Panama as well as K-12 educators to make this process easier and more intuitive. We are also seeking partnership with local and international organizations that teach coding to youth as part of their math, science, and media curriculums.

DSM: And the feedback?

RAC: The feedback from global scholars and local community members has been overwhelmingly positive. However, I am grateful to have received feedback from K-12 educators and users with no prior knowledge of the Congo tradition requesting differentiated audience-specific user guides and more contextual connections to allied Black diaspora cultural performance traditions in the Americas. With an interest in integrating Digital Portobelo into dual-language elementary curriculums, Dr. Stolte applied for, and received, an NEA Learning and Leadership grant that allowed her to travel to Portobelo in July of 2017 as a member of our team. With the assistance of the grant, she is working to establish relationships with K-12 educators in Panama; create dual-language pilot curriculums and curriculum guides based on Digital Portobelo for kindergarten, third, and fifth grade teachers; and introduce at least one of the curriculums into the classroom during the 2017 to 2018 academic year. The participation of educators, researchers, and community members with a vested interest in helping the project grow to better address the needs of their audiences is crucial to the project's longevity and relevance. I envisioned and collaboratively wrote the site's initial "script" and directed its first "performances." Now, I am excited to watch it extend beyond me.

Notes

1 The double Dutch rhythmic chant and song has been shared and transmitted across locations and generations in African American neighborhoods and cultures. In the 1930s, during the Depression era, children often jumped rope because the game required only a used clothesline to be played. By the late 1950s, however, a number of municipal and societal factors—such as the desire to keep children from playing in city streets and the availability of other games for children in upwardly mobile families—had decreased its popularity. However, jumping rope and double Dutch experienced a renaissance in the late 20th century, to the point that rope jumping became a competitive sport, with various double Dutch rope skipping leagues coming into existence around the world and tournaments being held throughout the year. www.britannica.com/topic/double-Dutch-game.
2 Ben Spatz is Senior Lecturer in Drama, Theatre and Performance at the University of Huddersfield; Arts and Humanities Research Council Leadership Fellow (2016–2018); author of *What a Body Can Do: Technique as Knowledge, Practice as Research* (Routledge 2015); convener of the Embodied Research Working Group within the International Federation for Theatre Research; and editor of the *Journal of Embodied Research*, a peer-reviewed video journal launching in 2017 from Open Library of Humanities. His research focuses on the transmission and innovation of embodied knowledge across physical culture, performing arts, and everyday life. In New York City, Ben has performed and shown work at New York Live Arts, Abrons Arts Center, Movement Research at Judson Church, and Lincoln Center's Rubenstein Atrium. He is an experienced performer and teacher of physical and vocal training for actors, drawing on a wide range of cultural and pedagogical sources. Ben lived in Poland from 2003 to 2005 as an apprentice performer at the Centre for Theatre Practices Gardzienice and a

Fulbright Fellow at the Grotowski Institute in Wroclaw. This is the content of an email correspondence between Ben and myself, September 4, 2017.
3 For the babies born deaf, speech is significantly dependent on touch and sight. High levels of family involvement have been found to produce greater language development outcomes in deaf and hard of hearing children. Drawing from a large body of research, there is a clear argument favoring the use of sign language with all children, regardless of their hearing status. This argument is based on three basic points: early language learning experiences affect other areas of development and are critical to children's future success; sign language provides the earliest possible mode through which children can learn expressive language skills; all children can benefit from the use of sign language, with no risk to other language skills. http://deafchildren.org/knowledge-center/parents-and-families/early-visual-language.
4 This reflects the years I lived in Ghana from 1998 to 2000 with ongoing and extended stays beyond this time over a ten-year period. The Ghana fieldwork is captured in my book, *Acts of Activism*. See Bibliography.
5 Affordances: the qualities or properties of an object that define its possible uses or make clear how it can or should be used. We sit or stand on a chair because those affordances are fairly obvious (Scott Lafee, *San Diego Union-Tribune*, 15 August 1993). An affordance is a resource or support that the environment offers an animal; the animal in turn must possess the capabilities to perceive it and to use it. (Eleanor J. Gibson et al. in *The MIT Encyclopedia of the Cognitive Sciences*, 1999). www.merriam-webster.com/dictionary/affordance
6 Abruni refers to a white person or foreigners.
7 Leisure has often been defined as a quality of experience or as free time. Free time is time spent away from business, work, job hunting, domestic chores, and education, as well as necessary activities such as eating and sleeping. From a research perspective, this approach has the advantages of being quantifiable and comparable over time and place. Leisure as experience usually emphasizes dimensions of perceived freedom and choice. It is done for "its own sake," for the quality of experience and involvement. Other classic definitions include Thorstein Veblen's (1899) of "nonproductive consumption of time." Different disciplines have definitions reflecting their common issues: for example, sociology on social forces and contexts and psychology as mental and emotional states and conditions (https://en.wikipedia.org/wiki/Leisure).
8 The Lindy Hop is an American dance that was born in Harlem, New York City in 1928 and has evolved since then with the jazz music of that time. It was very popular during the Swing era of the late 1930s and early 1940s. Lindy was a fusion of many dances that preceded it or were popular during its development but is mainly based on jazz, tap, breakaway, and Charleston. It is frequently described as a jazz dance and is a member of the swing dance family. In its development, the Lindy Hop combined elements of both partnered and solo dancing by using the movements and improvisation of African American dances along with the formal eight-count structure of European partner dances—most clearly illustrated in the Lindy's basic step, the swingout. In this step's open position, each dancer is generally connected hand-to-hand; in its closed position, leads and follows are connected as though in an embrace on one side and holding hands on the other (https://en.wikipedia.org/wiki/Lindy_Hop).

Chapter 2

Improvisation

The inherited body we bring to performance practice

> Discussions of acting technique, for the most part, continue to assume a neutral or unmarked body that transcends or ignores divisions of race, gender, and ability. Meanwhile, those who theorize identity are often working from a strategic essentialism that prioritizes indentitarian categories over a recognition of how embodied technique moves between bodies and practices. I propose that an epistemology of practice can be the basis for a conceptual framework within which "acting" and "identity" might come into more thorough and rigorous dialogue. To see acting and identity as contiguous, however, we must recognize the extent to which socialization and vocational training intersect in what Randy Martin calls the "composite body" of technique (1998: 139). This means, on the one hand, that the sedimentation of acting technique in the body contributes to and can even transform a person's identity; and, on the other hand, that identity itself is trained and practiced to a large degree as embodied technique.
>
> (Spatz 2015: 157)

This discussion of transmitted and embodied knowledge deepens the relevance of identity as well as the social, political, and aesthetic ramifications of acting and creating performances. We bring our embodied techniques with us in rehearsal and to the stage. These inherited techniques constitute our identities, and they arguably shape our bodies and musculature (Hamera 2007). The *composite body* is a meeting of acting and performance techniques with the socially transmitted knowledges of those embodied techniques that constitute our identities. How these layers of techniques are reciprocally conjoined, mutually respected, rigorously learned, negotiated, and enacted is the challenge and alchemy of aesthetic practice as well as the intellectual labor in theorizing about it. This is of special interest in developing performances based on fieldwork experiences: from oral histories and interview data to a range of field encounters, observations, and interventions we must decipher and interpret a matrix of socially embedded techniques and the performances that exceed them into "contiguous" techniques of improvisation, acting, movement, devised performance, and symbolic communication (Spatz 2015). All of which offer extended and experimental forms of collaboration and discovery. Bringing this conceptualization of the composite body into performed ethnography opens a useful vocabulary and more precise insights that recognize within the performer's body there inhere limitless inherited knowledges and practices that constitute ways of vocalization, gesture, action, and attitude that will intersect performance technique. The embodied techniques and practices learned and enacted in our everyday lives and that are inscribed upon our nervous systems, musculature, hearts, and minds are the very resources and residues that not only structure our identities, but are inseparable elements of every performance we make and that makes us. In 1892, the African American intellectual and orator, Anna Julia Cooper, was the first woman to speak in public, proclaiming: "when and where I enter, in the quiet, undisputed dignity of my womanhood, without suing or special patronage, then and there the whole Negro race enters with me" (Cooper in Giddens 1984). We may add to her statement by underscoring that when and where we enter our embodied techniques enter with us; they enter with us into performance practices that hold contested histories and social epistemologies across communities, both admonished and revered. And, as embodied techniques are malleable to the social practices they structure in everyday life, these same embodied techniques also become malleable to the performance techniques and practices they learn and embody anew. In summary: (1) To honor the intersection of socially inherited techniques and practices with those techniques and practices of acting and performance aesthetics is at the core of performed ethnography. We not only bring different kinds of bodies into the performance frame, but we bring a different network of direct and indirect knowledges to extend, critique, and reimagine the frame itself. This further invokes new knowledges of performance practice. (2) To honor the learned lineage of everyday technique is to pay attention to what different bodies can do marked by geographies and hierarchies of race, sexuality, class, gender, and spaces that deepen and complicate uncomplicated notions of identities beyond surface appearances and token substitutions. We are witness to identity layered by pathways of belonging. (3) To appreciate how practices are structured by infinite resonances of techniques, within the bodies of actors, is to invoke freedom, trust, and a space for the actor's conscious and unconscious choices from small gesture to grand action. Actors are free to trust—spontaneously or by design—their limitless reservoir of embodied techniques, both realized and unrealized. (4) Because all techniques are malleable up to a point and "move between bodies and practices" the actor's identity can affect performance techniques just as performance techniques can affect the actor's identity. It is often stated that we change performance as performance changes us. How we more precisely excavate the seeds and complex mutuality of this "change" is through the recognition and research of practice and the content of their techniques. The following is an example of how this discussion and the four points above can be understood and illustrated through improvisation when different bodies and identities perform the same task—to walk and to wait—first as a specific character and then as themselves. There are two parts to the exercise, and in each part, it should be emphasized that the actors will first perform a specific character. The characters (e.g., an angry person, a person in pain, a narcissist, a joyful person) should not be played as stereotypes, caricatures, or parodies but with sincerity, naturalistically, as real or honest depictions. When the character scene comes to an end, the actors will then repeat the scene performing as themselves.

In the two rounds of part one, each actor (one by one) will walk for a period of time in the following environments: (1) down a crowded street; (2) along a quiet beach; and (3) through a fancy, upscale clothing boutique. In two rounds of part two, the actors are waiting together as strangers for a period of time until each one enters their individual ride of choice (e.g., bus, taxi, friend or relative, chauffeur, or bus). The questions and observations for this exercise include:

Part One: Walking

- In each round as the actors portrayed a character and performed as themselves what did you observe in their posture or gait in the three environments?
- What did you observe in their attitude, disposition, or expression in the three environments?
- What gestural activity—same or different—did you notice as the actor played the character and then performed as themselves?
- How would you describe the physicality of the actors when playing a character in contrast to performing as themselves?

Part Two: Waiting

- How would you describe the form, quality, or personality of each of the actors' bodies while they were waiting? What was the same and different about them?
- Did you notice anything distinctive or idiosyncratic in the way they attained or gained access to their ride?
- How did each actor respond to others around them?

Note: This exercise can be revised to meet your own purposes with different character types and situations. The purpose is to compare how the body employs different techniques in different situations or contexts when performing as characters and as themselves. The purpose is also to determine how the influence of performing sincerely, as a specific kind of body influences, the performance of yourself when directly following the character performance.

Yes–No

- Start opposite a partner. One of you says yes, and the other says no.
- Try every way you can to get through to your partner using your one word.
- Use your voice, your body, your gestures. Argue, plead, cajole, yell, cry—anything to get your partner to agree with you. But, at the same time, listen to your partner.
- Let yourself notice when you have come to the end of what you have to say, or when your partner gets through to you. When this happens, swap words.
- If your partner changes from yes to no or from no to yes, you must change too.
- Once you are both listening and reacting well to each other start to improvise: "yes, I want you to clean your room right now." Provide examples and be detailed.
- Even as situation, event, and character emerge, and even as you try as hard as you can to "win," keep listening for that moment when something changes. And always go with the change.
- Notice how your body choices affect the game: What happens if you go down on your knees? What happens if you turn and walk away? What happens if you touch your partner? And notice what effect your vocal choices have, too.
- Notice what closes you off from listening or noticing the beat changes. Notice what leaves you open.
- Try playing the game very strongly, but listening for beat changes one every line or almost every line. What do you have to do, physically and mentally, to play a moment strongly without becoming so attached to what you are doing that you are not really listening? Is it a matter of alternating between doing and listening, or is there a way in which to do and to listen at the same time?
- Now start over, beginning with your vowel and consonant work. Connect your body with your voice and then extend the phonemes into gibberish. Now start the Yes–No game again, in gibberish, making sure your body and sound work remain full. Then slide back into English.

Source: Stephen Wangh[1]

Key concepts in improvisational acting and performance

Jazz acting relies on technique and craft that are used to facilitate deep exploration. The ability to fully inhabit one's body, command of vocal variety and flexibility, familiarity with narrative styles, and structures, and understanding of multiple relationships with audiences are the technical strengths on which jazz acting builds. Such competency creates the safe strong parameters within which play and experimentation can flourish. In addition to these standard acting techniques, jazz acting insists on listening and spontaneity—that is where the deep exploration is housed. In theatrical jazz, standard acting techniques can easily become armor inhibiting the very listening and spontaneity that jazz acting demands. When technique becomes a way to display one's proficiency for the admiring gaze of audience, or when technique becomes a goal, technique can seriously impede jazz acting.

(Jones 2015: 165–168)

Believing that improvisation is as varied as life itself, how does one describe Everything? Start with the rudimentary communication, basic numbers, the beauty of rhythm, the formation of shapes, the very perception of colors, a development of emotional understanding, and the basic physical tasks? You need them all, and you need to master every one of them to improvise.

(Amy Sedaris from Jagodowski et al. 2015: xiii)

Improvisation is understood in relation to a constellation of terms: spontaneity, freedom, metaphor, flow, risk taking, play, bricolage, trust, hope, collaboration, and to make minute-by-minute change within a structure of changing rules. Improvisation involves a spontaneous creation of something new. As Rob Wallace states: "It requires skill and training, it can be learned, and it can fail horribly, precisely *because* there are tacit rules within the community of improvisers" (2015: 188). Our discussion of technique and practice now turns toward what a body can do and how that body brings what it can do into the tacit rules of improvisation. Improvisation and devised work transform the range of those techniques and practices observed and recorded in field data into a performance frame. Experiences in the field—from oral histories and interview data to autobiographical moments—are networks within networks of embodied practices and techniques that become a reservoir for creative collaboration. When improvisation and devised processes become the groundwork of ethnographic performance we embellish the emergent and the spontaneous both in the field and in rehearsal. These instances of emergence and spontaneity will hopefully evolve into full scenes, gestural fragments, vocal effects, movement pictures, and so on, for the final production. Improvisers, however, also embrace free-play that conjures spur-of-the-moment units of performance and action simply for the joy of creative expression invoking greater feeling, meaning, and purpose about the process that are not necessarily intended for the final production or public view. Improvisation and the devising process become resource materials that build the show, but they serve more than a utilitarian purpose. They enlighten us and help us care and learn more about each other; and, they encourage a greater affective investment in our performance enterprise.

The following are key terms that highlight improvisation and are of special value to performed ethnography.

Flow

> Our ecstasy in dance comes from the possible gift of freedom, the exhilarating moments that this exposing of bare energy can give us.
> (Cunningham 2015: 166)

> Your subconscious will suggest things which cannot be foreseen by anyone, not even by yourself, if you will but yield freely and completely to the inspiration of your own improvising spirit.
> (Chekhov 2015: 171)

Improvisation, understood as a paradox of structure and freedom, is often described through the concept of "flow." Improvisation depends on the inter-animating dynamics of both rules and unruliness that make flow possible. Flow being the "deep involvement in an activity for its own sake with a lack of ego and no sense of time … intrinsic gratification becomes overridden beyond extrinsic rewards … where you lose the sense of time" (Csikszentmihalyi 2015: 150). Fully mindful, in flow, you cannot be bored, worried, or distracted because you are engrossed by the present moment. This presence—the power of now—makes past and future recede but not disappear (Maslow 1971 in Csikszentmihalyi 2015). Flow is described as "a transcendence of individuality," "a self-forgetfulness," a "loss of ego," a "fusion with the world" (154). In flow, the ego gets "out of the way of what is happening" to surrender to "the moment before us" (141). We pay deep attention to the present moment and from there action emerges that serves the scene. "Rather than inventing characters out of thin air, we pay acute attention to discover the character we are already" (142). This happens less through convoluted effort and more through trusting the deep attention and surrender that are generated by flow. We also understand that flow involves actions that are within the abilities of those performing the actions in adherence to established structures of play: sports, ritual, dance, and other countless forms of creative activity. As play and playfulness become necessary qualities arising within the flow of improvisation these elements of play embrace various aspects of rules, structure, risk, freedom, and pleasure. This is a playfulness that energizes improvisational acts, where socially embodied techniques combined with the trained techniques of improvisation charged forth into spontaneity, insight, and surprise. For example, during rehearsal for a show based on my fieldwork in Ghana, West Africa, entitled: "Is It a Human Being or a Girl," we improvised with the subject of a debate among many Ghanaian rights activists on the issue of free trade versus fair trade. To capture the spirit of the debate, we improvised a range of symbolic and metaphorical actions, soon an emergence of play and abandon emerged, spinning into free motion with a spontaneity and discovery that set forth countless forms. The actors, engrossed in their collective immersion and embodied creations, were generatively lost in the moment of making new formations of embodied metaphors that were both translations and commentaries on the debate of free trade and fair trade. The improvisation—through play and flow—emerged into what we later called the African Waltz. It was a hybrid of Africa rhythmic dance, social be-bop, and European ballroom. Spontaneously, from the African Waltz improvisation, one dance partner emerged as the embodiment of free trade while the other responded as the symbol for fair trade. The dance partners improvised a physical or movement based call and contrasting response in a competitive and combative riff on fair trade against free trade. The African Waltz dance partners covered the stage with push and pull steps, of contention and resistance, all the while as ballroom partners. The dance emerged as both a take-off from Western ballroom waltz and West African dance forms. The African Waltz became a choreographic metaphor on trade policy critiques set forth by Ghanaian human rights activists. It was play, flow, and improvisation, within the freedom and structure of the rehearsal space, ballroom waltz steps, Western African dance rhythms and be-bop where we discovered and landed on the African Waltz as an embodiment and representation for the fair trade versus free trade debate documented from my fieldwork data.

Response(ability) and listening

It is the responsibility of the improviser to strive toward freedom of the imagination, of expression, of iteration, of technique, in ways that expand what it means to be human in unexpected form.

(Fischlin 2015: 292)

Allowing ourselves to be affected in the most sensible, logical and realistic way is an easier thing than trying to manufacture a response that doesn't make any sense.

(Jagodowski et al. 2015: 126)

Responsibility

It is said that with freedom comes responsibility. If responsibility is a hallmark of freedom, then responsibility and the ability to respond are also hallmarks of improvisation. In collaborative performance, the cycle of improvisational responses, from beginning to end, is based on each improviser's ability to respond to another improviser's response. It is also my responsibility as an improviser to open a path for your ability to respond. It is this ability to respond or response(ability) where trust emanates and paves the way for freedom. Kelly Oliver states: "We have an obligation not only to respond but also to respond in a way that opens up rather than closes off the possibility to respond by others" (Oliver 2001: 18–19).

Improvisers trust that their fellow improvisers will respond to their response and that response, in turn, will invoke another or face the fear of falling into silence. We remember that "Nothing is more frightening than the absence of an answer" (Bakhtin 1981: 111). For improvisers, this answer does not end the conversation, but it assures its continuance. You are not alone on stage to either fall or fail; you can trust that a response/ answer will come and continue to come. The response(ability) to the generative answer/response is a co-creation, co-dependence in these moments of creative and collaborative spontaneity (294): we pay attention to each other; we listen to each other. We pay attention and listen to cues constituted by time, space, and history. Our work rests on our connection and our mutual trust. This is a *relational labor* described by Susan Foster in the following ways: "our consciousness shifts from self in relation to group, to body in relation to body, to movement in relation to space and time, to past in relation to present, and to fragment in relation to developing whole" (Foster 2015: 402).

We can expect his relational labor to unsettle the expected. It will surprise its spectators as well as its improvisers. In the call and response of collaboration, each moment is new—each moment a potential surprise. Improvisation also invokes the otherwise and makes this present interesting as we live in it and make it an adventure into new things. This otherwise that rises from responsibility and the ability to respond within collaborative creation, is a work of honesty and imagination that involves greater risks for higher purposes. Responses invoke the unexpected and otherwise of improvisation and can generate what Richard Schechner calls "dark play" (2015: 392). Response(ability) does not mean keeping within expected responses. Rather, it is trusting a response will come that leads us to discovery, to the otherwise, and moreover into the terrain of dark play. It is the force of dissonance and dark play where subaltern imaginings are expressed. Here, discovery takes even riskier risks and where accustomed rules are broken for higher aims and more just rewards, and where the expected expands and is refigured toward larger horizons of what is possible. It is where responsibility breeds trust to take us toward higher aesthetic and political risks and where listening becomes a profound act of immersion.

Listening

The response(ability) and "relational labor" that improvisers share cannot flourish without deep listening. Jean-Luc Nancy asks the question: "What does it mean for a being to be immersed entirely in listening, formed by listening or in listening, listening with all his being?" (2015: 17). A foundation of improvisation and collaboration is the will and the pleasure to listen. Improvisation and devised performance requires a different kind of listening when working with others within the intensity of ethnographic performance, relational labor, and response(ability) and freedom. The collaborators enter a domain of attentiveness where they raise the stakes of listening with all their "being." Nancy states:

> What does *to be* listening, *to be* all ears, as one would say "to be in the world," mean? What does it mean to exist according to listening, for it and through it, what part of experience and truth is put into play? What is at play in listening, what resonates in it, what is the tone of listening or its timbre? Is even listening itself sonorous?
>
> (2015: 18)

Listening "with the whole body" (18) is to listen in the present; to listen here and now. To listen to what is before you—body to body—in this instance so you may hear the "soundings of otherness" (Fischlin 2015: 294). What we hear we hear now, even if the soundings are from the past or an imagined future—we are listening to them now. The emphasis on listening with the whole body as characteristic of present time is a profound sensory experience. Profound in that it is not simply the sense of hearing, but it is listening as a dynamic and complex layering of a multi-sensory engagement. For ethnographic listening in performance, we listen with our whole bodies that both begin with and exceed beyond the ears into memories and imagining from the field, of how certain sounds evoke images, smells, textures, and tastes.

If improvisation and devised performance "intensifies humanity" by "intensifying acts of communication," it begins with this need and pleasure of listening (Fischlin and Heble 2004). It is not until the improviser has been called to deep and alert listening that they can now make the call that then begs the response in the elaboration of turn-taking and dialogue that these performances require. Each moment is emboldened by listening anew, even within the familiar and timeworn. This reciprocal listening demonstrates an aptitude for an "ethics of co-creation" (Fischlin et al. 2013: 11). It is also the improvisers' ethics of trust that enables and generates response(ability) and risks and what Ellen Waterman calls "a democratic process, conducted in good faith" (Waterman 2015: 61). This democratic process not only supports risk-taking, but a freedom for all voices to feel invited and inspired by risks "without the dominating control and ego" that shut down the ability to respond where good improvisation thrives (61). Waterman states:

> The possibility of failure is always imminent, because the process demands such a high degree of self-exposure. Improvisation is most satisfying when the conditions of trust exist that allow participants to risk everything in the moment of performance ... It also positions improvisation as a site of dialogism-in-action, where we bring our personal histories and values into contact with others in a spirit of openness to change. What's at stake in improvisation, then, is nothing less than the possibility of personal transformation.
>
> (2015: 59)

Prompted by responsibility, listening, and trust this "dialogue-in-action" makes personal transformation possible because improvisers listen with their whole senses and their embodied techniques from worlds and experiences that are now carried forth into the improvisational moment. As improvisers fully attend to each other—in full body listening and trust—this personal transformation happens, as the call and response and the give and take, are manifest in "A small hint from a partner—a glace, a pause, a new or unexpected intonation, a movement, a sigh, or even a barely perceptible change of tempo" (Chekhov 2015: 173). Responsibility, listening, and trust are all contingent on the existential relationship to others. We are not ourselves without others. This familiar quote by Mikhail Bakhtin sums it up:

> Everything that pertains to me enters my consciousness, beginning with my name, from the external world through the mouths of others (my mother, and so forth), with their intonation, in their emotional and value assigning tonality. I realize myself initially through others: from them I receive words, forms, and tonalities for the formation of my initial idea of myself ... Just as body is formed initially in the mother's womb, a person's consciousness awakens wrapped in another's consciousness.
> (Bakhtin in Goodall 2000: 140)

For improvisational response(ability), listening and trust are reflected in the following example.

Two actors are each in an imaginary glass box on opposite ends of the stage. Neither can free themselves from the box without carefully listening to the cues of the other. A third actor, upstage between the other two actors, listens to the two downstage actors and stops them abruptly during their story describing how they were confined to the box with their added asides describing how they plan to escape. The actors take turns on cue from the interruptions of the third actor. The confined actors are describing why they are confined to the box as they are simultaneously describing how they plan to escape. The confined actors must keep talking until they are stopped by the third actor. Once interrupted, they must immediately stop and pause as they listen to the other confined actor take up where that story ended to continue what was said, and thereby bringing the story seamlessly to their own reason for confinement and their plans to escape until the third actor stops them and this pattern continues. They cannot stop their story of confinement or escape until the third actor is persuaded they have each told a full and compelling story. If the third actor ends the scene to early or too late a member of the audience may replace the third actor and take the seat.

The observances and questions around listening are as follows:

- How precisely did each actor listen to the other to combine the two distinct reasons for confinement, yet provide one seamless story? Provide specific examples.

- Did either actor appear not to listen to a significant detail of the confinement story of the other? Provide specific examples.
- Did each actor follow the escape plan of the other and include it seamlessly into their escape plan? Provide specific examples.
- Did either actor miss a significant detail of the other's escape plan that could have been included in their own? Provide specific examples.
- Did the third actor listen intently to the two actors for moments of strategic interruptions? Provide specific examples.

Energy

> All human relations are the result of the flow and circulation of energy—thermal energy, chemical energy, electrical energy, social energy. Social energy includes *affective energy* [emphasis mine], which can move between people. In our relationships, we constantly negotiate affective transfers. Just as we can train ourselves to be more attuned to photic, mechanical, or chemical energy in our environment, so too can we train ourselves to be more attuned to affective energy.
>
> (Kelly Oliver 2001: 14)

> One does not work on the body or voice, one works on energy (41). Theatre deals *not only in the compression of time, but in the intensification of energy* ... (27). There is considerable mileage in the idea of energizing the body through strenuous exercise on the principle that expenditure = investment, i.e., that energy begets energy. A valuable by-product of such work in the long term is physical stamina ... (27). What concerns me is not the generalized energy we get from such activities, but the particular way energy informs presence and movement on stage (28).
>
> (Callery 2002: 27–41)

The concentration of energy—focused and palpable—transfigures time within the parameters of a framed performance from the day in a dramatic life to the historical hero epic. The transfiguration of time is constituted by an "intensification of energy" that is physical and psychological in the way energy enlivens thought and action, mind and body. Energy is what makes the compression of theatrical time possible. Callery states "This is an energy that involves more than stamina and agility alone, but it is the connection between energy and awareness" (2001: 21). Energy as a mind–body connection and as a force that generates the nature of our stage presence is the source of the depth of our believability and the magic of being vastly interesting to watch. The qualities and measure of energy we bring to the stage—even if we are quiet, motionless, and still. It has been said that the hardest thing to do on stage is nothing; it is energy that makes this nothing compelling. Energy is infectious. It spreads across the stage to others, emboldening the tension and concentration among performers.

> Acceptance looks like a passive state, but it brings something entirely new into this world. That peace, a subtle energy vibration, is consciousness.
>
> (Tolle 2004)

> Energy moves in waves.
> Waves move in patterns.
> Patterns move in rhythms.
> A human being is just that ... energy, waves, patterns, rhythms.
> Nothing more. Nothing less.
> A dance.
>
> (Gabrielle Roth from www.5rhythms.com)

For improvisation, it is human energy that engenders rhythm and rhythm engenders human energy. This reciprocity is relational and affective; it is social and communal. These are the energy-rhythms resonating between actors, vibrating through the plot, arc, or sequence of the performance. They are the energy-rhythms pulsating across language, bodies, emotion, sound. Lecoq distinguishes between tempo and rhythm: "Tempo is geometrical, rhythm is organic. Tempo can be defined, while rhythm is difficult to grasp," He goes on to state, "It may be found in waiting, but also in action. To enter rhythm is, precisely, to enter the great driving force of life itself. Rhythm is at the root of everything, like a mystery" (Lecoq 2001: 32). Energy and rhythm invoke the quality of joy. Vsevolod Meyerhold states, "without an atmosphere of creative joy, of artistic *élan*, an actor never completely opens up" (Meyerhold in Callery 2002: 71). Callery states, "Grotowski used the same word, *élan* to describe the kind of upsurge of energy and spiritual drive with which actors should enter their 'line of physical action'" (71). Callery underscores the relationship between energy and concentration in "keeping absolute focus on the task in hand": Joy is what is being done in the now, in the present moment. Joy is more than play, but "the attitude of our work" (71). Callery describes the actor without *élan* in performance as being "unwatchable" and states, "an actor without *élan* in workshop or rehearsal is hard work for everyone else" (71).

The following is an example of action and rhythm in the space of stillness. Stillness is placed in contrast and combination with action and rhythm to demonstrate the profound importance of energy that is contained in stillness.

Three to four actors stand still on stage. There are four movement sequences or beats. There is music playing. First: The actors walk on stage. They stand still looking straight out into the audience without gesture, movement, or speech. Second: The actors move in free circular motions to the music. They stop on cue. They stand still with their profiles to the audience looking out at various corners of the stage. Third: The actors move with more speed and force in staccato rhythms to the music. They stop on cue and stand with their backs to the audience and their head in a three-quarter turn. Fourth: The actors move in slow, steady, smooth motions to the music. They stop and return to stand still looking straight out into the audience.

Questions and observations for this exercise include:

- What word—adjectives, nouns, verb—can be used for each rhythm or motion sequence? Describe why you chose a specific word.
- For each of the four sequences of stillness, how would you explain the presence of energy? What title of name would you give the energy within stillness for each actor and sequence?

Hope

Creative collaboration is the hope for what our collective imaginings will set loose. Hope is an "avatar of freedom—it is the imagination of freedom, the imagination of what the world might be like. Improvisation is a form of responsible hope" (Fischlin 2015: 293).

> Hope is also intimate liberation. It lives on under oppression in ways that ally it with intimate, sometimes unknowable acts of the imagination, flourishing even as it is constrained or deprived of enactment. It cannot be dissociated from spirit, conscience, creative being … Improvisation is a constant reminder that it is possible to hope—and to do so in response to conditions that seek to limit human potential and creativity.
>
> (Fischlin 2015: 293)

The quote shows us that we not only trust and hope for the improvisational call and response (through patterns and rhythms manifest in the collective contract) but this hope is also a hope toward a future. To perform ethnographic moments of improvisation, whether in the field or on stage, is to hope for consequential effects of significance and results.

Example of Trust: Two actors are sitting on a park bench feeding birds. They are given a topic of conversation from the audience and both actors must keep the conversation going without hesitation or pause for three to five minutes (or longer depending on the experience of the actors). The conversation must be evenly balanced between the two actors. They will trust the other to pick up and honor where they are taking the conversation with the hope it will lead to something unique, special, or interesting in some way and that will hold the attention of the audience (Figures 2.1–2.3).

Figure 2.1 Class improvisation. Performance studies students at Northwestern University improvise: "What to do with the tree?" Evolved into the trope of protection. D. S. Madison, photograph.

Figure 2.2 Class improvisation. Anthropology students at the University of Cape Town improvise a tableau of "What to do about the one who knows the truth?" D. S. Madison, photograph.

Figure 2.3 Class improvisation. Anthropology students at the University of Cape Town improvise a tableau on "The response to the song of the free bird." D. S. Madison, photograph.

Questions and observations:

- Was the conversation balanced? Did you ever feel uneasy that the actors were stuck or unsure?
- Did each actor honor what was offered by the other actor? Did you feel the actors trusted each other to respond?
- Did the scene fulfill—large or small—what is hoped for in an act of improvisation?

Examples

Warm ups: socially transmitted techniques and improvisation

- **Neutral position** is a beginning point—open and experimental—for movement possibilities. I use it here not to invoke the universal human or toward the disappearance of transmitted embodied techniques, but as a possible step into a composite body and to generate exploration of characters and physicality.
- **Articulation and framing of inherited embodied techniques.** This is similar to isolating moments through the neutral mask, because the focus here is on inherited and transmitted embodied techniques we deliberately and precisely re-perform them in workshop or rehearsal. We now have a conscious awareness of specific ways our body does things that we might heighten, mark, and carry over into the performance. For a workshop on embodied technique and practice, Jasmine Mahmoud,[2] sent the following call: "We invite embodied demonstrations to answer the famous question: What can a body do? Maximum duration is ten minutes. There is no minimum duration. Demonstrations may involve a single body or multiple bodies. Some possibilities that spring to mind: martial arts; folk songs or show tunes; dance improvisations; demonstrations of athletic prowess; monologues or performance art; displays of virtuosity or limitation or exposure or grace or failure; something only you can do with your tongue, elbow, spine, etc.; something tender; something weird. Our goal is to create a space in which a wide range of bodily capacities is demonstrated. Each may be impressive, exhausting, thoughtful, messy, beautiful, profound, or just plain silly. A wide range of tones and qualities is desirable."
- **Creating and re-creating movement phrases.** We emphasize movement phrases as comprised of elements, or micro movements and gestures, where there is a beginning, middle, and end forming a sequence of actions with a perceivable through line. Elements are constructed, deconstructed, and reconstructed to embellish, refine, or create new phrases.

- **Punctuation and marking.** As the movement phrases and cycles begin to evolve and encompass the performance, within these larger motions there are smaller moments or punctums that are instances, flashes, of extraordinariness. As we work and rehearse, we notice these instances, stop and interrupt this movement within a movement to remark and, most importantly, interrupt and embellish its power and significance. These are moments of "somatic impulses" to be secured and heightened.
- **The grid.** There are a series of straight lines, crisscrossing each other at 90-degree angles on the ground. Envision the floor as a giant sheet of graph paper. In the beginning, in each person's natural walk, the group travels along the lines of the imagined grid. Each person is free to move anywhere in the room within the grid. The group then moves along the grid alternating between fast paced and slow-motion walking. The group then moves in reverse. Each person in the group then takes two or three steps adding a half jump. This sequence is repeated. After the group is comfortable with walking along the grid in these varied formations, each person may choose to walk along the grid changing the sequence so that everyone is no longer doing the same movement. Everyone now is moving differently and making their own different choices while altering or adding their own gestures or movement style to the tempo, reverse, and jumps. As the movements get going and group members are moving differently and in interesting formations, someone outside the group will call "Freeze." After a few seconds, they will begin moving again. The movement is repeated with the freeze again. In the final stage, the group will continue various movement choices, within the grid, as each person now chooses when to individually freeze. In the final stage the group is all together moving along the grid at different walking tempos, in reverse, in half jumps, and freezes as they simultaneously add their own gestures and movement personalities or styles to the guidelines. The exercise is also very effective with vocal sounds and words.
- **Fluid sculptures.** Meyerhold, in his biomechanics, directed actors to sculpt themselves in three-dimensional space, moving like fluid sculptures, in non-verbal improvisation. Bodies generated meaning and story without dependence on words and dialogue. This goes back to the notion of movement progress: impulse to movement, to action, to gesture, to sound, and finally to word. Bodies moving through space, embraced by action and gesture, where sound becomes an outgrowth, symptom, and rhythm of the movement and where words are "dreamlike" and abstract has become a popular technique in excavating movement as well as physical narratives. This was beautifully done in a playback workshop. Fluid sculptures are dancing tableaux that represent a feeling, concept, or emotion. They are

one of the basic performance forms in Playback Theatre. After a memory or feeling is shared from an audience member, the actors step out one at a time to the center of the stage with a sound and movement, each reflecting an aspect of the teller's experience. After a beat or two, the next actor joins the first, connecting physically as one would in a three-dimensional sculpture (as in the machines game), adding a different sound and movement (a different texture), and embodying another aspect to the feeling or experience. This action continues until all the actors on stage are contributing to the sounding, moving sculpture. Once the last actor has joined, the sculpture continues moving for another couple of beats and then ends by all the actors stopping together and then acknowledging the teller with a glance. Fluid sculptures sometimes contain text as well as sounds (Fox 2010; Rowe 2007; Salas 1991).

Notes

1 From *An Acrobat of the Heart* (Wangh 2000: 167).
2 Jasmine Mamoud was a graduate student at the time, in the Department of Performance Studies. She lead the workshop on embodied technique and practice.

Chapter 3

Devised theatre

> I am interested in resonances, not continuities ... The work is about process. It is about the performers finding their way, bringing their distinctive gifts to the work and letting those gifts ring forward through the character or symbol or "figure," through the breath of the company. As Carlos is fond of saying, "Everything is already in the room."
>
> (Jones 2015: 14, 180)

Devised theatre can start with nothing and it can start with anything (Oddey 1994). Yes, it is about process, about the "breath of the company" discovering and exposing together and "finding their way" into a public performance. This is the collaborative process of making up the performance as you go, moment-to-moment, or scene-by-scene, with a group of people that share and shape their collective input into relational labor and collective production. Collaborators bring their varied ideas, expertise, and identities with them culminating their efforts into layers of content, form, style, and purpose to constitute the performance. The creative elements devisors choose from and negotiate are limitless, for example, images, themes, music, texts, paintings, movement, fantasy, sound, objects, and so forth. Although devised theatre is broadly defined, there are common threads that connect most work, as Alison Oddey states:

> Any definition of devised theatre must include *process* (finding the ways and means to share an artistic journey together), *collaborating* (working with others), *multi-vision* (integrating various views, beliefs, life experiences, and attitudes to changing world events), and the *creation* of an artistic product.
>
> (Oddey 1994: 3)

This "artistic journey" provides the opportunity for devisors to make impassioned performances that influence the circumstances, commitments, and concerns within their own lived experience and beyond. Because this work provides the opportunity for performance makers to reach across a range of art forms and methods, and because devised performance is continually and extemporaneously shape shifting these conceptualizations and collaborations, we must underscore the importance of process. Finding the ways and means to share an artistic journey is a process, like improvisation, that encompasses a structure, that is, a beginning, middle, and end, however linear or non-linear it may become. To develop this structure within our process, we must not shy away from the three "Rs": rules, roles, and responsibilities. When necessary, we may need guides and facilitators, with specific skills and talents, to enhance the process of collaboration and democratic decision-making as well as to maintain the schedule (149–151).

Ethnographic data and process

More aligned with adaptation than playwriting, ethnographers who stage their fieldwork data and experiences for local and/or global audiences will now charge the raw material of empirical moments into a performance frame that transforms those moments into a sensual, symbolic, rhetorical, and communicative event. The adaptation of fieldwork into an aesthetic performance is a deepening excavation of ethnographic data, methods, and analysis in specific ways:

First. Historic figures or significant individuals, whose words and actions were not present or accessible within the live encounters of field research, are now enlivened and represented through a range of staging techniques and aesthetic forms, making those identities present and accessible through the performance of letters, diaries, news clippings, memoirs, legends, gossip, and other textual, vernacular, and primary source material.

Second. The countless numbers of words that create both the encircling soundscapes and the silent reflections of fieldwork—from high theory to oral traditions—must be abbreviated into an "economic form" and "aesthetic shape" (Saldaña 2011: 70). From this range of in-depth interviews and participant observation to data analysis and field journaling, the abundance of words—heard and read—are now distilled, made more precise, coherent, and intelligible within the temporal framework of a performance event.

Third. Fieldwork is not simply a compilation of data to be analyzed, but it is now an opportunity to imagine other worlds and possibilities for human action both in its present moments and in its future (2011: 60). Performed ethnography is necessarily metaphoric, symbolic, and allegorical, opening the field site to alternative political, cultural, and social arrangement. This also makes it possible for devisors to imagine and illuminate the unspoken and hidden sub-texts happening in the field to inform and affect the lifeworlds of local interlocutors as well as the world views across public audiences.

Fourth. The performance, particularly when it is within the field site, becomes a means of communal participation, healing, and advocacy. Devisors, comprised of community members or others who form an integral part of the ensemble, are opening communication channels of local knowledges and extended imaginings as they relate to their own living environments. Because the devising process requires collective invention through performative processes of experimentation and creation, local people are in command of their own stories and their own rhetorical power through the protection and effects of collaboration as well as the humanity and emotional force of a staged, public event.

Fifth. When fieldwork culminates in a devised performance, it becomes an expanded, interpretive layer of data analysis. Devisors are not only making an embodied performance, they are intellectually and theoretically asking questions, analyzing material, assessing information, and articulating assumptions. Devised performance is a collaborative method of embodied research through the transformation of field data into staged enactments. Devising is an epistemological journey where mind and body conjoin.

In summary, there is no singular or unchangeable structure or process for creating a devised performance; however, we may take up general principles, to be adapted and revised, to suit the needs of a performance or ensemble. Beginning with a deliberate process equips devisors with a map for their journey, even if the map changes to lead us down more unknown and uncharted pathways. Process provides a starting place for discoveries to evolve and collaborations to materialize with less frustration and time lost. Because each devised work is unique, and elements of the process will mix, blend, and reconfigure for the specific needs of an ensemble, the process requires ongoing substantiation and evaluation. Devised performance is wonderfully messy; more reason to embrace process and principles so the messiness is knowledgeable, playful, and generative rather than gratuitous, discouraging, and disappointing. Offered here, in four stages, is a synthesis of sorts for devised methods.

Suggested stages for devised performance

Stage one

> It is in this sense creative individuals live exemplary lives. They show how joyful and interesting complex symbolic activity is. They have struggled through the marshes of ignorance, deserts of disinterest, and with the help of parents and a few visionary teachers they have found themselves on the other side of the known. They have become pioneers of culture, models for what men and women of the future will be.
>
> (Csikszentmihalyi 2008: 125)

The starting point for a devised performance may vary from: (a) an individual or director, with a pre-determined topic or idea, wanting to devise with a group of people that are known or unknown to them with no determined opening date; (b) an established ensemble or company of devisors with a topic in mind and a scheduled opening date; (c) an ensemble or individual wanting to do a devised work with no determined topic or opening date; and (d) or combinations of the above.

Whether individual or group, and wherever you start from the circumstances listed above, the beginning stage is most often focused on information gathering that leads to further discovery of your *subject* or *topic*. Because passion and commitment are prerequisites in the research and exploration of your topic or subject, it follows that deep listening, shared support, and collaborative encouragement are also foundational.

If you are an individual, preliminary research on your own is most helpful before you meet with a possible ensemble to gain their interest and trust. If you have a topic in mind, you will not only need to describe yourself, your experience, and your approaches to collaboration, but you will also need to provide preliminary information on the topic: why you think it is especially suited for devised performance and how you envision staging. Providing sufficient context and background will begin communication and provide insight into who you are, why you are bringing them together, and how all of you might begin this process together. Keep in mind for this first meeting you will have preliminary research so your potential collaborators will have a basic understanding of you and the topic to decide to join or not. Once they have made the decision and you are now an ensemble, then the more layered, nuanced, felt-sensing, and embodied research begins through the collective sharing of textual materials, audio/visuals, fieldwork experiences, the explorations of improvisation, and so forth.

A schedule is needed. Because time is limited, organization is essential. To begin, discuss and form a consensus of the group's goals and objectives. It is best to determine a rehearsal schedule around specific objectives prompted by questions. For example:

- How many weeks are needed to rehearse from the first meeting to the opening performance?
- What are our collective objectives for each week or at each stage of our rehearsal schedule?
- When and how shall we regularly evaluate our objectives relative to our schedule?

Performing ethnography and stage one

Techniques for generating ideas are essential during these first stages. One method for generating productive and stimulating ideas takes the form of a communal idea board (Rohd 1998). The board involves the following: (1) Everyone contributes questions and ideas to form a visual image in the form of a simple list or enumeration, a collage, a mind map, or a cluster tree. The point is that all questions and ideas are arranged in a way for everyone to see as well as to compare, contrast, and invoke collective responses.

The subject of water

Water as life	Poverty and water	Water ecology
Human body as water	Race and water	History of water
Human qualities of water	Ownership of water	Water magicians
	Water as property	Water workers
Water as consciousness thinking and feeling	Water as profit	Poetics of water
	Stolen water	Water as beauty
Water justice	Hidden abodes	Language of water
Water democracy	Water disease and Guinea worm	Water and love
Water as human right		Water as performance
Capitalism and water	Spirituality of water	Water as destruction
Water wars	Respect for water	Water as feeling
Globalization and water	Water rituals	Water as light

(2) Depending on the number of members, the ensemble may divide up individually or in small groups for questions and ideas to be contemplated and refined in more depth. Within an assigned time-period, members come back together for the ensemble to respond, synthesize, and refine their ideas and questions. This may lead to open sharing and discussion or turning the ideas into an added layer of creative forms such as book or song titles, a six-word story, a sketched image, and more.

Song titles

Water, Hear Me Pray
Water is the Boss of Me
Disrespect Water/Disrespect Me
Water Love
Take Me to the Water
Magic Water Man
Thirsty and Water Gone for Good
Water Dance

Book titles

Water Wars and Stolen Lives: Who Owns Our Water?
Political Economy of Water in the Quest for Thirst and Riches
Climate Change and the Disappearance of Water
Water and the History of Migration
When Water Gets Angry: Disturbing the Ecology of Earth and Water
Water as Poetry: The Language of Water across the World
Water Rituals and Rites: Water as a Human Right
Water and Desert: Climate Change and Human Will

Six-word stories

Water prays for our protection today
Steal my water be cursed forever
Water brought love yesterday and returned
Water washed earth then beauty came
Water dancer smothered the rain thieves
She spoke water and it rained

48 Embodied technique and practice

My water body healed your pain
Hear the water speak forgotten stories

(3) If sharing postings and this level of creative forms produce even more ideas, the ensemble may decide to create a second visual posting to further concretize topics as well as formulating their collective goals and purpose. This visual board may take the form of a synthesis of the initial boards and postings and look more like a mosaic or collage of words and images in an admixture of shapes, forms, texts, colors, and impressions.

Improvisation in stage one: building concepts, ideas, and topics

As an alternative, or in addition to collective postings, to generate initial ideas, the group might employ improvisation to further enhance discussion and to put more embodied action into topics and concepts. Improvisation also allows the group closer insight into various performance abilities and styles as well as

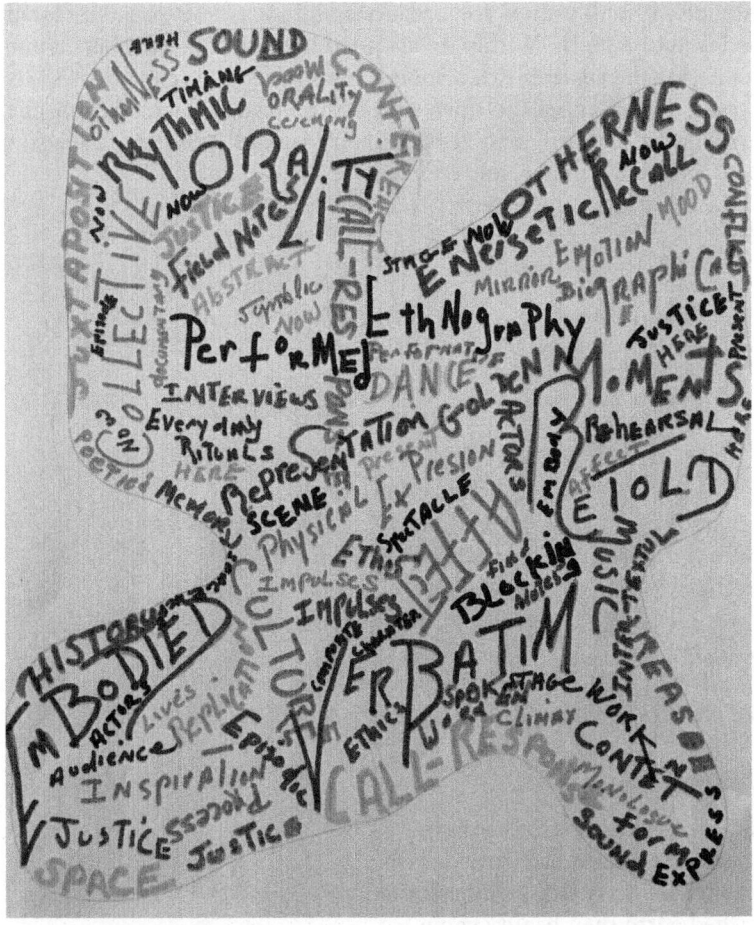

Figure 3.1 An example of a word cloud reflecting concepts, methods, and sensations related to performed ethnography.

Devised theatre 49

Figure 3.2 A word cloud reflecting intersections of performance, technique, communication, and ethnography.

creating stage pictures of topics and how these images can evolve into story and movement to make performance scenarios. Pre-production improvisation adds in discovering various methods and techniques that group members might not otherwise share or know about each other as well as clarifying their collective purpose, fine tuning the topic, formulating parameters of the work, and identifying alternative research forms and locations.

The following are prompts from popular improvisation exercises that are meant to be extended, revised, and multiplied as you discover new uses for them. Keep in mind these are improvisational seeds to sprout in various creative directions.

Image, sound, text[1]

In a small group, one person at a time "sculpts" their idea by positioning the bodies of other actors to create an image or tableau.[2] Each image becomes an interpretative response to a theme or idea. From the starting image, the sculptor may add other elements:

(A) One or more rhythmic movements to be contained within the image. The rhythm of the movement(s) is created through repetition, turn-taking, simultaneity, or various combinations.

(B) A word, phrase, or vocal sound that has been excerpted from a text is now added to the movement. The utterances are in coordination with the movement and can also be expressed through repetition, alternating voices, in chorus, or in various combinations.

(C) An object has been placed in a specific location at the beginning of the scene and ends up in a different location by the end of the scene.

Another member of the group repeats this exercise until each group member has taken their turn as a sculptor. Because each proceeding sculpture-movement-sound expression is different from the one preceding it—like a slideshow—the group will need to collaborate in creating transitions between each image to flow from one sculpture-movement-sound to the next. The transitions can be wildly creative by adding another layer of expressive sound, imagery, and movement to serve as flowing intervals between each sculpture-movement-sound tableau.

Taking shape[3]

Stand in a circle. One person runs into the center of the circle and makes and holds a shape representing an idea. They then utter a word, phrase, or sound to represent that idea while continuing to hold the shape. Another person runs into the center of the circle and adds a shape and sound to the first, while some part of both their bodies are touching and thereby making a new shape. They both hold the shape while a third person enters the center, adding another dimension to the shape. A fourth enters, adding to the three figures, until the whole group has formed one collective shape and sound that simultaneously represents their collective ideas.

Object, topic, and story

An object is placed on stage. The improvisers are given a prompt in the form of a word, concept, or topic, for example, "Homelessness," "Bullying," "The Joy of Living," "Mindfulness," "Poverty," "Coffee," "New York City," "War and Peace," "Cinderella," and so on, it can be any anything. One-by-one each improviser enters the stage, picks up the object and does something with the object that relates, in some way—directly or indirectly—to the prompt. Each improviser speaks for no more than twelve words[4] during their scene. The entire scene should take no longer than 60 seconds. Each improviser then places the object down anywhere they choose and exits the stage. The next improviser enters and picks up the object where it was placed from the previous scene and continues with each improviser saying and doing different things with the same object and the same prompt.

Next step sculptures[5]

Like image, sound, text, each person "sculpts" their idea. The other group members are "clay" and the sculptor positions them into a still image of the sculptor's idea. This is all done in silence. The sculptor places themself inside the image. It is important that everyone remembers their positions in the first image before the next sculptor creates the next image. Each person in the group sculpts their idea. Finally, the group flows through each of the images, from beginning to end, like a "slideshow." After the images, have cycled through the first time, the group will cycle through the images again, this time with each sculptor (still inside the image) stating a title for their image. The group holds the image for another beat and then transitions to the next picture.

***

The point here is to collectively determine your topic as well as to clarify, concretize, and/or extend the original topic. It is also a method of consensus in the complicated and often contentious task of developing and identifying the first steps of the devising process.

Stage two

> We analyzed and interpreted data cognitively, corporally and figuratively. In doing so, our understanding of our research project grew and seeped through our skin, into our bodies to be reassembled, restored, and re-inscribed. These enacted embodiments of each other were constructed assemblages through which we explored our ideas, thoughts and feelings about our research inter-subjectively.
>
> (Ackroyd and O'Toole 2010: 93)

It is during this stage where specific research criteria and information gathering are discussed and where this discussion leads to identifying and dividing up areas and points of interest for further exploration and future staging. Individuals or research partners will collect relevant information, insights, and inspiration on their area of interest. The next step will be to share their findings with the full ensemble. This is a show-and-tell moment that can escalate into an energetic exchange of stimulating ideas, thereby igniting a creative gold mine of things to include and consider for the final performance. Information and research sources may include a treasure trove of materials from film, photography, and paintings to newspapers, poetry, and fieldwork journals.

Performed ethnography and stage two

In staging field data, there are five domains we will take up in stage two:

First. When interviews are conducted by the director, adapter, or ensemble members, it is important to come to a consensus on the interview protocol and in determining key interview questions that will adhere to or invoke themes, topics, movements, images, and soundscapes to be developed in rehearsals and during the devising process (Saldaña 2011: 28). Key factors to consider during fieldwork, and the interview process, when communicating with field participants, interviewees, and interlocutors: (1) Describe to them the performance in as much available detail as possible as it relates to process, purpose, genre, and format. You may ask yourself: How shall I describe what we intend the performance to look like, our purpose in devising it, and who our anticipated audience will be? (2) Clarify consent. Make sure field participants understand their words and actions will be represented, in some manner, on stage. You will decide if consent should take the form of an institutional contract, tape recorded agreement, signed letter, verbal agreement, or if the form and nature of consent should evolve organically from the interactions and experiences in the field. (3) Inquire if there are specific concerns about the performance and how they will be represented. You will determine a protocol if participants should change their mind or if there is a substantial disagreement about the script or moving forward with rehearsals. (4) Including interlocutors and interviewees as collaborators in the process and as ensemble members in effectively contributing to staging and representation. The ensemble must develop methods and principles to assure that voices and opinions from field participants are heard, and the collaborative process is genuinely equitable. It is important that no one is made to feel less ownership in the project or less valuable than any other member of the group.

Second. Being mindful of storied experiences and identifying those collected stories, from interview data and field encounters, that are particularly conducive to inter-textual materials, such as biographical data, projected images, installations, symbolic movement, sound effects, and so forth. This means paying attention to various types of questions that invoke, emphasize, or comprise the following: opinion/advice, feeling/emotion, knowledge/skill, sensory/descriptive, background/demographic, behavior/action, story/once-upon-a-time, and so forth. One question that is intentionally meant to garner a specific response, may, instead, open multiple responses and combinations, but not necessarily the one expected. For example: the interviewer asks a question intended to obtain information on background or demographics; however, the interviewee does not directly or explicitly address demographics or background but, instead, reveals more about personal emotion, affect, value, and individual experience. The response to the question ends up being a story; it is a story about a time, place, value, affect, and experience. However, it is *no less* factual (relative to demographics and background) but more subjectively remembered and plotted. The answer provided demographic information that was constituted by narration. Demographic facts were inside the felt-sensing story, waiting to be excavated. This is not to say that all narration is neatly linear in a beginning, middle, and end sequence. Devisors take up how various genres of narration culminate in a range of performance choices by adding intertextual elements. These elements become theatrical tools for devisors as they continue to craft field stories and expressions from epic plots to small fragments.

Third. Waiting for devisors are countless documents and objects that comprise the zeitgeist of field spaces both vast and local. These documentary materials are evidenced and resonate in letters, diaries, vernacular expressions, local news, poetry, musical forms, news reports, architecture, photographs, film and video footage, legal documents, adornments, personal, domestic, public artifacts, and so forth. This is where we are reminded that ethnography is a sensory endeavor where we must also reckon with and be inspired by those instances of over-stimulus. It is the abiding ethos of fieldwork where we are surrounded by an abundance of elements that constitute spirit, mood, and affect inseparably from culture, knowledge, and history. Embracing a swath of documentary materials provides illuminating evidence and revelatory memories for words spoken in the field to be later theatrically contextualized on staged.

Fourth. Sharing "golden moments" from fieldwork.[6] As we begin to select verbatim excerpts, from interviews and field notes, to share with the group a few staging examples might include: composite monologues, experimenting with alternating phrases from choral poetry and song lyrics to spoken word and call–response sermons as well as juxtaposing multiple interviews with overlapping or rhythmic interview questions and interview answers.

Fifth. From verbatim transcripts and field notes, ensemble members begin to design movements and physical expressions from these textual materials ranging from literal movements that mirror or replicate textual data, on one end, and abstract, impressionist, and physical impulses, on the other. Improvisation enters again, at this moment, as method and inspiration for the research to move the body and set words into symbolic action. It is through improvisation where field moments and research data are turned into play and discovery with more affect and more energetically realized.

***

At the core of our process, as we move from stage two, we are reminded of improvisation as the groundwork of devised performance and that it is also a dynamic of information gathering. Whether you begin as an established company or as an individual (hoping to find a group of devisors to work with) this conjoining of topic, research, and improvisation is invaluable to moving our process forward to the next steps.

Workshop: stage two

PING CHONG: LIMITATIONS AND WALKING THE ROOM

In a workshop with Ping Chong, he emphasized that "within limitation there is a lot of invention."[7] The invention that limitation can invoke was demonstrated in the workshop by how we make (1) shapes in space; (2) sound in space; and (3) movement inside movement. Chong began with the act of walking, and it was through walking where participants, in Chong's words, began "breaking down elements to make a performance." It was on Ping Chong's workshop that I have based the following three exercises.

Exercise one. Sound and limitation: "walk the room". Walk naturally with hands down, face looking straight ahead, and, most importantly, listen to the sound and the pace of your feet and the feet of others in the room. Pay attention to the sound of footsteps throughout the entire walking exercise. First, walk through the space, not too fast or too slow, at a medium or neutral pace—everyone should be walking at the same pace. Walk simply and mindfully, listening carefully to the sound of your steps and others around you. You are walking in a relaxed alertness. Spend several minutes walking the space and listening. Next, walk along the walls, again at a medium pace, listening to the steps and the pacing. Continue to walk along the walls listening in a quiet, calm, relaxed alertness. Finally, walk in the center of the space at the same medium pace with everyone else. Make sure there is a balanced distance between each of you with no large gaps or clumps. Continue listening to all the pace and steps, focus on maintaining a unified pace. Keep walking the center, calm and alert, listening and feeling the collective walking as a collaborative performance.

Exercise two. In exercise two we will add the following elements to the neutral walk: (a) reverse; (b) fast; (c) slow; (d) levels; (e) half jumps; and (f) freeze.

First, the group will begin neutral walk and then turn and walk in reverse. Continue walking in reverse at a medium pace, paying attention to the space around you while listening to your footsteps and the footsteps of others. The workshop or group leader with then call "forward" to signal the change from the reverse walk to a forward walk. The command will alternate between "reverse" and "forward" with everyone still paying attention to the sound and space around them. Second, after the group is relatively comfortable with "forward and reverse," you will now add "fast" and "slow." Alternating all four choices with a combination of directions, for example, some walk fast forward, some walk slow forward, some walk fast reverse, and some slow reverse. Walkers are instructed to change within these four combinations, still mindful of the sounds and spaces between them. Third, freeze is added to the combinations with differing combinations of walkers freezing at certain moments (one person freezes; two or three will freeze; all freeze, etc.). The calls of forward, reverse, fast, slow, and freeze create interesting movement compositions especially when walkers are paying attention to the sound and space around them. As you are walking, your face always remains expressionless. Finally, levels and then half jumps are added. The result is a performance where combinations, contrasts, and alternations of all these elements constitute a lively and interesting movement composition where contrasting elements, by individual walkers, are embodied in open space, along the walls, in the center, or in combinations of the three.

Exercise three. A group will be given time to make a performance (the time for preparation depends on the skill and experience of the group and the length of the rehearsal or workshop). This assignment can be adjusted or revised to meet the needs and purpose of participants. From the elements of forward, reverse, fast, slow, levels, half jumps, and freeze, create a movement piece adding a compilation of sound, gesture, and quotes from your field data. The key is to compose these various walking elements to accompany words and sounds from the field, putting excerpts from field data in motion through the design of bodies moving in space. With the walking exercise, you are experimenting with movement, sounds, and words that may include music, added sound effects, and more layering of word and phrases. This exercise invites you to focus on sequences, phrasing, simultaneity of movement and text, contrasting movements using starts, stops, and tableaus, and how all this enhances moments and impressions from the field.

Circle story[8]

A collective story is created as one person after another adds one word at a time (including "a," "and," "the") building toward a sentence, then into a beginning story, developing the dramatic middle and, finally, the end. Hannah Fox offers another form of the circle story in the "cliff-hanger paragraph." This can also be done after the group has warmed up from the one-word story. In the cliff-hanger, each person begins to tell a brief story then cuts it off in the middle of a sentence. Fox provides this example: "They came to the bottom of a very large mountain and suddenly heard" (Fox 2010: 109). The next person continues from the cliff-hanger and then cuts their story off. This continues full circle with the story ending in a cliff-hanger. The third version of the circle story is what Fox calls the 1-2-3-4-5 formula. The first person says one word, the next person adds the next two words, third person adds three words, and so forth. After the fifth person adds five words, the next person goes back to one word or down to four words. When I have done the three renditions of these circle stories with ethnographers, each person draws from their own fieldwork encounter to build the story. Everyone adds their different field experience to the circle while still composing an intelligible and interesting story.

Better to hear you with!

This is another storytelling exercise from Hannah Fox that is particularly useful for ethnographers. The listener stands between two storytellers, one on the right and the other on the left of the listener Three people stand in a line where all three are facing the audience. Together and on cue, the storytellers tell their different stories to the audience, simultaneously at the same pace and volume. The middle person listens for as many details as possible from both stories. After a minute or two, the presenters stop, and the listener tells the audience what they heard from the storytellers. This exercise is a wonderful way of sharpening attention and listening skills as well as practicing how to refine and condense field stories and experiences. It is also useful in thinking about how this exercise can be revised and redesigned for staging overlapping and simultaneous narration.

* * *

With the topic decided, research guiding ideas, and improvisation putting flesh on the bones of embodied process, we can now move to stage three of more focused rehearsals, drafting the performance, and developing the script or score.

Stage three

> By devising and improvising around particular stories, events, and characters, the spoken word was transformed from being the story of a character into a multi-layered text of many characters, some changing from historical stereotypes to contemporary representations. ... The performance was in parts biographical, epic, naturalistic, and occasionally expressionistic, all contained in a flexible episodic storytelling framework. It accommodated other expressive forms such as music, dance, poetry, re-enactment and multi-media. This resulted in an interdisciplinary, integrative style that utilized the creative skills of collaborating artists and of members of the community. The approach integrated intensive rehearsals with moments of reflection on work in progress. Thus, both our thinking and doing were subject to change. Reflection was critical to the creative and social process and included how the team worked as a group as well as what this said about the team and the nature of the project.
>
> (Ackroyd and O'Toole 2010: 178, 180)

> I noticed that most of the ethnodramas I've read have been written in such diverse dramatic and theatrical forms as the revue, rant, radio drama, performance art, story theatre, reader's theatre, participation theatre, simulated lecture, and ritual. It's a bit ironic that slice-of-life scripts about human social reality, constructed with the conventions of realism or naturalism, are quite few.
>
> (Saldaña 2011: 207)

Performed ethnography lends itself to far-reaching inter-textuality in the multiple forms and varied theatricalities it takes up. The joy of adapting "slice-of-life" performances is that in the very act of adaptation you are not confined to one genre but open to the infinite possibilities of how to signify, (re)present, and shape life.

It is during the third stage of rehearsals, where characters, content, form, and style begin to take shape as well as the overriding performance concept. This is an intensive collaborative phase where the ensemble works in an exchange of shared direction and insights and/or away in groups with specific prompts and themes to bring back to the ensemble for refinement and elaboration. Now, we are moving toward a score or final script. This is also the stage where site specific performances move their rehearsals to the physical space or visual environments where the work is ultimately presented. Although it is not always possible to work on site at this stage, considerations and alternative adjustments should be worked out now.

Performed ethnography and stage three

It is at this stage where we begin to identify the implications and subtext of our data. We bring to the surface, to conjoin and juxtapose, the many conversations across field sites of ensemble members. Our collective data now takes up dramatic form. We rehearse and improvise a range of field interactions. We turn toward the expressions, sentiments, and embodiments of interlocutors to begin designing a collaborative score. We pay special attention to how all this is constituted through dialogue and dialogic encounters. Adapting and devising dialogue can be particularly challenging. Johnny Saldaña offers suggestions for staging cross-cutting dialogue, purposeful banter, and choral exchange. In *cross-cutting dialogue*, voices shift variously through interconnecting expressions, points of emphasis, alternating patterns, rhythms, contrast, and so forth. The questions become: What unique vocal arrangements can be discovered across our collective voices? How does cross-cutting affect and amplify our field data? *Purposeful banter*. The challenge is to transcend two people who appear to be engaged in light-hearted teasing or romantic flirting into a compelling and thoughtful exchange that is laden with serious and consequential implications. The questions become: What is revealed in the exchange? What are the specific elements that make the exchange compelling relative to attitude, disposition, tension, secrets, circumstance, revelation, values, and so on (108). *Choral exchange*. Here we add to cross-cutting and highlight a multiplicity of voices as they form varied arrangements of individual and collective expressions. Saldaña explains:

> The effect is a cascade of multiple thoughts and impressions, used most often to highlight the diversity of possible perspectives about an issue, at other times, the technique can be used purposefully for dramatic effect when the rapidity of utterances creates a sense of ironic juxtaposition, comic cacophony, or surrealistic chaos. Think of choral exchange as a form of *vocal collage* that provides a heightened sense of omniscient insight about the characters or issues for audiences.
>
> (Saldaña 2011: 109)

This "vocal collage" can take a variety of forms and it reminds of how the voice and voices in combinations can offer a range of special effects and sonic imaginings. Ethnographic dialogue is more of a triad or culmination of choral voices, bodies in motion, and field sounds and words. We work toward an alchemy of balance where movement makes words more heartfelt and interesting at one end while words make movement more heartfelt and interesting on the other.

In these final stages of devising, we are beginning to see and feel what the show will be. Continuing to develop the performance through ensemble sharing and improvisation, we now begin to finalize the script or score. This stage concretizes the overall direction of the piece, orders the segments, scenarios, scenes, and, if needed, sets the storyline. The score will note the content of each scene to submit to the costume and light design. We are nearing the end of rehearsals that determine the style, movement, characters, figures, concept, cues, and script. After this stage, rehearsals are less about discovering new ideas and materials and more about run-throughs of determined ideas and materials. Devised performance is always a journey of creation and experimentation, so your run-throughs are still flexible and open for certain changes. We know new insights often come after a show has opened, whether it be a comment from the audience or a revelation or observation from the actors or director. We do not need to resist all changes in the final stages; sometimes they can make profound improvements. But these changes are small and nuanced rather than foundational and structural. Too many changes can leave members feeling nervous, frustrated, and off-balance. Feeling open to improvement is one thing, but feeling nervous about someone upending weeks of foundational work is another. As we end stage three, the passion and commitment in scripting a devised performance over time must be balanced by reasoned consistence on one end and reasoned changes on the other. There are always exceptions to almost every rule in devised performance but hopefully they are by consensus and necessary. As we concretize the performance into a script form, we are made more aware of the many aesthetic and theatrical dimensions that encompassed our devised work.

> We used a range of performance techniques including improvisation, character development, role play, symbolism, manipulation of dramatic elements, scriptwriting and rehearsal processed to explore and transform verbatim data. Space, contrast, conflict, climax, timing, tension, mood, rhythm, sound, symbol, focus, and language were used to provoke intellectual and emotional responses in the audiences. Rather than relying on a reading of the selected verbatim text, as performer-researcher we manipulated the space, the actors and dramatic elements to construct an interpretation of the data and our research findings through our theatrical text.
>
> (Ackroyd and O'Toole 2010: 91)

This culmination into a "theatrical text" can be summarized in three overriding features:

First. We now know how the show looks and feels. We fine tune the ways specific ethnographic elements generate and constitute dimensions of embodiment, representation, and aesthetics, for example, oral histories that unveil the biographical and autobiographical; storytelling frameworks that capture the epic in content and the episodic in form, presentational styles that embellish elements of naturalism while juxtaposing moments of expressionism; intercutting music, dance, sound, multimedia, interactive-installation, and more.

Second. We attend to how the assemblage of ethnographic elements are now plotted into a format that has evolved into a performance collage that is simultaneously in keeping with theatrical revue, cultural and quotidian ritual, dramatic episode, rhetorical custom, and more.

Third. The script becomes a docudrama from creative collaborations that are inspired when fieldwork becomes the source material for devised theatre that is in keeping with the techniques of physical theatre where "the paradigm of progressing" evolves from "impulse to movement to action to gesture to sound to word" (Callery 2002: 8).

The following are thought questions for stage three that can be amended for your specific purposes:

- What is this performance about?
- How do we want our audience to feel as they witness different moments in this work?
- Who is our audience?
- How did we both attain and revise our goals and objectives?
- What is the subtext and underlying thread or current throughout the work?
- How are the source materials, that is, interviews, field journals, research data, and so on, serving the work and how is the work serving the source materials?
- How can we describe what our performance did?
- What discoveries did we make?
- As we are mindful of our devising process, what discoveries have we made about working together relative to the purpose and effectiveness of the performance?

Workshop: stage three

Picture map[9]

Select a story or theme from interview data and transpose it into a drawing—sketch or colors—that represents a visual story or picture map. Create a staged replica of the picture map by adding movement and words as bodies move across the replicated scene to plot the story with dialogue and movement.

The flowing phrase

The group will compile a series of words, phrases, or sentences based on discussions and personal sentiments expressed by the ensemble. The compilation will take the form of poetry, prose, or narrative that reflects a particular theme. The compilation is divided into segments where each segment is choreographed into a specific group movement. The movements may range from literal replications, abstract associations, symbolic or metaphorical interpretations, and so forth. After all the movements are choreographed for each segment in the compilation, a moving wordscape is developed. The wordscape may be sung, spoken, or sounded in a combination of vocal and movement arrangements with movement and text reciprocally punctuating each other. The group will begin the movement wordscape on one side of the stage area and end on the other. It should feel like a flowing trajectory of movement and words.

Descriptive and expressive scene

The group constructs a seed or outline from the devised themes. The outline is performed in two styles: (a) literally/descriptively and (b) symbolically/suggestively. For both the literal and symbolic performances, the group will have only two to three lines in the beginning, the midway point, and the ending. The seed of the plot is fleshed out and expanded through the two different styles and key textual features that will be expanded and polished as rehearsals progress.

Scene with objects

A seed plot or outline is now developed into a scenario using an object. This is an improvisation that is first done in complete silence. It includes three beats: first, an object is found; second, the actor discovers how the object can be used or a purpose it serves; third, the object is taken away or lost; fourth, the actor(s) create an ending for the scenario. This is a story that builds toward a clear beginning, middle, and end. After the silent scenario is performed, and the beats are established through the improvisation, the scenario will be repeated. The second time the actor(s) will add words and texts from field data.

In summary

> Jazz encourages an experience that is beyond the expectation of linearity (fixed) and a mechanized timelessness (predictable), and moves into a now time that is relational (improvised) and body-centered (vulnerable).
> (Jones 2015: 11)

The processes and stages of transforming field data into devised performance are an experience comparable to a jazz aesthetic. This "now time" that is all at once relational, vulnerable, self-sensing, and improvised, forms key ingredients that inspire devisors and bring forth the performance. From stage one to stage three, there is no perfect, fixed, or complete rule that devisors cannot adjust or improvise to their own needs and purposes. And, again, please take them for yourself and make them useful to you. What is outlined here is more akin to prompts and principles to be used as tools for your work. This brief summary serves as key take-away points for this section:

First. The devising process strives to meet the goals, resources, talents, and intentions of its idiosyncratic devisors as it thrives on flexibility and spontaneity. The stages are to be cut, pasted, and inserted into whatever is most useful for the group and the work.

Second. Devisors have limited time, therefore, flexibility withstanding, it remains important to create a rehearsal schedule that is in conjunction with your collective goals and objectives. This also means to mark key deadlines for your set design and the written cues for the sound and light designers as well as media segments.

Third. During the beginning stages of research, your independent findings, conducted with partners (if not through ensemble sharing), are then brought back to the full ensemble for discussion, brainstorming, and collaboration. How the research will be edited, adapted, and translated into a performance is most effective through question techniques, communal posting, and improvisation.

Fourth. The script is developed during a designated rehearsal span of discussion, play, discovery, experimentation, and improvisation. As improvisations develop, devisors will begin to mark what they want to keep, cut, and revise—placing scenes and beats into sequence—like the editing process for authors of written drafts (Saldaña 2011). The difference is this editing process is accomplished through collaborative movement—feet moving in space with others across the floor—with your whole body in rehearsal. Gradually, you are forming your script during rehearsals by scoring your blocking, movement sequences, images, sound, vocals, dialogue, and so forth (Figures 3.1–3.3).

We will now turn from the general process of staging devised performance to the special significance of movement. The next section takes up specific movement techniques that will guide and enhance our physicality work.

Interview with Honey Pot Performance

Honey Pot Performance describe themselves as a creative Afro-diasporic feminist collaborative committed to documenting and interrogating fringe subjectivities amidst the pressures of contemporary global life.

Honey Pot Performance enlists modes of creative expressivity to examine the nuances of human relationships including the ways we negotiate identity, belonging and difference in our lives and cultural memberships. Dismantling the vestiges of oppressive social relationships is part of the work. Through

Figure 3.3 Class improvisation. Devising variations of fear in the woods in formations of lines and levels. D. S. Madison, photograph.

Figure 3.4 Class improvisation. Cape Town. Devising the idea "which history is inside the book?" D. S. Madison, photograph.

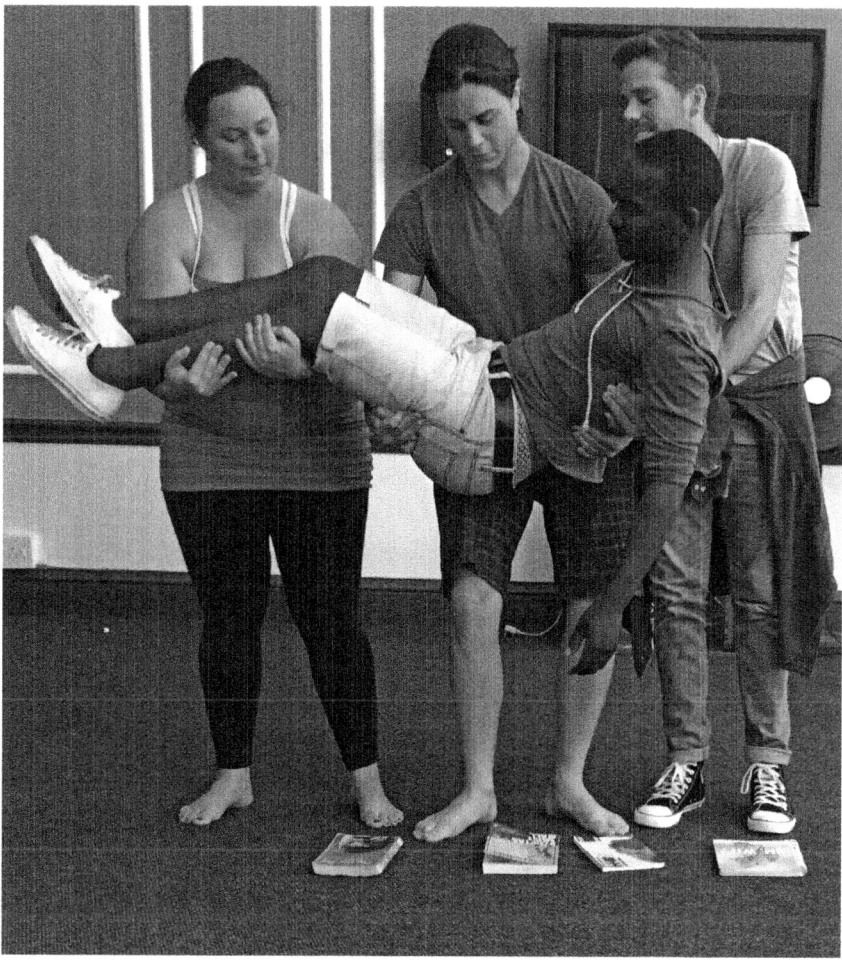

Figure 3.5 Class improvisation. Cape Town. Carrying a truth of history. D. S. Madison, photograph.

critical performance, public humanities programming, and deep community engagement, we emphasize everyday ways of valuing the human.

> Following in the footsteps of cultural workers such as Zora Neale Hurston, Beryl McBurnie, Pearl Primus and Katherine Dunham, Honey Pot Performance forefronts African diasporic performance traditions. We draw upon a central notion found in performance studies, Black feminist discourse and sociology: non-Western, everyday popular and/ or folk forms of cultural performance are valuable sites of knowledge production and cultural capital for subjectivities that often exist outside of mainstream communities.
>
> Honey Pot Performance[10]

Honey Pot interview with D. Soyini Madison, Meida T. McNeal, Abra M. Johnson, and Felicia Holman

Meida: Our relationship and the way that we came into performance as an ensemble has been organic and improvised. I think it began with friendship. We were all performers in different ways and realized we wanted to make something together. Our first creation was Bag Ladies. It was an improvisational process. We literally sat together in my living room with a bottle of wine and recorded conversations about books, poetry, and other various readings that were meaningful to us and we brought up question around Black diaspora belonging as well as our ideas and experiences about place and space. This way of talking together, sharing, and exchange is integral to our process. We've recorded many conversations, edited them, and built a performance.

Soyini: Your performance of Bag Ladies arose from your conversations.

Felicia: We are uber Erykah Badu fans. She is our matron saint. Around that time her song "Bag Ladies" was magical for us. We were thinking about this idea of baggage and the narratives of our respective and collective identities in the USA and in the Black diaspora. We wanted the performance to reflect Erykah's song and the diasporic sense of baggage.

Abra: Improvisation is this kind of structured unstructuring. It's making room for other forms of engagement outside of us. Through improvisation we are consciously thinking about who is going to be watching, what might their response be, how can we have a space that's open for them to participate? Improvisation is part of our process of creating work, but it also becomes the performed work, the final performance. But, our improvisational work is also continuously emerging before our audiences. One example is the hugs at the beginning of our performance of Juke Cry Hand Clap. An improvisational moment emerged in the way we began that piece.

Felicia: Juke Cry Hand Clap was our 2014 feature.

Abra: At the beginning of that show, we literally go out into the audience and start to hug people.

Soyini: What inspired that improvisational moment?

Abra: Being House-heads[11] here in Chicago, and from stories we accumulated in workshops and interviews, we knew that in House music spaces people were hugged. People received love and tolerance in House spaces they were not necessarily getting anywhere else. And so we greeted each other that way. When you go to a House party, you see people you haven't seen for a while and most people know each other or come from different camps that know each other. So, when you walk into a House party it's always a big "Hey!" with a big hug. We wanted to bring our audience into the reality of a House music space, and it was impromptu and

	people's responses were: "Are they about to come and touch us?" That was really a strong moment
Abra:	*In the beginning of the show, we're dancing, we're remembering the stories, and the House spaces, and then we suddenly stop and we just hug people. It actually ruptures and disrupts that flow of the moment.*
Meida:	*It broke that fourth wall*
Abra:	*The more scripted our work, the more we start to improvise*
Soyini:	*Yes, it goes back to that idea of the structuring unstructured nature of improvisation that Abra mentioned.*
Felecia:	*As Afro-diasporic Afro-feminism, there's this continuum, this lineage, and that's a through line in our work as well. We are privileged to have this legacy. You can see it in something like the "dozens,"12 being able to "riff" or you "picking down" when "I'm putting up." This legacy is also reflected in proximity, eye contact, tone of voice. This is all raw material and inherently improvisational.*
Soyini:	*These are embodied techniques of improvisation transmitted through Black cultural practices and performances of insult, boasting, joke and storytelling, and so much more. Tell me about your rehearsal process.*
Felicia:	*We have open rehearsals. We have public "works in progress" showings. We don't necessarily have the closed studio practice. We open our process to incorporate community feedback that brings a visceral understanding and engagement with the work. This is an added layer to our improvisational process. We begin with a template, conversational frame, or narrative to invoke a large opening for people to improvise.*
Soyini:	*You take collaboration and community seriously in extending your improvisational and collaborative process to community engagement and performance making. How do you balance or turn your more intimate or ensemble moments of improvisation to then open it up to more public involvement?*
Meida:	*With Juke Cry Hand Clap there were months we performed variations of flocking, because in House there are recognizable or common movements and vocabulary, but sometimes the emphasis is on the individual body. And so, we did a lot of following and flocking each other to spark pop-up movement qualities. These movements evoked memories, scenes, and stories of House culture, and made a future performance.*
Felicia:	*This is our experience of making art and loving art here in Chicago. House music and the House scene are our roots. All these ways House has fed us creatively and socially, we wanted to celebrate and document. Particularly in this epoch of pop culture where so much local meaning and invention is getting appropriated and erased. We wanted to make sure, from real authentic*

	female House-heads to say to the world: "Yo," this is our Chicago experience, and our experience is not just a vacuum, but it is a continuum. It is a valuable social practice.
Abra:	*Chicago House is such a critical expression and we recognize it as our own. House encompasses several generations, especially for people of color and LGBTQ people of color. House is the post disco era where Chicago begins to blend all these formative sounds into something contemporary.*
Felicia:	*For people who know this city, House is very much a part of Chicago's history. People talk about Chicago blues and jazz, but for a couple of generations of folk, you must also talk about House. So, for us who were born and raised, second- and third-generation House-heads, we were born and raised in this music and sub-culture that folks created before us. Bronx has hip-hop but for us it's House music. We were raised, steeped in House, and came into the realization that House was a part of everything we do, the way we talk, the way we dress, the way we look at stuff aesthetically, the way we identify with each, the way we have a certain consciousness about our Chicago identity. All of it is firmly rooted House subculture.*
Meida:	*We collected names of specific historical sites in Chicago, and we divided all of it into eight categories, social club spaces or anything connected to House venues where House is central to these spaces. The map cuts across the 20th century and you can see how the Chicago landscape changes, decade by decade. We combine places, stories, notable Chicago figures, and so forth (Figures 3.4–3.6).*
Felecia:	*We held monthly parties, and in our monthly parties we gathered information from the public. We posted big maps of Chicagoland.*

Figure 3.6 Honey Pot Performance: the mapping sessions.

Figure 3.7 Honey Pot Performance: the mapping sessions.

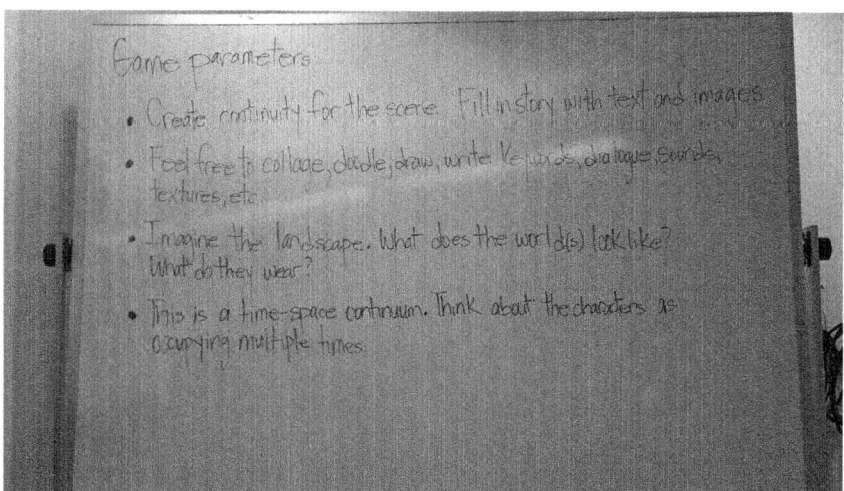

Figure 3.8 Honey Pot Performance: the mapping sessions.

	We included questionnaires where we were asking people about their experiences with House. Our monthly sessions were basically a workshop, but it was also like a party. They were held on Friday nights.
Meida:	*We also played House music to evoke that visceral House thing.*
Felicia:	*House music in concert with different themes. It was blues, House, and gospel.*
Abra:	*These were our mapping sessions.*
Soyini:	*Wow, you were also excavating and performing history. What was it like to be there in the mapping sessions?*
Felicia:	*We posted maps up on the wall with a series of questions that served as prompts: What is House to you? What was your first House party? What current events were happening at the time you were going to House parties? Do you still engage in House culture? How did House influence your style? What did you wear? What kind of hairstyles? How did House influence your mobility? What did you travel for House parties and music? What prominent people do you remember on the House scene?*
Abra:	*Literally, we took the city and broke it into wall-sized quadrants. We then took Post-it notes and asked people to write the places where they partied, or where family members partied, or anybody they could remember. They placed the Posts-it on the map.*
Meida:	*It evolved into a collective remembering. We offered another section where individuals could write stories of their experiences with House. And all this included music and dancing.*
Soyini:	*So, you really told the history of the city at these parties?*
Felicia:	*It was great! People posted their stories. Read them. It was all shared.*
Soyini:	*The stories were also maps? Narrative or story maps of House sub-culture?*
Felicia:	*Yes, and they also tape their stories to the wall maps, reading each other's stories marked by locations on the land map.*
Meida:	*This was not a conventional land map. They were small story maps of language, memory, and history, mapped onto the Chicagoland wall map with its quadrants*
Abra:	*Telling the social and political history of Chicago from the late 70s until now. We were marking those city spaces of our grandparents and parents who were migrants and immigrants to Chicago and the way they passed on their social spaces to us.*
Meida:	*It was a mirror of Chicago politics as well as the municipal codes that started to shape neighborhood demarcations and migrations into the city and from neighborhood to neighborhood.*
Abra:	*House was blossoming. Then, Mayor Harold Washington13 dies, right? And, then, there's this whole bunch of stuff—city politics— that starts to happen. Now, venues need liquor licenses. And, there*

	was the start of Cubs night games, right? So, when Wrigley Field started having games at night, everything in and around Medusa's began to change.
Soyini:	Medusa's was a teenage dance club and city-wide gathering for House-heads and House sub-culture located in Wrigleyville, Lakeview?
Voice:	Yes, and everything around Medusa's stopped catering to teenagers. Now it was all about people who had Cubs baseball tickets.
Abra:	That effectively begins to shut down, by association, so many venues and scenes for House many of which were also a concert space for House music.
Voice:	The venues either shut down or they change their format.
Abra:	We have the death of one mayor—Harold Washington, then an interim mayor, then the installation of a new mayor with a new focus, all within a five-year period. Within a five-year period, many of the spaces dried up and raids started happening.
Soyini:	So, you are creating this performance around the legacy of this music from beginning to end where people come into this collaborative space and share their history of House. Now, these community members are as much a part of the primary research as your own memories as well as any kind of textural or archival material. Okay. What happens as they are remembering their stories and putting them on the map board? It seems you are making yet another performance of those performances.
Felicia:	Yes, and that all becomes the source material that we take into the studio and build upon.
Abra:	That was Juke Cry Hand Clap.
Meida:	It is a similar technique with our current work: Masking Her. We have what we call Black Feminist Futures workshops. This is the name of a series of workshops where we had written up characters in an Afro-futuristic14 narrative. We hold these public workshops where we work in collaboration with community members to create characters and narratives.
Soyini:	This is your collaborative, improvisational process: creating public workshops to create public performances.
Meida:	We collaboratively blend stories—our stories and community stories.
Soyini:	So you all are like collaboration on speed? [laughter]
Soyini:	Yes, collaboration, on collaboration, on collaboration. So even after you collaborate, you collaborate with a wider public. Then you make a performance. Moreover, it seems that even within your final performances, the final product becomes an improvisational collaboration.
Felicia:	Yes. The process of Masking Her was so beautiful.

Soyini: *What made it beautiful?*

Felecia: *First, we call it Black Feminist Futures and people showed up. A core group of people who just kept showing up. And, we had such a wide age range, people from 20 to 80, men and women.*

Soyini: *Seeing people show up is a beautiful thing, especially intergenerationally and for that topic.*

Abra: *It was a once a month, six-month process, with six different workshop events. For each session we performed excerpts from our most recent work in progress. People would then break up into small groups and talked together. Next, they wrote responses to our performances.*

Feleica: *Before they broke into groups we offered prompts like: How would you describe the world of this character? What do they look like? How do they sound? How do they move? How do they meet? Questions like this.*

Abra: *But, in each instance we're focused on moving the story along. We're now at the point where we are gathering it all up to finish the story.*

Meida: *Yes, we bring all these stories and imaginings together and create one script world.*

Soyini: *And, once again you become facilitators and curators of collective stories, collaboratively and improvisationally. But with the Black Feminist Futures workshops, you are entering into a different genre of story, less on memory and history and more on imagination and speculation. Even though these different genres can never be totally different and separate they remain distinctive.*

Felicia: *Yes, this is our first foray into a speculative fiction format. We are excavating heroines and meta-heroines through these collective characters and how they navigate hostile and surreal environments. So, it's still rooted in what we know, but also much of what we don't know.*

Meida: *We began thinking about Masking Her by having conversations about our treasured writers and formative texts. We talked about the theories, fiction, poetry, and our personal philosophies that propel us forward and remind us that we will make it through the hardest challenges. We identified passages from these conversations and we each wrote a piece of fiction from a passage. And from the admixture of conversations and writings, we began piecing it all into a collage of sorts. We were contemplating what all these story pieces might mean.*

Soyini: *This process was clearly different from the story map and your existential connection with House music. Tell me more about how the workshops assisted in this process?*

Felecia: *I didn't read comic books or sci-fi or anything like that. But, with this kind of performance making, you can dream outside of yourself. The workshops really helped me put flesh on my characters.*

Abra: *Characters and the order of characters were formed from the workshops.*

Felecia: *As we shared the progression of performance there was an inherent vulnerability we bring to our process.*

Soyini: *Why do you choose this way? Why don't you all create it yourselves, and get it ready, and have it done?*

Felecia: *It is part of our agency as Afro-feminists, as Afro-diasporic advocates, that we create art that is a platform for ourselves and other creatives in a community and through community. I think that's really why we got together, not just that we love each other and love the work that we do, but we are all of like minds in that we have to advocate for public, collaborative work. And we risk vulnerability.*

Meida: *And, there's healing in the collective responses to our performances. In* Ladies Ring Shout, *we held weekly workshops for women of color who were feeling the pressures of the economy.*

Soyini: *This was during the awful recession. So many people were suffering.*

Meida: *Yes. During that economic downturn, we held the workshops as a creative means to deal with the pressure, poverty, and feelings we didn't quite have language for, or didn't have a safe space to express how messy and fucked up the economic struggles were for so many of us.*

Soyini: *How has political economy transformed your performance making?*

Meida: *The times are different, but in a lot of ways that's exactly what* Masking Her *is doing. It is opening up the space for people to use fiction, or speculative fiction, to express their feelings and transform those feelings into stories that heal. We are evolving into the next stage of whatever we are. And, we're trying to figure out what that is. It's an exciting moment to know that we spent all these many years building relationships, designing and devising processes, into what we hope will become, a more articulated, or codified method.*

Soyini: *But, right now if you could articulate what that codified method is becoming, how would you describe it?*

Meida: *I know it's something that's fluid and movable but it still has a spine to it.*

Felecia: *Experimental, intersectional, dynamic embodied storytelling. We incorporate critical performance, public humanities, and community engagement. It's very much about community-based techniques. I think you used the word democratic. I think that's pretty much what we're going for. Not that we don't trust ourselves to make work. But, really recognizing the responsibility of these bags that we carry, right? So it's another evolution of being a bag lady, right? So that we recognize that there are certain legacies we carry or that people will interpret no matter what we do. But we also*

	feel responsible to people who are generous enough to give us their stories. We're responsible to them. That is a way to stay connected to them and to bring them into the making of the work.
Abra:	*People feel really invested in our work. I saw that with* Masking Her, *but I also saw that with* Ladies Ring Shout. *People were there for us and with us. After being a part of that process, they turned up and showed out for us.*
Aisha:	*It is very much shared. We hear this in the feedback. We wouldn't be doing this for this long, openly calling ourselves Black feminists, if we weren't committed to community building. And even all the stuff, I don't like to say it: we endured.*
All:	*[Laughter] No, there was some endurance!*
Felecia:	*The women that came before us, women who created a space for us to be, to work, to create—we consistently go back to their words and work. I literally woke up at five in the morning thinking about Gloria Anzaldúa. I went through all my books, until I finally found that PDF, "How to Tame a Wild Tongue," in chapter five of* Borderlands. *It was written 40 years ago and it's still relevant for me right now in 2016. Still relevant right now to all the stories that we hear. I mean* Ladies Ring Shout *was about lack and about struggle under the economic recession. A good friend of mine who just got married, had her PhD, her husband at the time had his PhD, and they were living from house to house. They couldn't find jobs. They were homeless, but also ashamed. The amount of shame—saying it out loud—we can't admit it. It's so shameful to say that I'm broke. "I love what I do, but I'm broke; and this economy is terrible. All these people were going through this economic struggle with us."*
Abra:	*Having these conversations around economy, labor, value, shame, and saying to yourself: "Oh, I've done all the right things that's prescribed: I've been a good citizen, finished school, law abiding, blah blah blah, ... but I'm still broke and my future is precarious." It became a more expansive discussion about political economy and mobile homelessness, beyond our own demographic. It was a commonality of struggle across ethnicity and geography. It became an interrogation of nation and economy. This is what the performative project of* Ladies Ring Shout—*armed with Gloria Anzaldúa—was about.*
Aisha:	*But going back to your question about identifying as feminist. For me, my identity came from the model of my immigrant grandmothers, aunts, and mother who raised me. It was from growing up in a household of freedom fighters and being exposed to Harriet Tubman and Sojourner, Cecil and Assata. No one told me I should be a feminist. This is the identity I claimed for myself after being a young woman with these examples. It made sense to me.*
Meida:	*And performance makes it all real.*

Case study two: the digital in dialogic performance across two continents

Description

Through email correspondences and Skype, two friends began collaborating on an idea to bring stories about the human relationship to water, as a global phenomenon, into public view in the form of a transnational performance. Together, they adapted and directed a performance between Ghana, West Africa and the USA, North America. The performance evolved into a live-digital performance simultaneously viewed across West Africa and North America with audiences and performers interacting with each other in real time. The live-digital performance was presented in three parts. Each part was digitally recorded in both countries where the performance in one country was digitally integrated into the live performance of the other. Each of the three parts consisted of alternating elements of liveness, in the home country, with elements of the digital (live fed) in the partner country and projected on a screen. The three parts consisted of the following:

(1) Imagery of the six-word story. Stories comprising six words, from a range of experiences and perspectives on water democracy were collected and narrated alongside photographic images, of water scenes, from each country. The multiple stories were curated into digital snapshots or "postcards" where the photographs, accompanied by the six words, became talking pictures or storied images.
(2) Dancing the narrative. The six-word stories were followed by longer three- to five-minute narrative poems on struggles over water as a human right. The narrative poems were expressed through choral readings and dance. The dances formed an interpretive arch where movement underscored the choral reading from the beginning, middle, and end of the narrative poem.
(3) Exchanging audiences and exchanging water stories. At the end of the performance, both audiences were invited to share memories and feelings, evoked from the show, of their personal relationship and encounter with water as a human right. The idea was for audiences, across the Atlantic, to be witness to the responses of each other regarding the performance exchange as well as their cross-cultural and geo-political experience with water.

Process and contents of the digital-live performance

The script. The collaboration between John in New Orleans (USA) and Kofi in Tamale (Ghana, West Africa) began when they met at an international conference on water democracy. A friendship developed and the two decided that upon returning to their home counties, they would set a schedule to create a transnational performance about water as a human right. John and Kofi, through a combination of email, Skype, and FaceTime, outlined their script of three parts and decided on a set of three joint rehearsals through video conferencing and life feeds.

The rehearsals. The rehearsals consisted of single rehearsals (within the home country) and joint rehearsals (live streaming to include both countries). The single rehearsals focused on: (1) following the script outline; (2) devising and developing the three sections; and (3) integrating cues, pauses, stops, and starts for the interactive moments of live streaming with their performance partners across the Atlantic Ocean. The joint rehearsals focused on: (1) coordinating and setting up live video streaming between New Orleans and Tamale; (2) rehearsing interactive cues and collaborative performance moments with on-screen, international partners; and (3) perfecting the timing and fluidity of words, images, and movements across the distances of two different time zones, cultures, and mediums of live and digital interplay.

The show. Imagery of the six-word story comprised four intervals. Each country taking turns between the live and projected imagery. For example, Tamale began with a photographic image projected on screen of local people drawing water from a nearby pond with a voice-over of a six-word story "We reach for water and live." The Tamale performers were sculpted on stage to replicate the photograph. The Tamale performance with voice-over, screen projection, and with the Tamale actors' sculpted positions were all live streamed across a large projection in New Orleans, where the New Orleans performers also assumed the position of the Tamale photograph. The Tamale performers and audience were also able to see the New Orleans actors replicate the Tamale photograph on a smaller downstage. New Orleans then projected a photographic image of a flood scene from Katrina with the voice-over: "Floods cry out in angry waters," while the actors in both New Orleans and Tamale were sculpted on stage replicating the image. This section continued alternating images and voice-overs through live streaming. Dancing the narrative was more detailed in its interdependence between the international partners. For example, the New Orleans performers created a narrative poem depicting the relationship between the overflowing oceans, flooding, and climate change. In the choral reading, actors dramatically moved about the stage to underscore the arc of the poem and specific points of emphasis. As the poem was being dramatized in a choral stage-reading in New Orleans, it was simultaneously performed by dancers in Tamale. The dancers in Tamale were live streamed to a New Orleans audience and the choral readers were live streamed to a Tamale audience. Exchanging audiences and exchanging water stories. The length of the show was approximately one hour to leave time for a second hour of audience exchange between the two global cities. In this section, audience and performers, saw and heard each other as they shared stories and exchanged experiences of water from a range of perspectives, from privatization, trade policies, and poverty to climate change, water customs and culture.

Reflections

In reflection, John and Kofi felt the show was a success, but they were concerned about its sustainability and efficacy. They videotaped the third section of the audience exchange, but did not have an effective videotape of the first and second section of the interactive performance. They decided to re-stage the performance, adding suggestions and critiques from trusted audience members, colleagues, and performing artists from both continents, who saw the first performance and who were invested in the beauty and efficacy of applied theatre. A professional videographer was hired on both continents to produce two videotapes—from the perspective of a live Ghanaian audience and a live USA audience. Kofi and John hoped the video would serve as an example of what works and does not work in the intermix of digital-live, transnational, and collaborative theatre as well as some of the pressing issues circling water democracy and climate change. John and Kofi also understood that their collaboration was just the beginning. They felt there was so much more to explore that centers on the political, artistic, and technical possibilities of transnational, collaborative performance.

Notes

1 This is a rendition of Augusto Boal's moving sculptures.
2 The other actors are "clay" and the sculptor "molds" their bodies in several ways, for example: by touching and physical placement; explanation of what the image should look like without touching; demonstrating through the sculptor's own body; a volunteer demonstrating where the image can be repeated or replicated.
3 This is a popular warm-up that I'm specifically drawing from Viewpoints. See Viewpoints section.
4 Each ensemble may choose their own number of words that can be more or fewer than 12. I chose 12 because it seems to be the number that is most clear and precise without being too little or too much.
5 Hannah Fox, *Zoomy Zoomy: Improv Games and Exercises for Groups* (2010: 118).
6 Saldaña describes those reports from the field that are in some way memorable or extraordinary as "golden moments." He goes on to state: "I search for artful

moments, not just activism. And every time I go to the theatre I search for entertainment, not just meaning" (211). It seems that "golden moments" are those moments that are all at once artful and meaningful.

7 Ping Chong + Company creates theatre that crosses boundaries of identity, community, and form. The work encompasses puppetry, dance, documentary theatre, and other experimental theatre forms. While our projects explore a wide variety of subject matter, from a hidden genocide in Africa to class struggles in America to modernization in China to the massive displacement of refugees in modern wars, the common thread is a unifying commitment to artistic innovation and social responsibility. As an artist who has shifted between multiple worlds, identities, and communities, Artistic Director Ping Chong has honed a collaborative creative method that examines the fluidity of identity and fosters cross-cultural exchange. Ping Chong approaches theatre-making as a generative artist, working with a team to develop productions through an extended and organic multi-year process. Ping Chong + Company serves as an artistic incubator for the projects it undertakes and then seeks out producing and presenting partners to extend the range of its projects (www.pingchong.org/interdisciplinary-performance). This example is drawn from a workshop given by Ping Chong at Northwestern University in January 2014, where he described the capacity of limitations as a means for creative invention.

8 From *Zoomy Zoomy* by Hannah Fox. Hannah Fox is artistic director of Big Apple Playback Theatre. Fox leads dance and theatre workshops across Europe and Latin America. Many of the exercises in this section are drawn from *Zoomy Zoomy: Improv Games and Exercises for Groups* (2010). See bibliography. Fox is the daughter of Jo Salas and Jonathan Fox, the founders of Playback Theatre.

9 The picture map is a popular exercise in devising ethnographic performance see Johnny Saldaña (2011).

10 Honey Pot Performance is a creative Afro-diasporic feminist collaborative committed to documenting and interrogating fringe subjectivities amidst the pressures of contemporary global life. Honey Pot Performance enlists modes of creative expressivity to examine the nuances of human relationships including the ways we negotiate identity, belonging and difference in our lives and cultural memberships. Dismantling the vestiges of oppressive social relationships is part of the work. Through critical performance, public humanities programming, and deep community engagement, we emphasize everyday ways of valuing the human (http://honeypotperformance.com/about/).

11 House music (named "House Music" after The Warehouse club in Chicago where it originated in the early 1980s) is a style of electronic dance music that was developed by dance club DJs in Chicago that were influenced by early to mid-1970s dance music as spun by DJs in New York, and spread to Detroit, New York, and eventually Europe. House music is strongly influenced by elements of the early to mid 1970s soul- and funk-infused dance music style of disco. House music takes disco's use of a prominent bass drum on every beat and developed a new style by mixing in a heavy electronic synthesizer bassline, electronic drums, electronic effects, funk and pop samples, and reverb- or delay-enhanced vocals. The common element of house music is a prominent kick drum on every beat (also known as a four-to-the-floor beat), usually generated by a drum machine or sampler. The kick drum sound is augmented by various kick fills and extended dropouts. The drum track is filled out with hihat cymbal patterns on the eighth-note offbeats, and a snare drum or clap sound on beats two and four of every bar. This pattern is derived from so-called "four-on-the-floor" dance drumbeats of the 1960s and especially the 1970s disco drummers. Producers commonly layer sampled drum sounds to achieve a more complex sound, filling out the audio spectrum and tailoring the mix for large club sound

systems. House music is uptempo music for dancing and has a tempo range of between 118 and 135 bpm. Producers use many different sound sources for bass sounds in house music, from continuous, repeating electronically-generated lines sequenced on a synthesizer such as a Roland TB-303 to studio recordings or samples of live electric bassists, or simply filtered-down samples from whole stereo recordings (from classic funk tracks or any other song). Electronically-generated sounds and samples of recordings from genres such as jazz, blues, and synth pop are often added to the foundation of the drum beat and synth bass line. House songs may also include disco or soul-style and gospel vocals and additional percussion. Techno and trance, which developed alongside house music, share this basic beat infrastructure, but they usually eschew house's live-music-influenced feel and Black or Latin music influences in favor of more synthetic sound sources and approach (www.urbandictionary.com/define.php=House+Music).

12 A game of put-downs: the rapid, ritualistic exchange of insults, often targeting family members. The rhetorical contest of playing or shooting the dozens (also known as *capping, ranking,* and *sounding*) (www.thoughtco.com/the-dozens-game-of-insults-169041).

13 Harold Lee Washington (April 15, 1922–November 25, 1987) was a lawyer and politician from the state of Illinois who was elected as the 41st mayor of Chicago. Washington was noted as the first African American to be elected as mayor of Chicago in February 1983. Washington served as mayor from April 29, 1983 until his death on November 25, 1987.

14 Afrofuturism is a cultural and aesthetic theory and practice that combines elements of science fiction, historical fiction, fantasy, Afrocentricity, magic realism, history, and current events, with non-Western cosmologies to critique the present-day dilemmas of people of color and to revise, interrogate, and re-examine the historical events of the past.

Chapter 4

Movement and scenes of body work

> A simple movement can transform a banal object into something else.
> (Lecoq 2001: 98)[1]

With a focus on movement-centered performance, we think of the progression as building from impulse to movement, to action, to gesture, to sound, and finally to word (Callery 2002). There is a school of thought that contends before the body enters movement, or before a focus on movement and its precision can take place, the performer shall begin in "neutral position." This notion of neutral position is a contested one, and, if taken literally, can be deeply problematic. Coming from the point of view that our postures, movements, and ways of doing things are *not* neutral but are constituted by social, cultural, and psychological dispositions and identities, the idea of "neutral position" requires explication, particularly considering Spatz's discussion on transmitted knowledges and embodied techniques. Meyerhold described the neutral position as feet parallel, hands down by hips, fingers pointing to floor, eyes looking toward a point in the distance. Here, neutral position is less about contested and contesting identity and more about a position of stillness. It is to be motionless, *alongside* and *with* our embodied identities, in this trans-identitarian position or "placement" of our body. The social body is "still" and open for possibilities of what a "composite" body can do in performance. It is getting ready for other things our bodies can do, and in other ways, and across other identities, without dishonoring or attempting to erase our own inherited body knowledges. Lecoq described neutrality as precognitive existence before language and as the state of being "simply human." Lecoq states neutrality as the "embodiment of the existential within all of us, the collective, universal, or generic human" (2001: 34). The emphasis for our purposes is less on the "universal human" as an achievable state of being, but, in many ways, the opposite. I employ Lecoq's work on expressionless masks or neutral mask to demonstrate what is and is not universal about embodied movement. This mask work powerfully places our focus on movement from a range of differences and commonalities as well as inheritances and techniques that are broadly playful while being a means of exploring old and new movement habits and techniques. In neutral mask, the attention of spectators is inclined to focus more on the body and what it is doing. And, for performers, the focus is more on movement intentions and how movements are accomplished. Working with masks, whether in the form of a neutral mask or whatever available form of full or partial face masking—cloth covering or paper cut-out, bag with eye holes, and so on—physicality becomes more focused, heightened, and re-imagined because: (1) both large and small movements become more apparent and obvious to be developed and refined; (2) movements are more easily isolated in order to build control, tension, and energy; and (3) engrained gestural habits and unconscious movement patterns are more noticeable, demarcated and embellished, or lessened and changed for the purpose of character and scene. This also means that the masked body is more apparent and movement patterns and techniques become more apparent and therefore open for the merging and re-composition required for character building in addition to the motions, rhythms, or stillness of a performance frame.

Warm-up improvisations for neutral mask

1. The museum, the thief, and the sleeping guard

In neutral mask, the thief enters the museum and closely examines, through mime gestures and movements, an array of beautiful objects. With the expressiveness of their whole body, the thief touches and attends to each object with interest and intensity, demonstrating their intrigue with the objects. A guard is sleeping nearby. The thief must find the one and only object he is searching for quickly—without waking the guard. Each time the guard turns and makes a noise the thief freezes until the guard quiets down. After a few moments of searching and examining the objects in the room, between freezes when the guard moves, the thief quickly and quietly leaves the room as the guard is about to awake and catch him.

***

2. The first snow and play time

In neutral mask, actors become small children playing in mounds of snow with oversized boots and heavy coats. They are throwing snowballs at each other as they dodge balls, get hit, fall, get back up, make more snowballs while continuously getting hit again, and so forth. Remember, the snow is heavy and high, you are small and encumbered by big boots and coats against the quick, playful motion of throwing, hitting, and getting hit and starting all over again.

***

3. Talking hands (one person)

In neutral mask, you are "telling," with your hands and arms, a fairytale or myth. It is not important if your audience is familiar with the story, but it is important that you know the story and can provide, with hand and arm motions, drama and precision to key moments in the story.

***

4. You and the bee

In neutral mask, you are walking through the park on a very nice day and enjoying the weather when you pass a flower garden. You pick up one flower from the garden and notice a bee on the leaf. You don't know what to do. The bee starts buzzing around the flower, and you become afraid thinking the bee is going to bite you. You begin to swat the bee, but it comes at you, closer and closer and you try to get away from it, swatting it away as it keeps coming, but it is coming in all directions and you frantically try to get the bee to go away. It stings you, you react with great pain and then it goes away. You walk off the stage.

***

5. The happy sandwich

In neutral mask, you are sitting down reading a book and begin to feel very hungry. You decide to get up and prepare a sandwich. You prepare the sandwich and then sit down to eat with great anticipation and excitement to take a bite into your delicious sandwich. But your phone rings. With hesitation, you put the sandwich down to pick up your phone. Someone on the other line is saying something to you and you have very, very strong reactions. You put the phone down and run off the stage, leaving the sandwich on the table.

***

Note: The purpose of these neutral mask improvisations is to put the body intensely in motions that require various situations, actions, and responses. These are exercises meant to warm up the ensemble: to feel more free with their bodies, less uninhibited, and imaginatively playful in preparation for more direct movement experimentation related to the devised topic and themes. Each of these exercises can be extended and revised to add many more neutral mask warm-ups to your list.

Efforts and factors from Laban/Bartenieff

> The astonishing structure of the body and the amazing actions it can perform are some of the greatest miracles of existence. Each phase of a movement, every small transference of weight, every single gesture of any part of the body reveals some feature of our inner life.
>
> (Rudolf Laban)

Rudolf Laban[2] developed an extensive system for the observation, notation, interpretation, and performance of human movement. Laban contributes another method in keeping with psychophysical acting or the outward expression of inner feelings and intent.[3] Laban's *Four Movement Factors* and *Eight Basic Efforts of Action* are particularly helpful as a starting point in generating a range of literal and symbolic movements to create character action and behavior, specifically to design movements that reflect the yearnings and inner life of a character or persona: Laban's conceptualization of Choreutics—specific movements constituted by inner feelings, reflections, determinations of the will, and a range of emotional impulses—reflects much of the scope of Laban's system. However, it is far more extensive and detailed for the purposes of this book, therefore I will focus more narrowly on his formulation of efforts and factors (EF). He believed these factors and efforts entail all human movement.

The factors

According to Laban, all human movement is constituted by four basic factors. Each of these four factors is composed of two sub-factors that are opposite to each other. Movement emanates from these four factors and their sub-sets where more movement can be created, designed, and reimagined when we are aware of the factors and skillfully apply them in our work. The factors and their subsets are listed below:

Direction (sometimes referred to as *Space*)
    Direct > the straight path, uninterrupted, unswerving
    Indirect > the curved path, bend, meander
Speed (sometimes referred to as *Time*)
    Sudden > instantaneous, swift, unexpected
    Sustained > ongoing, continual, prolonged
Weight (sometimes referred to as *Strength*)
    Heavy > hefty, dense, or forceful
    Light > wispy, weightless, or delicate
Flow (sometimes referred to as *Fluid*)
    Bound > constrained, fettered, restrained
    Free > unconfined, open, unbound

The efforts

To illustrate factors as human action, Laban added eight efforts that enact and embody each Factor. These efforts demonstrate what factors look like and how we use them from day to day or how we can create symbolic movement from them. Because the eight efforts are embodiments of factors, they illuminate direction, speed, weight, and flow with more intention, sensory awareness, and context. The eight efforts are: *Pressing; Wringing; Gliding; Floating; Thrusting; Slashing; Dabbing; Flickering*.

Table 4.1 summarizes the eight efforts and their corresponding factors.

Table 4.1 A summary of the eight effort actions

Effort	Direction	Speed	Weight	Flow
Punch	Direct	Quick	Heavy	Bound vigorous, jolt, lunge, thrust, spurt, impact
Slash	Indirect	Quick	Heavy	Free sprawl, swipe tear, fling splash, throw
Dab	Direct	Quick	Light	Bound dart, crisp spritely, points staccato, tap
Flick	Indirect	Quick	Light	Free quiver, crisp whisk, flutter twitch, leap
Press	Direct	Sustained	Heavy	Bound pull, firm deliberate squeeze, sturdy
Wring	Indirect	Sustained	Heavy	Bound writhe, screw gnarled, knotted
Glide	Direct	Sustained	Light	Free smooth, calm soothing, linger, stroking
Float	Indirect	Sustained	Light	Free gentle, undulate, hover, soft, vaporous

Listed below are a selection of improvisations, games, and exercises I found most helpful when teaching efforts and factors to students and workshop participants who were most concerned with how to create different forms or types of movement and, moreover, how to make such movements and gestures more interesting, authentic, and meaningful in performance. The following exercises and games are intended to put Laban's efforts and factors into action as well as to spark further ideas for designing moment. The following will also generate ideas and to warm up the ensemble for interactive play, collaboration, and physical movements for scene work and for the adaptation of field data.

Improvisation exercises for *efforts and factors*

6. *Floating: indirect, sustained, light, free*

Begin with everyone standing alone in a space.

(a) Make shapes that only include angles, lines, and hard edges (use more than arms, use your whole body).

(b) Translate the angular shapes into curves
(c) Combine lines and curves (isolate different body parts, having one in a straight line and another in a gentle curve). Create contrast, juxtaposition, and tension in your various shapes.
(d) Pay attention to how you are making a shape, stopping, then starting a new one. Try to keep the movement fluid, so one shape leads to the next, so the process is of one shape evolving into another.
(e) Add changes to the tempo and pay attention to how tempo leads to different shapes.
(f) Work in groups of two and experiment with larger groups. The two actors are connecting and responding physically as in a three-dimensional sculpture adding another movement and embodying another dimension—this is a back and forthing or a call and response of fluid movements as one move flows into the next.

* * *

7. Punching: direct, quick, heavy, bound

This was once a popular childhood game where two players, facing each other extend the palms of their hands out in front of each other facing down. They look straight into each other's eyes and cannot look down at their hands. The first player places both palms under the palms of the second player. Each focused on the eyes of the other. The first player quickly flips his hand to tap the top of the second player's hands before they can pull back. The second player quickly tries to pull back their hands to avoid being tapped. The first player keeps going until the second player gets tapped. The players take turns back and forth when the other player is tapped. This is more of a light "hit" than a punch, but remains direct, quick, heavy, and bound, while not intended to hurt or cause pain to the other player. It is a wonderful exercise in focus, stillness, concentration, and in waking-up the brain and the reflexes.

* * *

8. Slashing: indirect, quick, heavy, free

With your bare hands as your only weapon, you and your fellow villagers must slash through multitudes of crawling death vines encircling and closing-in on your village at every angle. The vines grow and multiply surrounding your village and blocking out the light. As everything becomes darker, you can hardly see in front of you. No one can push back the vines; you can only slash through with your hands that act as swords with the hope that the sun's light will appear leading you to an opening. Once you cut through the vines, and create a small opening of light, everyone can slash their way through to escape.

* * *

9. Dabbing: direct, quick, light, bound[4]

The goal here is to lightly dab your partner in the small of their back while preventing them from touching you in the small of your back. Clive Barker states, "Most people find this very difficult because it is essentially a horseplay game using blind energy ... they attack at the same time, or defend at the same time and so are never within reach of their opponent's back." Barker suggests playing this game in at least two groups to see how others play. After watching others play you might come up with new "strategies." This game is another reflex game to practice and awaken your attention, reflexes, and responses. Barker asserts performance "is about response and not statement," he says, "it is about a continuing process of ... response ... rather than a series of dogmatic or fixed statements which are ultimately boring."

10. Flickering: indirect, quick, light, free[5]

This is a balance exercise. Make a tail with toilet paper about 24 inches long. Tuck the tail into your waist-band at the back. The object of the game is to take the other person's tail. Once your tail is taken, you are out of the game. It is important that there should be no running and no standing with your back against the wall. Barker states the value of this game exceeds play because we are making theatre, for Barker it is "the way that you face the other people, the way you sneak up on them; it is about the way that you attempt to provoke your opponents ... thus placing themselves off balance, and then you can steal their tail." He goes on to state:

> This is about the center-line that runs from behind the eye, through the larynx, the pelvis and into the ankle bone. This is also what helps release the actor's voice. Coming into line relaxes the breathing and releases the imagination and the instinct.

***

11. Pressing: direct, sustained, heavy, bound

You will imagine there is a large door. Take time to imagine and determine its dimensions, color, texture, and so forth. See and feel the door. You are trying to hear what the person on the other side of the door is doing. You begin by pressing your ear to the door, then the side of your face, then you place your hands and arms on the door to get closer, then the whole side of your body. You realize the person on the other side of the door wants to enter. You now press your whole body against the door to keep them from entering. They overpower you and push the door open. You step back and stare at them with such force, as though your eyes were pressing back at them. They feel your eyes pressing back at them and lean back. They freeze and do not enter.

***

12. Wringing: indirect, sustained, heavy, bound

The Interview

The trains were running late so you are late for a job interview. As you were walking from the train to the building of the interview there is a sudden downpour. You finally enter the interview room. You sit down and you are alone, waiting for the interview to begin. You are nervous, dripping wet, and upset. You attempt to wring dry parts of your clothes. The interviewer comes into the room. You stop wringing your clothes. You and the interviewer exchange greetings and begin talking about the weather. Although you are trying to be calm and impressive, throughout the conversation you are nervous and begin twisting and turning in wringing gestures with your hands, arms, feet, legs, and torso. Throughout your nervous wringing movement, the interviewer is trying to twist open, with great dramatic gesture, a water bottle cap. Both of you are trying to carry on a serious conversation, throughout the wringing movements, not acknowledging the wringing gestures of the other.

***

13. Gliding: direct, sustained, light, free

A "pirate" sits in a chair, blindfolded, in front of the room. There are coins placed on the ground in front and surrounding the pirate. A group of no more than six participants are standing several feet away in front of the chair who will attempt to steal the pirates treasure. They are given the signal and each one begins to move up silently in a light, gliding motion, closer and closer, directly toward the coins. Once they pick up the coins, they move back to the starting point. This must all be done without the pirate hearing someone near, coming or going. If someone is heard approaching or moving away, the person in the chair will point in the direction of that individual. That individual must then go back to the starting point and begin again. Someone must stand behind the chair to determine if the pointing is accurately directed at a specific individual and who must start again. This is an excellent exercise in sustainment, lightness, and direction. A gliding motion to capture the coins is the aim. Barker warns that the reason people give themselves away is because "they don't sustain their movement but move in blocks, stopping and starting."[6]

***

These games and exercises are intended as starting points in their continued creation. They are warm-ups to generate more movements and gestures to spark ideas for devisors as they match content with action. From the tiniest gesture to the grandest spectacle, efforts and factors help us imagine more precise and deliberate action in the design and creation of physical theatre.

Body, Effort, Shape, and Space or BESS

Irmgard Bartenieff[7] was a dancer, physiotherapist, and student of Laban. One of her contributions to Laban's work was her conceptualization of BESS (Body, Effort, Shape, and Space). Bartenieff's addition to Laban's work is much more detailed and extensive than I can offer here, so I will focus on BESS and the insightful questions it invokes not only for efforts and factors, but how we continue to design movement generally. I will examine Body, Effort, Shape, and Space through a compilation of thought questions followed by exercises that respond to the questions directly. It is important to note that the questions I enumerate in the four elements of BESS are addressed, answered, and illuminated in the exercises that follow them.

Body. How do our body and vocal rhythms connect with the rhythms of our breath? How does our head align with our spine? Does our spine—from head to tail—slope over more horizontally or stand up more vertically? How does our abdomen or core contribute to our balance, stability, and mobility? How does our lower body support our weight and guide the quality of our movement in and through space? How does our upper body and lower body synchronize and connect in movement and in stillness?

Effort. What is the relationship between human energy and human effort? How can Laban's eight efforts serve as prompts to create movement phrases and physicality in performance? Why is every effort constituted by *Weight* (heavy or light), *Flow* (bound or free), *Speed* (sudden or sustained), and *Direction* (direct or indirect)? What is the significance of efforts and factors toward the infinite possibilities of shape?

Shape. Barteneiff stated, "Movement goes out into space and creates shapes." Why would she emphasize breath as integral to this? When our body moves in patterns that are like the rhythm of our breath, why does she describe these movements as general dimensions of growing/shrinking? Why does she define growing/shrinking as a vertical dimension of lengthening/shortening and a horizontal dimension of widening/narrowing as well as a sagittal dimension of bulging/hollowing? According to Bartenieff, when bodies move or "grow toward" something, or in the direction of somewhere, we may then think of shape qualities as "openings" and "closings." How then is it helpful in performance to think about "moving toward" as opening and closing in the following ways: vertical as rising/sinking; horizontal as spreading/enclosing; sagittal as advancing/retreating? Using Laban's efforts/factors and Bartenieff's BESS, how can we think of shape as a three dimensional and co-creative process of linear forms, arc-like pathways, curving figures, and altering dimensions that are all motivated by our environment as well as our relations with others and our self-needs?

Space. How can we merge our inherited embodied techniques—our identities and personal kinesphere—in thinking of space as infinitely real and infinitely imaginary constituted by endless levels, pathways, crossings, diagonals, spirals, planes, and dimensions of the vertical, horizontal, and sagittal?

The following workshops are both an embodiment of the questions and a response to them.

Improvisational exercises for BESS

14. Walking through BESS

Four actors are positioned on stage. Each actor depicts a still image or sculpture representing Barteneiff's Body, Effort, Shape, and Space. The four actors cover the stage with space between them. Each actor represents a passage into their specific element. The **Body** actor creates a fluid sculpture with five continuous points of emphasis: (1) breath replenishing the body; (2) flowing into the belly button or core as source of balance and stability; (3) legs holding up the body, guiding its movements, flowing into (4) alternating motion and stillness, and ending in the original position of stillness. The **Effort** actor's fluid sculpture takes up movement interpretations of heaviness then lightness; of flowing freely through the stage then being restricted or bound; of flowing in a direct path toward a location then taking an indirect path back; of flowing into slow motion and then moving suddenly into fast motion—alternating—then back into the original position. **Shape** actors move ... growing/shrinking, that is: a vertical dimension of lengthening/shortening; a horizontal dimension of widening/narrowing; and a sagittal dimension of bulging/hollowing. When bodies move or "grow toward" something, or in the direction of somewhere, "openings" and "closings." **Space** actor—real and imaginary with endless levels, pathways, crossings, diagonals, spirals, planes, and dimensions of the vertical, horizontal, and sagittal.

* * *

15. Tableau with objects

Write or choose lines from a text that address a theme, subject, or quote. With an emphasis in the distinction among Body, Effort, and Shape, create three tableaus depicting three different placements of an object. Each tableau should flow to the next seamlessly while voicing your lines. The lines, the movement/transitions, and the tableaus must be in coordination and in sync with each other. The tableaus are not in freeze positions but held in soft pauses (two to three seconds). Before the scene begins, the object is pre-arranged on stage in the same place for every scene.

* * *

16. Repetition of BESS

Repetition and movement (re)cycle. With an emphasis on body, effort, shape, and space, include repetition to make a distinction among the four categories. Whether we conjoin movement phrases or frame them in isolation we may employ repetition as a means of emphasis, meaning, and affect. Attention here is on the generative recycling of movement through repetitions or re-appearances. It is what Henry Louis Gates describes as "repetition with a difference."[8]

***

17. Circle, clump, line

The focus here is on shape and space. A group of at least four performers enter the space and form a circle. Once the circle is made, they immediately form a clump. From the clump, they form a line. The sequence is repeated, but this time the actors make a change in the circle, clump, line so it looks different from the first. They create a third sequence, again, with a different kind of circle, another clump, and another line. Once the group is familiar with the repetition, they will freely move, without instruction, from one of the three formations to the other. The rule is that all participants are moving in the same formation. Viewpoints asserts that movers getting "from one formation to the next is the point of the improvisation. Allow the group to find as many permutations of circles, lines, and clumps as possible. Notice how relationships and events seem to unfold naturally and effortlessly" (Bogart and Landau 2005).

***

18. Story in a box (Madison)

Enter the space with a feeling of deep ambivalence and hesitancy.
Slowly open the piece of paper you have folded in your hand and stare down at it intensely.
Fold the paper back up, but this time, fold it as small as you possibly can.
Place the folded paper in the box on a table.
Close the box—it will not close—after three tries you can close it
Walk away. Stop. Think. Slowly look back at the box.
Walk over to the box and attempt to lift the box from the table. You cannot. It is stuck.
Using all your strength, attempt to open the box again. It is stuck.
Look at your audience. Stand still and pause (about 10 seconds).
Go to the box. Lift it from the table. Walk away. Name where elements of body, effort, shape, and space constituted this performance.

***

In summary, Barteniff's BESS and Laban's Eight Efforts and Four Factors broaden and refine our movement vocabulary and our physical and gestural choices in several ways: First, by adding deliberate choices to the mix of impulses and intuition by employing efforts and factors as prompts. Second, by encouraging us to be more conscious of our inherited body techniques that we carry with us in the creation of a particular character or persona while being mindful of body, effort, shape, and space. Third, by providing a theory and set of practices to help us intersect, compose, contrast, or match our embodied techniques and identities with that of the character or figure needed to build the performance. Fourth, by expanding our knowledge of performance and movement techniques, we can then imagine, design, and interpret new ways to enrich character and development, processes of adaptation, and to physicalize the fantastical and non-human with more intention and confidence.

The 5Rhythms from Gabrielle Roth[9]

Your body is the ground metaphor of your life, the expression of your existence ... So many of us are not in our bodies, at home and vibrantly present there. *Nor are we in touch with the basic rhythms that constitute our bodily life.* We live outside ourselves—in our heads, our memories, our longings—absentee landlords of our own estate. My way back into life was ecstatic dance. I reentered my body by learning to move myself, to dance my own dance from the inside out, not the outside in.

(Gabrielle Roth interview 2007)[10]

Gabrielle Roth's 5Rhythms are an invitation to the "basic rhythms that constitute our bodily life." At the core of the practice is the belief that everything is energy, and moves in waves, patterns, and rhythms. Roth believed the 5Rhythms place the body in motion to quiet and still the mind. The 5Rhythms are: (1) Flowing; (2) Staccato; (3) Chaos; (4) Lyrical; and (5) Stillness. When danced in sequence, the Rhythms are described as a "Wave." I include the 5Rhythms in our discussion because they provide a pathway to embody BESS as well as efforts/factors through joyful and vibrant dance forms. The following is a description of each of the 5Rhythms as it relates to efforts/factors and BESS.

Flowing. Bodies extemporaneously dance fluidly, unrushed, and continuous. The fluidity of the body resembles smooth circles rather than sharp angles; the body moves out in space in soft graceful extensions rather than sudden or forceful projections; the body moves in pauses and slow beginnings rather than abrupt stops and starts.

Example. To warm up into fluid rhythm, begin by walking the room in a slow even pace, calm your mind and pay attention to your foot-steps moving across the floor and how your feet, ankles, legs, and entire body feels as you walk. After a while, begin to walk in round, circular pathways gently turning left, right, moving backwards, and pausing from time to time. Focus internally on your own body and imagine your body as weightless, floating in space as you circle and pause the various directions. If gentle, fluid music is available, let the music and your imagination carry you over waves of water, smoothly and gently, in all directions. Feeling comfortable in the weightlessness of your body flowing like water, pay deep attention to your own body—ignoring anyone or anything outside of it—listen and attend to the music and your body as it moves light and fluid as water. It is important to be mindful and present with your own flowing body and the wonder and power of your arms, legs, head, torso, and the muscles, bones, and music. If your mind wanders off to other bodies or how they are moving in the room, or any element outside yourself, gently bring your attention back to the gliding, indirect lightness of your flowing body as a form of meditation. Feel free to allow the gentle fluidity of your body to move extemporaneously in any direction or form, in a flowing dance. Explore spontaneously the dancing flow of your body in space.

Staccato. On the other side of flow, the percussive draws upon the weight, balance, and strength of the feet with emotional power. Staccato is described as "the fierce teacher of boundaries" and as the "protector and ambassador of our fluid being." (Roth, 5rhythms.com) This is a rhythm of definition, clarity, quick stops, starts, and bold angles.

Example. From flowing dance, the ensemble will pause, and after a few seconds, they are asked to turn the pause into a freeze. The body, in freeze position, becomes more tense, exact, and heavy. No longer moving in circular paths, guided by the gentle force of a water stream, they are now walking on a grid. Imagine the floor to be a bold black grid of perfect squares and hard angles. You have the same directional prompts as flow, but with opposite force. Your walking is no longer flowing but mechanically sharp and straight, no longer light but heavy, no longer flowing but direct, and no longer in soft curves but precise angles. Your mind now focuses on staccato movements and you are less meditative and more deliberate and intentional with your movement. In staccato, your movements of left, right, forward, backward, levels, and freezes are alert to precision, quickness, and angularity. The ensemble dances in staccato with sharp, fierce, quick, angular, direct, and bold movements. Your body moves in the rhythm of percussive patterns, resonating with the strength, force, and musicality of the traditional drum. Imagine the intensity of dancing for communal protection, ancestral blessings, and rain from the heavens.

Chaos. From stark borders and edges of Staccato, you now move to the feeling of boundless freedom. You release and let the body go where it wants and where it can move in any manner and in any direction. In Chaos, you must move "faster than you can think." The head, spine, hips, arms, and feet are on a wild and spontaneous reverie into unknown motion. A motion that comes from impulse and energy. There is overflowing of cathartic energy to feel free in this moment. "Chaos breaks us free of our illusions and throws us headfirst into the beat ... Chaos is the gateway to the big mind."

Example. Coming out of Staccato, the ensemble is asked to freeze. You now move from a deliberate and alert focus on angles, edges, and the grid to a free focus, or non-focus, where your mind moves less on either meditation or alertness, but toward abandonment of thinking to an acclamation of impulse. You are less in your head and more completely in freeing your body to move on reflex and instinct. Moving at your own pace, because chaos does require speed, you move to the pace and tempo of your own intuitive rhythms and desire. Like with all the rhythms you are focused inward; in chaos dance you move without forethought but with instinctive invention and exploration—do not deliberate, do not pause—move with openness and freedom, suddenly and expansively, everywhere and bravely: shake, reach, circle, forward, backward, sideways, arms discovering space along with feet, abdomen, buttocks, legs, head, and neck. You move to the rhythms of the music or the musicality of your own feelings and impulses and "dance like nobody is watching."

Lyrical. The transition from Chaos into lyric is a turn from defined motion and strict lines into a flexibility of movement choices that encompasses a combination of rhythms. Flow, staccato, and chaos are all welcomed in lyric rhythm so that our inner feelings and reflections are expressed outwardly however we choose to dance them. Roth described Lyric as an articulation of our deepest self in space and time. Lyric is a dynamic of our personal ethos, like a song or poem, open for others to experience yet an expression that is unique to us. When we dance in lyric our movements are unobstructed by categories and genre. We choose and combine freely to tell our version of truth. "The Lyrical is expansive and connects us to our humanity, timeless rhythms, repetitions, patterns and cycles."

Example. Coming out of the freeze from chaos, you will now move into the choreography of your inner feelings and personal story through lyric. What you are feeling in this moment, or what you want to feel, or who you are, or who you wish to be are expressed in lyric. It is a creation of your inner monologue—stream of consciousness—manifest through your improvisational movement creation. Lyric can be part flow, part, staccato, and part chaos—any combination you choose to declare your thoughts, feelings, imaginings, and hopes.

Stillness. The ensemble will pause for a few seconds in lyric. Take a breath; everything is now slower and sustained. You are still in motion with a quiet, calm energy.

> Moving in Stillness and being still in motion fuses the accumulation of our bodies' life experiences into our true wisdom. Eventually we dissolve into sitting meditation, where all the other Rhythms of our journey converge in the vital resonance of Stillness.[11]

Example. Coming out of the Lyric freeze you will now find a position of comfort: standing, lying, or sitting where your body is most at rest and peace. The focus here is to be still in your body while gathering calm, still energy. This is not an inattentive or dead stillness; it is a stillness of tranquil energy and awareness. It is the moment where serene energy is aligned with your breath. In stillness, we honor our breath and we are fully present and observant of the motion and sensation of our breathing. In this breathing meditation we are in union with the peace, quiet, and internal rhythm of our breath.

Discussion questions

After the 5Rhythms, participants most often want to talk and check in with each other about the experience. This leads to discussion of how they are feeling in their bodies and in community with each other. I often start out with this open question that takes flight in countless and heartfelt responses: What did you feel? This question can take hours of mouth-dropping discussions—altogether surprising, humorous, and poignant. Other related prompts might include: What was your body "saying"? What did you see in your thoughts? Could you "dance like nobody was watching"? Where did you go? How do you feel now?

Augusto Boal[12] and Newspaper Theatre

Newspaper Theatre

> [A] Jazz practice is whatever our "literal" art practice may be (writing, painting, choreographing, etc.) *and* is simultaneously our expansive response to any limitation in life … The texts in a jazz aesthetic imagine time as coterminous realms … Worlds interact across time and space, and characters often move in and out of temporal, spatial, and psychic sites.
>
> (Jones 2015)

> Living Newspapers brought current issues—ones readers might encounter in the news—to life on the stage. Rather than illustrating such problems through dramatic narratives following one or two plot lines with a beginning, middle, and end, in which the audience comes to know and empathize with particular characters. Newspaper Theatre (NPT) invoked questions that troubled and re-invisioned the news report. They presented viewers with multiple viewpoints in relatively quick succession drawn from diverse sources, including photographs, graphs, and charts, in an effort to educate, unsettle, and call audience members to action. Living Newspapers were, furthermore, presentational. In other words, they shattered the fourth wall … Similar to a jazz aesthetic, Newspaper Theatre (NPT) interprets feelings, experiences, and story into endless forms and possibilities, for example, narrative drama, improvised fragments, readers' theatre,[13] dance and symbolic movement, comic satire, solo performance, and so forth. It is the Brazilian director, teacher, and activist, Augusto Boal, whose NPT approach is particularly useful for devisors because it encompasses these forms and more by transforming any piece of news, narrative fiction, or non-dramatic texts into twelve performative techniques. I distinctively use the term

Theater of the oppressed (from http://beautifultrouble.org/theory/theater-of-the-oppressed)

Image Theater. Invites spect-actors to form a tableau of frozen poses to capture a moment in time dramatizing an oppressive situation. The image then becomes a source of critical reflection, facilitated by various kinds of interventions: spect-actors may be asked to depict an ideal image of liberation from that oppression, and then a sequence of transition images required to reach it, or to reshape an image to show different perspectives.

Forum Theater. A performance or scene that dramatizes a situation, with a terribly oppressive ending that spect-actors cannot be satisfied with. After an initial performance, it is shown again, however this time the spectators become spect-actors and can at any point yell "freeze" and step on stage to replace the protagonist(s) and take the situation in different directions. Theater thus becomes rehearsal for real-world action. Legislative theater takes forum theater to the government and asks spect-actors to not only attempt interventions on stage, but to write down the successful interventions into suggestions for legislation and hand them in to the elected officials in the room.

Invisible Theater. A performance that masquerades as reality, performed in a public space. The objective is to unsettle passive social relations and spark critical dialogue among the spect-actors, who never learn that they are part of a play. Augusto Boal said of one invisible theater intervention, "The actor became the spectator of the spectator who had become an actor, so the fiction and reality were overlapping."

performative as an intervention in its intent to demarcate unjust power structures and hidden abodes of oppression, masked in objective or neutral language and representations. NPT constitutes performative techniques as it also constitutes another genre of performance praxis. Boal's Twelve Techniques in Action.

(Musher 2015)

SIMPLE READING

We begin with a straight and simple reading without emphasis or emotion. The live presence of a body (or bodies) reading from a text in a performance space is the only presentational element. The point here is to read "out loud" where every word is understood and heard clearly while making no attempt to necessarily convey emotions or feelings. The presence of bodies reading in specific position on stage holds inherent dramatic qualities, especially juxtaposed to reports of extreme events and circumstances. In a simple reading, human behavior in its most unforgettable and poignant moments—for good or bad—is effective by contrast.

I. Aleppo[14]

Actor One enters stage left and **Actor Two** enters stage right. **Actor One** holds a newspaper and **Actor Two** holds a cell phone. At the beginning of the scene, **Actor One** remains stage left and **Actor Two** remains stage right. As the scene continues, the Actors change positions at key points during the news report, yet continue to read without expression. The timing of the alternating reading is without pause as though speaking in one voice.

	(Actor One enters stage left and reads from the newspaper)
Actor One:	Activists and rebels in the besieged city say mass executions have begun
	(As Actor One reads, Actor Two enters reading immediately after Actor One)
Actor Two:	children are burned alive as Assad's Iranian- and Russian-backed forces move in.
Actor One:	The United Nations' top human rights official on Tuesday charged the US and other countries
Actor Two:	with collectively wringing their hands in the face of the
Actor One:	wanton slaughter of men, women and children in Aleppo
	(Actors continue to read, changing positions further downstage, facing each other reading.)
Actor Two:	These are false claims. The Arab Syrian army can never do this and we have never done it in our army's history.
Actor One:	The official Syrian news agency SANA instead lay blame for atrocities in Aleppo on the rebels,
Actor Two:	alleging that eight people were killed and 47 were injured in regime-held areas after the opposition bombed them.
	(Both Actors turn to read facing out to the audience)
Actor one:	Most of the victims were women and children …
Actor Two:	Decrying the crushing of Aleppo,
Actor One:	the immeasurably terrifying toll on its people,
Actor Two:	the bloodshed,
Actor One:	the wanton slaughter of men, women and children,
Actor Two:	the destruction,
Actor One:	the Jordanian-born UN official warned,
Actor Two:	We are nowhere near the end of this cruel conflict.
Actor One:	Dozens of bodies reportedly litter the streets of a number of east Aleppo neighborhoods, with residents unable to retrieve them due to the intense bombardment
Actor Two:	and fear of being shot,

Actor One:	the UN had reports that at least 82 civilians,
Actor Two:	including 11 women
Actor One:	and 13 children in four neighborhoods—
	(The Actors now move freely back and forth across the stage as they name the four neighborhoods)
Actor One:	Bustan al-Qasr,
Actor Two:	al-Ferdous
Actor One:	al-Kallaseh
Actor Two:	al-Saleheen.
	(Both Actors abruptly stop in position and pause)
Actor One:	The White Helmets, a volunteer rescue group, described Aleppo as being
Actor One and Two:	"like hell."
	(pause, then the Actors continue reading moving to their original positions stage right/left)
Actor Two:	The streets and destroyed buildings "are full of dead bodies,"
Actor One:	The rescue service was reported to be totally paralyzed by the assault.
Actor Two:	And those who survive the air raids could not be helped.
Actor One:	"Women and children—their screams can be heard underneath the rubble.
Actor Two:	Unfortunately, there is nothing we can do to get them out.
Actor One:	Everyone is panicking.
Actor One:	There is great fear.
Actor Two:	Everyone can only think of himself, not about others."
	(Actor One moves downstage center and reads)
Actor One:	This morning 20 women committed suicide in order not to be raped.
Actor Two:	Seventy-nine of them were executed at the barricades.
Actor One:	The rest—everyone under 40—were taken to warehouses that look more like internment camps.
Actor Two:	"They face an unknown fate," he said.
Actor One:	"What can happen next, if the international community continues to collectively wring its hands can be much more dangerous" …
	(Actor Two comes downstage center to stand next to Actor One and reads)
Actor Two:	"We cannot let this continue."
Actor One:	"We cannot let this continue."
	(End of Scene)

The simple reading in its non-expressive, non-feeling, and robotic tone is in contrast to the emotions and human tragedy of the report in an attempt to render the story more pronounced and impactful, invoking emotions, sensory responses, from the original occurrence unhindered by theatrics or expressions beyond the presence of the human body and voice on the stage

MATERIALIZING THE ABSTRACT

For Boal, the "abstract" here means to neutralize unjust or graphic news elements as ambiguous, non-specific, or innocuous. To materialize the abstract is to make apparent, explicit, graphic, and vivid what the news report either diminishes or ignores, for example, the evidence of torture, the violence of systemic racism, the economic inequity of gender, and so forth that are underemphasized or become vague and convoluted.

TEXT OUT OF CONTEXT

A news story is performed out of context relative to the events, space, or time in which it occurred. The purpose here is to contrast, deepen, or underscore the context of the news event overlooked by the report. The following example demonstrates how Newspaper Theatre is effective beyond news reports and can be used to stage other types of texts. The next example employs elements of materiality and context to stage an ethnographic moment centering on internal questions of ethics and self-reflections that fieldworkers most often confront.

II. Me and my shadow[15]

R1 and **R2** represent the ethnographer who is depicted on stage as having two identities in the characterizations of Recorder One [upstage left] and Recorder Two [downstage right]. They are facing each other across the opposite ends of the stage. Upstage of **R1** and **R2** are two large screens that resemble large walls surrounding them. The screen images capture a series of ethnographic locations, maps, and abstract symbols. Sound effects underscore the tension between **R1** and **R2** and the internal tension that necessarily affects the self-reflexive ethnographer.

(An old map of South Africa, during the Apartheid era, is projected on both screens. South African music is softly played in the background. The actors are speaking from an ambiguous location—a place out of place and a time out of time—that is the deeply internal space of their consciousness)

R1: In KwaZulu-Natal, South Africa, they arrested Mr. Sule and put him in a prison cell. He had stolen water.[16]
R2: What happened?
R1: Mr. Sule earned 100 rand per month selling water, but eventually he could not afford to payed the water bill. He also had to pay for food and shelter for his family and school fees for his children. His family needed water and he could no longer

	stand by and watch his children beg for it. Mr. Sule made an illegal connection to the supply pipe. When it was discovered, the police came and put him in jail.
R2:	What does Mr. Sule have to do with you? What are you doing here in Ghana? *(The music stops and the screens go black. In the center of the screen is a small, faint picture of ocean waves)*
R1:	It's about water … I need to know more … I need to do …
R2:	(Mockingly) Water … I neeeed to know … I need to do … what is it you need to know … to do? *(The dots in the middle of the screens are becoming larger as the dialogue progresses, and the sound of ocean waves builds as the tension between R1 and R2 becomes more intense)*
R1:	There are big people with big money who want to own the water.
R2:	And???
R1:	AND they want to sell it!
R2:	And???
R1:	AND they want to manage it and make a profit.
R2:	Annnnnnd???
R1:	AND there will be people who can **NOT** afford to pay for it. *(The small dot has now grown larger to cover the screen showing large ocean waves with the sound of waves now clearly heard almost covering the voices of the actors, causing them to speak louder over the ocean waves)*
R2:	Ohhhhhhh … But, what has that got to do with you, nosey woman! Stay out of other people's business. PROFIT and PRIVATIZATION have always been the twins of progress! You know what they say: "God provided the water, but not the pipes." *(The screens are completely black and there is silence. Standing in front of each screen is a dancer. During the following dialogue the dancers interpret the words of the Recorders. The dance is almost mime-like in its literal interpretation of the words. The movement takes on the affect and temperament of the dialogue)*
R1:	There will be people who cannot afford to pay for it!!
R2:	Read my lips: *(emphasize each word)* W A T E R B U S I N E--
S	— m-a-n-a-g-e-m-e-n-t // d-i-s-t-r-i-b-u-t-i-o-n // m-a-i-n-t-e-n-a-n-c-e // s-a-n-i-t-a-t-i-o-n. PIPES! PIPES! PIPES! Water is not free!
R1:	*(preachy)* Water Cannot Be Owned! Water is a public good. The public will manage it, the public should profit from it, the public …
R2:	*(She laughs)* The public/schmub-lic! … Hah! *(as if reading a headline, then becomes very, very sarcastic!)*. The public in the Developing World Economies, oh that public has been VERY successful, so efficient, so honest and so concerned about the

public good—Yes, yes, getting water to alllllll the people allllll the time, concerned about alllll its poor citizens, never an ounce of corruption or waste or just NOT knowing what the hell they're doing ... yes, leave it to the governments of these countries, after all they have done SO well *(dramatic change in attitude)* ... done soooo well.

R1: You don't understand. You haven't been paying attention to ... it is ... it is ... let me explain ... the problem is ...

R2: The PROBLEM is the public sector has done so well as the water pipes break down everywhere; as the water collectors take money from the people and put that money in their own pockets, as the government water companies over-charge, mis-charge, under-charge, or don't charge for water they mis-manage, while all the while making a messy waste of natural resources. Some people around here haven't had water flowing from their pipes in weeks! Months!

R1: You are not looking below the surface! You don't know what you're talking about. You don't know anything ... It is more complex, it is more complex ...

R2: *(Mocking in a high voice)* "It is more complex, it is more complex ..." Maybe if the Big people come, with their Big plans, and their Big money, and their Big pipes, and their Big teams, and their Big, Big, Big, Big promises maybe people in this country can get some water ... clean, fresh, EFFICIENT water.

R1: You don't understand what is really going on. You are missing the point. You don't understand.

R2: Then make me understand! Help me understand! Tell me what I need to know and do! Tell me the TRUTH! You are here taking up space and getting in the way ... Tell me what is the truth and what needs to be done ...

R1: *(She is grasping for words and thinking hard)* The truth is ... The problem ... hmm ... It's complex ...

R2: *(Exasperated)* What is COMPLEX?!
(The dancers exit the screens and two different videos are projected on both screens of women and children fetching water from local ponds)

R1: I'm learning ... It's here, I've got to get to ... I'm here ... I will be here.

R2: Learn what you came here to learn! Don't give me slogans and platitudes! I am so tired of slogans and platitudes? Can you say something different and More! Recorder! There is no replacement for water! NO Replacement!

R2 and R1: There is more to know here ... I will be here ...

R1: I will be here.

R2: I will be here ... we

R1:   We
R2:   We must.
R1
and R2: We must.
         (Video stops on image of women and children fetching water from ponds as R1 and R2 face each other and freeze in place)
         (End of Scene)

Although this example does not provide a news story to demonstrate how performance can concretize, materialize, and make evident significant information made abstract or vague in news reports. Nor does it take a news story out of context. The example shows us how "materializing the abstract" and "taking a text out of context" can be used in staging an ethnographic dilemma. The ethnographer is outside the context of the field and on the stage before an audience, inside the dueling consciousness of her own mind. The one ethnographer becomes a bifurcated character before an audience. Furthermore, questions of ethics and the demand for self-reflection relative to our own intent and purposes can often be ephemeral, hard to grasp, and inaccessible. The mode of "materializing the abstract" brings these abstract ideas to the surface through explicit questions between R1 and R2.

PARALLEL READING

This is an intertextual approach where the news report is interwoven and parallel to other representational forms. These parallel texts may take an abundance of forms: actual digital images or film footage; a range of live performance genres; sonic effects from recorded music, and soundscapes; ethnographic sound documentation; literary and poetic frameworks; dance and symbolic movement; representations of paintings, sculptures, and material culture; and so forth. The purpose of parallel reading is to provide an added form and communicative domain to that of the text and to open a path to a range of the aesthetic and rhetorical choices.

CROSSED READING

The crossed readings can also take many forms and vocal arrangements from choral reading; alternating words and/or phrases; repetition, tempo, and duration of voices; debate or argumentation. These alternating readings—for comparison, contrast, or emphasis—to expand the information or effects of the article, for example, context, point of view, rhetorical power, journalistic value, and so forth.

REINFORCEMENT READING

The news item is aided or reinforced by adding extra elements, such as: "audio/visuals, jingles, advertising, publicity materials." In Example III, we move from an ethnographic reflection and return to a news story. This scene also moves from digital imagery and visual projections to a focus on vocality and sonics. It is through voice and sound effects that the crossed reading is made pronounced.

III. Dakota pipeline: we will pray for you; we love you[17]

A group of actors form a **Chorus** and they are "flocking" and creating a collage of vocal sound effects during the entire dialogue between **Actor One** and **Actor Two**. Between the **Chorus** gliding together as a group [or as a flock of birds], they will stop at intervals and pause, from their combined/contrasting body positions, as they form various tableaus that resemble a human sculpture.

(The Chorus is together in a clump to stay warm, they are freezing cold with their arms wrapped around their individual bodies to stave off the freezing water being [imaginatively] sprayed at them. In a cluster of voices, some repeating "pop-pop-pop" while others alternate and repeat, "We love you—We will pray for you—We love you." The Chorus moves upstage and then circles around and through the Actors. As the scene begins, the chorus is upstage center and the Actors, with their backs to the audience, are downstage center right and left facing the chorus. As the Actors speak, the Chorus whispers its words and continues to move in circular patters around the Actors. There is a hologram projected across the stage. The hologram is a map depicting the planned layout for the pipeline installations and its connections across the land area. The stage is lit by the hologram as the two actors move in and out of the light and the pipeline map is projected across their face and bodies)

Actor One: ... people walking through the dark of a winter North Dakota night

Actor Two: some of them so cold, and sprayed with water for so long, that their clothes were frozen to their body and crunching as they walked.

Actor One: you could hear this crunching sound and this pop-pop-pop, and people yelling [to the police],

Actor Two: "We'll pray for you! We love you!"

Actor One: As police unleashed streams of icy water Sunday night against Dakota Access pipeline demonstrators, Linda Black Elk, a member of the Standing Rock Medic and Healer Council, was helping care for injured demonstrators.

Actor Two: The council estimated that 300 people were treated for injuries, including 26 who were taken to area hospitals.

Actor One: Medic and Healer Council, released a statement pleading with police to halt the use of water cannons.

Actor Two:	"As medical professionals, we are concerned for the real risk of loss of life due to severe hypothermia under these conditions,"
Actor One:	When asked in a press conference Monday about the use of water cannons, Morton County Sheriff Kyle Kirchmeier said,
Actor Two:	"We don't have water cannons," ... "This is just a fire hose. It was sprayed more as a mist, and we didn't want to get it directly on them, but we wanted to make sure to use it as a measure to help keep everybody safe,"
	(The hologram transforms to the scene of the water hoses being sprayed on the protestors, while the chorus is still making whispers of "pop-pop-pop" and "I love you; I will pray for you.")
Actor One:	"We're just not going to let people and protesters in large groups come in and threaten officers. That's not happening."
Actor Two:	Medics on the ground said the demonstrators they observed were unarmed and largely nonviolent
Actor One:	Noah Morris was another medic at the scene, he said ...
Actor Two:	They were just hosing people down with their water cannon that continued for the entirety of the four hours I was out there watching, ... the rivers and creeks nearby had started to crust over with ice.
Actor Two:	As he and his medical team flushed the eyes of people sprayed with tear gas, the water and milk of magnesia they used turned to black ice when it dripped to the ground
	*(The **Chorus** moves out from the clump and spreads out across the stage to fill the stage space. During the following section **Chorus** members echo words from the news story as they mime varying gestures to heal and respond to the "wounds" on their body. Each member is creating their own unique and continuous "wound movement" throughout the scene. A hologram is now projected on the stage floor projecting a river. A general blue cast lighting effect now fills the stage.)*
Actor Two:	In a statement to the *Los Angeles Times*, the sheriff's department denied using concussion grenades
C1:	*(wound movement)* Denied. Concussion grenades
C2:	*(wound movement)* Denied
Actor One:	and suggested the injury was caused by explosives allegedly used by protesters.
C3:	*(wound movement)* Injury. Injury. Allegedly used by protesters. Allegedly used.
Actor Two:	The Medic and Healer Council responded,
C4:	*(wound movement)* The Medic and Healer Council.
Actor One:	These statements are refuted by several eyewitnesses who watched police intentionally throw concussion grenades at unarmed people,

C5:	*(wound movement)* Who watched police intentionally
C6:	*(wound movement)* throw concussion grenades at the unarmed …
Actor Two:	There is a charring of flesh at the wound site,
C1:	*(wound movement)* throw concussion grenades at unarmed
C2:	*(wound movement)* at unarmed people
Actor One:	and by the grenade pieces that have been removed from her arm in surgery
C3:	(wound movement) From
C4:	(wound movement) Her
C5:	(wound movement) Arm
Actor Two:	and will be saved for legal proceedings."
C6:	*(wound movement)* and will be saved
The Chorus:	*(In a cluster of voices, some repeating "pop-pop-pop," while others alternate and repeat, "We love you—We will pray for you—We love you," the* **Chorus** *comes back together, as in the opening scene, in a clump to stay warm. They are again freezing cold with their arms wrapped around their individual body to stave off the freezing. The* **Chorus** *moves upstage and then circles around and through the* **Actors.** *As the scene ends the chorus is upstage center and the* **Actors,** *with their backs to the audience, are downstage center right and left facing the* **Chorus.**) *(End of scene)*

The chorus creates vocal background music, rippling echoes, and contrasting chants to demonstrate the range of sounds that can be imagined for crossed and reinforced readings. As the chorus "flocks" toward certain points on the stage to emphasize key passages from the reading, the hologram works as a parallel reading in visual form. The words of the news-text become a sonic and visual double telling of the text through modes of crossed, reinforced, and parallel readings that follow unexpected choices.

HISTORICAL READING

The news item is supplemented specifically by relevant historical material. Historical reading is unique in that it may include the other forms of Newspaper Theatre: parallel, crossed, complementary, rhythmic, improvisation, and so forth with the stipulation being that these forms are at the service of illuminating historical information.

RHYTHMICAL READING

We discover the musicality of words in the article through a focus on rhythm and beat. The words are now transformed, more akin to poetry and/or song than the original prose text. The words become lyrics punctuated by the musicality of rhythm and beats to form a new sensation for the reader where reading invokes a feeling of movement.

IV. Traveling stories

R1 and **R2** go back and forth in a less contested dialogue than the one in the previous exercise. This is an ethnographic rhythmical reading centering on the notion of "truth." This time, the **Recorders** are reaching for a greater sense of ethnographic purpose through questions of interpretation and the notion of multiple truths that are simultaneously harmful on one end and liberating on another. Through history and a rhythmic poetics, they contemplate these tensions and attempt to resolve them. During the scene, various images of their fieldwork sites are projected on the two large encompassing screens, providing the illusion of being inside the field. **R1** and **R2** are moving freely about the stage in all directions stopping and starting improvisationally at their own pace.

R2: Historical fact. In 1807, Britain used its naval power and its diplomatic muscle to outlaw trade in slaves by its citizens and to begin a campaign to stop the international trade in slaves. The importation of slaves into the United States was outlawed in 1808. These efforts, however, were not successful until the 1860s because of the continued demand for plantation labor in the New World

R1: Truth is elusive

R2: But it demands our attention

R1: It doesn't stay in one place or breathe inside one story

R2: But, it can. We've got to find those one places and those one stories. We've got to search. Truth demands our attention in the multitudes of its yearnings. We've got to fight for it. We are not alone

R1: Can we see and listen deeply, past the obtuse blindness of appearances and the paralyzing silence of too much noise

R2: Historical truth. Toward the end of the classical era, larger regional kingdoms had formed in West Africa, one of which was the Kingdom of Ghana, north of what is today the nation of Ghana.

R1: Historical truth. Before its fall at the beginning of the 10th century Ashanti migrants moved southward and founded several nation-states, including the first empire of Bono founded in the 11th century and for which the Brong-Ahafo of Ashantiland is named.

R2: Deep past the Lies reborn again and again by the greedy and the lazy

R1: We will search for Truth in the multitudes of the one story

R2: The one story that is always here and there and in the everywhere details of life lived on the hard, edge blade of truth's teeth

R1: It will hurt, it always does. Because truth's blade cuts deep, deep at the skin and bone of what it implies

R1: The implication

R2: Yes. The implication that breaks your heart and demands the search for more truth. More truth. More

R1: Historical fact. Republic of Ghana, is a unitary presidential constitutional democracy, located along the Gulf of Guinea and Atlantic Ocean, in the subregion of West Africa.

R2: Historical fact. Spanning a land mass of 238,535 km^2, Ghana is bordered by the Ivory Coast in the west, Burkina Faso in the north, Togo in the east and the Gulf of Guinea and Atlantic Ocean in the south. *Ghana* means "Warrior King" in the Soninke language.

R1: Do we feel our hearts breaking from the teeth

R2: Sometimes. But more than breaking, we feel our heart swelling as if it is about to burst open into flame

R1: Burst from what

R2: Burst from the fear and hope of finding the right question to spark the right story that will unleash an avalanche of truth

R1: Bursting from the fear and hope of how we will carry these stories back, so they will not soften the teeth of truth or dull its blade

R2: We are bursting from how we will listen and wrap words around the stories that we must carry back

R1: Back home

R2: Back here

R1: Back everywhere. The words we wrap around Truth's teeth will fly past us and carry themselves beyond our reach. We make Retold stories

R2: Every Retold story becomes a traveling story. Retold far beyond the presence of our own body

R1: Retold for truth's sake? To harden the teeth and sharpen the blade

R2: Yes. Our hearts are bursting and not breaking from the weight of the search, the weight of the question, the implication, but most of all, most of all, from the weight of carrying these truths truly

R1: Yes, beyond our reaches and beyond the starting point of the one true story

R2: What give us the right to search for true stories? How can we hang words upon them?

R1: We are not of this place. This is not our home

R2: Historical fact. The territory of present-day Ghana has been inhabited for millennia, with the first permanent state dating back to the 11th century. Numerous kingdoms and empires emerged over the centuries, of which the most powerful was the Kingdom of Ashanti.
Beginning in the 15th century, numerous European powers contested the area for trading rights, with the British ultimately establishing control of the coast by the late 19th century.

R1: Historical fact. Following over a century of native resistance, Ghana's current borders were established by the 1900s as the British Gold Coast. On 6 March 1957, it became the first sub-Saharan African nation to become independent of European colonization.
R2: We live in the richest country in the world
R1: That is a fact. What should we do about it?
R2: Use it like a blade on fire against its own flame
R1: For Truth's sake?
R2: Yes, and for the sake of hearts on the verge of exploding
R1
  and R2: Yes, and for the sake of hearts on the verge of exploding.
 (End of Scene)

The historical passages are inserted between the lyricism of the "truth" so that the prose of history and the poetics in search of the one "true story" form a rhythmic call and response. History is embellished by poetry and vice versa. There are four movement and vocal transitions between R1 and R2 that highlight abstract thought and material reality. This mode is most poignantly illustrated through spoken word and oral history performance.

COMPLEMENTARY READING

The purpose here is to add relevant material omitted from the news article. These complementary materials can be strategically inserted into the article demonstrating the contrast or difference between their inclusion as opposed to their exclusion in the manner the news is interpreted and represented in the original article. The complementary readings may come from your own research, experience, or other news sources,

INSERTION INTO THE ACTUAL CONTEXT[18]

The news story is placed within a performance frame that depicts the actual context of the story, not available or less accessible in the news. Through the insertion of a performance mode, the news story exceeds the experience of reading and now becomes a sensory encounter with the time, space, and/or circumstances of the news subject.

IMPROVISATION

A theme or news story is now made into a subject for improvisation. Improvisation offers the widest choices for Newspaper Theatre, for example, dance or symbolic movement, comic dialogue or monologue, narrative scenarios, performance art or tableau, song lyrics and musical renditions, or any improvisational act within a performance frame that is prompted by a news event or selected text.

V. Together across borders[19]

There are three locations, including both live and digital performances, where two large screens are placed. Different audiences are in each separate location. The screens project live feed or pre-taped recordings, depending on the technical capacity or preferences of the ensemble. The first location presented here is "Dakota" that takes place in woods, forest, or prairie. The second location, as mentioned in the news report, represents Wells Fargo Bank or a staged replica of the bank. The third location is the Waldorf Astoria or a staged replica of the hotel.

#1. DAKOTA

Beat One:
Three actors form a triangle; they are outside surrounded by trees or prairie flora. Two actors are positioned left and right with a third actor who is elevated, upstage center. The downstage actors chant and sing excerpts of songs from the Dakota Pipeline protests as they hold a small vase and pour drops of water on the ground surrounding the trees or prairie plants. The center stage actor performs an indigenous dance circling around the other actors and the three points of the triangle. The two actors place down their water and join the dancer. At the end of the dance the three actors position themselves at various points on the land against the backdrop of the flora.

Beat Two:
A video appears on both screens showing a protest at a Wells Fargo Bank in New York City. The live actors use improvisation to interact with the projected image of the Wells Fargo protest. They use vocal and movement cues to echo and replicate the protesters at the bank to be virtually with them.

Beat Three:
At the end of the video, the actors improvise from the pantheon of indigenous myths and narrative a reflection on the power of water. A second video now appears on the two screens. The actors move to the audience area to watch the screen.

Beat Four:
From the audience area the live actors, again, improvise movement and vocal cues to be virtually present and interactive with the Waldorf Astoria protestors.

Beat Five:
The video ends and the performers invite the audience to come into the performance space to join them in song and dance. Small vases of water are passed among audience members for each to pour drops of water on the trees and plants.

#2. WELLS FARGO BANK, NEW YORK

This performance takes place in the original protest site or in a public space constructed as the virtual Wells Fargo Bank, depending on the ensemble's resources and access. Screens positioned on the site play a live stream or recorded video of the "Dakota" performance. In a live performance, two actors come from the audience section and stand downstage of each screen. An image of the Oceti Sakowin Camp at Standing Rock in North Dakota is projected on the two screens.

Actor One [as Broadcast Reporter]:   In New York City, close to 100 people protested outside Wells Fargo's 15th annual pipeline symposium to demand Wells Fargo and other banks stop investing in the $3.8 billion Dakota Access pipeline. This is Rachel Marco-Havens of Earth Guardians.

Actor Two [as Rachel Marco-Havens]:   We're standing here today in front of the Waldorf Astoria, traditionally this has held the 1 percent for as long as it's been standing. Inside, there are pipeline investors, and I just met one. And I met three, and they all say they don't care about what happens to the people along the lines of the extractive industry. We are here because water is life. We are here because we must stand in solidarity across Turtle Island to take care of each other and to stop this fossil fuel infrastructure and to recognize that we can transition to renewable now. We must defund these corporations.

The screen now shows the "Dakota" folktale performance (live streamed or recorded). The two live actors now mirror the actions of the Dakota folktale performance as they are virtually performing with the actors on screen. At the end of the improvisation, the live performers join the audience. A different video (live streamed or recorded) is now shown of the Waldorf Astoria protest. As the video ends, the two actors invite the audience to join in the song and dance resembling the Dakota performance as they are given small vases to drop water into the plants placed along the performance area.

#3. WALDORF ASTORIA, NEW YORK

This performance takes place in the original protest site or in a public space constructed as the Waldorf Asteria, depending on the resources and access of the ensemble. Screens positioned on the site play (a live stream or recorded) video of the "Dakota" performance. The live performance of two actors is downstage of one large screen with a projection of the Oceti Sakowin Camp at Standing Rock.

Actor One [as Broadcast Reporter]:   On Sunday, the U.S. Army Corps of Engineers denied Energy Transfer Partners, the company behind the pipeline, a permit to drill under the Missouri River, halting construction for now. This is Rocio Velandia at the New York City protest reacting to the news.

Actor Two [as Rocio Velandia]: They had announced that they were going to stop, but we saw it just like a war tactic to disperse and confuse. But we are the indigenous peoples of Mother Earth, and we are used to the injustices against our people. We know how to survive. We have been here for thousands of years, and we will remain. And whatever happens to the indigenous people is actually happening to everyone on Earth. We have to understand that when the water is gone, we will all be gone.

Beat Three:

The projection of the Wells Fargo Bank Protest is (live streamed or pre-recorded) on the screen as the actors present an improvisation mirroring the actions of the bank protest, interacting with the actions on screen, in a virtual ensemble performance.

The Bank protest fades out as the last scene of the Dakota performance comes into view. A second screen now shows the last scene of the Bank protest. Now, in all three sites audience and actors sing, dance, and chant together, live and virtually, as they pass and share small vases to drop water into the plants placed along the performance area.

***

These examples are listed to spark more ideas and to imagine other arrangements from Boal's twelve modes of NPT. Countless modes of staging any text—from poetry, novels, and newspaper reports to ethnographic data, oral histories, field interviews, and more—can be generated from NPT. Boal intended this technique to be a method of intervention and protest where the "Theatre of the Oppressed" can then counteract forms of hegemony and exploitation where counter-hegemonic action can now embrace distortion on one hand and honor a free press, which is celebrated to underscore the machinations of the powerful, on the other. Newspaper Theatre is not only meant to unveil the discrepancies and falsehoods of news reporting and other textual materials, but is also to underscore and honor those news reports and textual materials that excavate the truth and enlighten the public. Boal's modes of Newspaper Theatre are much like a jazz aesthetic in that they are improvisational, layered with techniques and forms, and like "theatrical jazz" they embrace "rebellious identities" (Jones 2015: 33). We turn and conclude with a jazz aesthetic commentary from Jones: "The propensity for transformation connects theatrical jazz to social change and social justice. Theatrical jazz transformation is built on truth telling present-tenseness, and dedication to joy, hope, and life." She goes on to state, "To tell the truth in the present moment means an acknowledgment of a host of social devastations" (2015: 211) (Figures 4.1–4.3).

Figure 4.1 Labor Rites. Efforts and factors in the labor of factory work. Choreography by Joel Valentin-Martinez. Photograph by Rafi Letzter.

Figure 4.2 Labor Rites. Rhythms of chaos as the devil punishes Sisyphus. Choreography by Joel Valentin-Martinez. Photograph by Rafi Letzter.

110 Embodied technique and practice

Figure 4.3 Labor Rites. Newspaper Theatre as Wise Clowns witness the journalist write his story in the present while imagining it unfolding before their eyes. Upstage actors read the article in future time. Photograph by Rafi Letzter.

Notes

1 Jacques Lacoq is regarded as one of the 20th century's most influential teachers of the physical art of acting. He was born December 15 in Paris, France and participated and trained in various sports as a child and as a young man. During the Second World War, he began exploring gymnastics, mime, movement, and dance with a group who used performance to express their opposition to the German occupation of France. After the war, Lecoq then studied mime with Jean Daste (a former pupil of the acclaimed teacher of mime, Jacques Copeau), who introduced him to masked performance and Japanese Noh theatre. He left Grenoble and spent six months teaching mask work in Germany, before accepting another teaching position at the University of Padua in Italy. He spent eight years in Italy teaching and working as a creative practitioner and discovered the traditional and popular Italian theatre style of *Commedia dell'arte* as well as the tradition of masked chorus work developed in Ancient Greek tragedy. He returned to Paris in 1956 and opened his own school, the Ecole Internationale de Mime et de Théâtre, which has had many homes in Paris over the years but has continued to attract large numbers of students from all over the world. Lecoq also toured with demonstrations of his physical art of the actor and periodically conducted classes in Britain that had an enormous impact on the development of British theatre. He was awarded the prestigious Légion d'Honneur in 1982 and continued to take classes at his school right up to the day before his death on January 19, 1999. Lecoq's work and research has mainly been disseminated through the training he has conducted with the many students who have attended his classes and demonstrations overseas or his classes at his school in Paris. This may be why a myth is often circulated that suggests his methods were somehow secretive or reserved only for his students. However, he has published numerous articles

and interviews, edited a text in French entitled *Le Théâtre du Geste* (1987) and his book, *The Moving Body* (translated and published in English posthumously in 2000), outlines a number of his philosophies and approaches. The texts he has produced also indicate why it is so difficult for students to pass on his teachings. They explain that the training is very practical and very specific for each student because every actor's body and mind has accumulated different tensions and conditioned responses. Lecoq's training methods therefore focus on releasing pre-conditioned views of acting and bringing an actor's attention back to "playing" (https://resource.acu.edu.au/siryan/Academy/theatres/lecoq,jacques.htm).

2 Rudolf Laban was born in Bratislava, Hungary, in 1879. He was an architect and painter and became fascinated with rituals, folklore, mythology, dancing, art, and mathematics. He saw life as a dynamic movement experience. He founded several dance/movement schools in Germany and in 1930 became Director of Movement at the State Theatres in Berlin. Eventually, however, the Nazis banned his notation and books. Laban fled to Paris and later travelled to England where he turned his energies to education and improving the efficiency and harmony of the industrial workforce. He died in 1958. Laban looked upon movement as a two-way language process through which the body could communicate by giving and receiving messages. He believed that movement stems from the inter-dependence of body, mind, and spirit, and he understood that our inner life relates to the outer world. Laban created a theoretical language in order to help the observer understand and record movement objectively. This is still widely used in many fields of the movement/dance and therapy worlds. In the therapeutic field, studying and using the basic fundamentals of Laban movement, these come under the titles of body, space, relationship, and effort, and enables one to obtain a greater understanding of one's own movement patterns and preferences. It helps to increase observation skills of others and to record and assess the movement needs of clients in the clinical setting (www.sesame-institute.org/movement-rudolf-laban).

3 From *Acting: Psychophysical Phenomenon and Process*, edited by Phillip B. Zarrilli, Jerri Daboo, and Rebecca Loukes: "Given our focus on acting as psychophysical phenomenon and process, we use the compound term 'psychophysical' to mark the dialectical engagement of the actor's bodymind in the 'inner' and 'outer' process that constitute specific approaches to acting. We view the phenomenon of acting as an embodied, inter-subjective, inter-corporeal, experiential process of attending to and enacting tasks/actions, and of sensing, perceiving, feeling, remembering, and imaging—all shaped by historically and culturally specific assumptions and/or paradigms. Therefore, one of our purposes is to investigate and interrogate these specific modes of experience and engagement of the actor as they have been shaped by historically and culturally specific paradigms. We also step back from these specific discussions to strategically consider more general questions about acting."

4 This exercise was taken from Clive Barker's *Theatre Games* (1978) with an accompanying DVD that includes Barker leading a workshop of his games at the University of Warwick, UK, in Spring 2003, with a group of participants. Barker worked with Joan Littlewood's Theatre Workshop (1955). He directed at the Royal Court, for the German National Theatre, and lectured and directed across the USA and Europe. He was joint editor of *New Theatre Quarterly*.

5 See Barker (2010).
6 See Barker (2010).
7 Irmgard Bartenieff (1900–1981), dancer, choreographer, and pioneering physiotherapist, attained worldwide renown as the foremost authority in the United States on the work of Rudolf Laban, whose methods of notation and analysis of human movement she developed and adapted. In 1943, Bartenieff graduated from New York University's Physical Therapy Program, and over the next several

years worked as a therapist in several New York area hospitals where Bartenieff helped rehabilitate victims of the polio epidemic. In 1965, the renown folklorist, Alan Lomax approached Bartenieff about joining his Performance Style and Culture Research Project, conducted through the Anthropology Department of Columbia University. Bartenieff was teaching courses in the Effort/Shape program at the Dance Notation Bureau and together, she and Lomax along with some of her students, collaborated in creating the method of cross-cultural dance analysis known as Choreometrics. In chapter 10 of Lomax's book, *Folk Song, Style and Culture* (1968), Lomax, Bartenieff, and Paulay (one of her students) describe the origin and meaning of the term: "In order to distinguish the level of this comparative study of movement from the levels where previous investigators have worked, we have given the method a freshly coined designation, Choreometrics, meaning the measure of dance, or dance as a measure of culture" (223). They wrote: "Choreometrics tests the proposition that dance is the most repetitious, redundant, and formally organized system of body communication present in a culture ... The dance is composed of those gestures, postures, movements, and movement qualities most characteristic and most essential to the activity of everyday, and thus crucial to cultural continuity. By treating these elements redundantly and formally, dance becomes an effective organizer of joint motor activity. Dance supplies the metronome to meter and regulates, or orders the energy and attention of groups of people, and thereby acquires the weight of general community approval. Thus dance functions to establish and renew consensus at moments when a society, without further discussion or explanation, is ready to act in concert" (224) (www.culturalequity.org/alanlomax/ce_alanlomax_profile_irmgard_bartenieff.php).

8 Described with more detail in his book: *Monkey: A Theory of African American Literary Fiction* (2014). See bibliography.
9 The 5Rhythms are further elucidated by a series of four maps. The maps foreground embodiment, affect, life cycles, and archetypal themes across the 5Rhythms. The *first* map, "Waves," constitutes all the rhythms, danced in sequence, with a focus on the body as a vessel of wisdom and memory. Each rhythm evolves into the next as a continuous evocation and expression of embodied intelligence, experience, and memory. Gabrielle Roth reminds us that the body knows things and remembers things. The wave opens the path, at each stage, for these knowledges to be set into motion. The *second* map, "Heartbeat," is directed toward our heartfelt emotions and how the overarching wave, patterns, and energies of the 5Rhythms can open our hearts and tap into our emotional core and what Roth referred to as the *spontaneous heart*. This map is concerned specifically with the body as carrier of emotion and how we hold fear, anger, sadness, joy, and compassion to then transform all those emotions into movement. The *third* map, "Cycles," directs us to an embodied contemplation of our life cycles: birth, childhood, puberty, maturity, and death. This map invokes a moving story of our lives and the internal imprints—consequences or influences—each cycle has upon our body, mind, and spirit. "We make connections, reweave threads, let go of the hurt and humiliations. We get real." She goes on to state: "We honor the people and events that have shaped who we are and the challenges and gifts they left us with and reinvent our inherited self into somebody we truly want to be." This cycle manifests both our personal memories and their release—both present time and possible futures. In the *fourth* map, "Mirrors," we watch and become witness to, what Roth called, our *ego characters*. The moving body is also a contemplative body. Without judgment, we see ourselves as we respond, enact, and embody various roles that we play and replay throughout our life cycles. Movement in the mirror stage can be both action and enlivened stillness, in gestures that evoke self-reflection of the ego and its characters, while calling upon an authenticity of the self or embodied realizations of how we might move

in the world more generously open to others. These notes were drawn from www.5rhythms.com.
10　Gabrielle Roth (1941–2012). The guiding principle behind Roth's work was her theory of the 5Rhythms. Roth grew up on the East Coast. Possessed by "a hunger for rituals of spirit," as she described it in her book *Sweat Your Prayers*, she became fascinated by the two poles of body and spirit represented by ballet and religion. She was seven when she glimpsed a ballerina through the window of a dance school and made up her mind that that was what she wanted to do. Religion held just as large a place in her young life. On Sundays, she hid in the bushes outside the local fundamentalist church, enraptured by the passionate rhythms of preaching and singing. She continued dancing through college, to rock 'n' roll as well as ballet, until an old knee injury stopped her. Doctors told her she would never dance again. Roth gave up dancing. "I had been cruelly cut off from a deep and beautiful part of myself," she later wrote in her book. She was thrown into a deep depression. She retreated to Big Sur, California, to participate in group therapy at the famous Esalen Institute. Before long, she had joined the institute's staff as a masseuse. When director Fritz Perls discovered Roth had once taught movement therapy in a mental hospital, he asked her to teach it to Esalen therapy groups. The turning point came one evening at an institute social event. Live percussionists were pounding out rhythms and Roth found herself on the dance floor in spite of her knee. The music took over completely. By the time she came back to herself, she was exhausted and drenched in sweat. Time had cured her wound. She later said that the experience taught her that humans have a natural craving for ecstatic experience and one way of satisfying it was through dance. She devoted herself to uncovering "the flow of each person's energy." That would be the key to her emerging knowledge. The form the knowledge eventually took was the 5Rhythms. Roth explained in an interview with Amazon. com. "The language of movement is rhythm. Rhythm is our mother tongue, and everything is moving in a beat, in a pulse, in a pattern, in a cycle, in a wave. I began to notice that as people surrendered to their dance, their soul became more visible. And when that energy was visible, one could see the patterns of rhythm that were natural to the soul. These five rhythms are Flowing, Staccato, Chaos, Lyrical, and Stillness. And each one is like a state of being" (www.musicianguide.com/biographies/1608002429/Gabrielle-Roth.html#ixzz29gUnl0of).
11　www.5rhythms.com.
12　Augusto Boal was raised in Rio de Janeiro. He was formally trained in chemical engineering and attended Columbia University in the late 1940s and early 1950s. Although his interest and participation in theatre began at an early age, it was just after he finished his degree at Columbia that he was asked to return to Brazil to work with the Arena Theatre in São Paulo. Prior to his experimentation, and following tradition, audiences were invited to discuss a play at the end of the performance. In so doing, according to Boal, they remained viewers and "reactors" to the action before them. In the 1960s, Boal developed a process whereby audience members could stop a performance and suggest different actions for the character experiencing oppression, and the actor playing that character would then carry out the audience suggestions. But in a now legendary development, a woman in the audience once was so outraged the actor could not understand her suggestion that she came onto the stage and showed what she meant. For Boal, this was the birth of the spect-actor (not spectator) and his theatre was transformed. He began inviting audience members with suggestions for change onto the stage to demonstrate their ideas. In so doing, he discovered that through this participation, the audience members became empowered not only to imagine change but to actually practice that change, reflect collectively on the suggestion, and thereby become empowered to generate social action. Theatre became a practical vehicle for grass-roots activism. His work at the Arena Theatre led

to his experimentation with new forms of theatre that would have an extraordinary impact on traditional practice. Because of Boal's work, he drew attention as a cultural activist. But the military coups in Brazil during the 1960s looked upon all such activity as a threat. Walking home from an Arena performance of Brecht's *The Resistible Rise of Arturo Ui* Boal directed in 1971, Boal was kidnapped off the street, arrested, tortured, and eventually exiled to Argentina, then self-exiled to Europe. In Argentina in 1973, he published his first major theatre text, *The Theatre of the Oppressed* (Routledge Press). While in Paris, Boal continued for a dozen years to teach his revolutionary approach to theatre, establishing several Centers for the Theatre of the Oppressed. In 1981, he organized the first International Festival of the Theatre of the Oppressed in Paris. Following the removal of the military junta in Brazil, Boal returned to Rio de Janeiro in 1986. He has established a major Center for the Theatre of the Oppressed there (CTO – Rio) and has formed over a dozen companies that develop community-based performances. The vehicles for these presentations are primarily Forum Theater and Image Theater. Forum Theater relies upon presentation of short scenes that represent problems of a given community such as gender for a conference on women or racial stereotyping for a class on racism. Audience members interact by replacing characters in scenes and by improvising new solutions to the problems being presented. Image Theater uses individuals to sculpt events and relationships sometimes to the accompaniment of a narrative. Reference from Doug Paterson at http://ptoweb.org/aboutpto/a-brief-biography-of-augusto-boal/.

13 Reader's Theatre is a performance form where actors do not memorize their lines. In early renditions of Reader's Theatre, actors relied primarily on vocal expression to convey the text in place of full sets, costumes, intricate blocking, and movement. This was referred to as performance of literature because it emphasized the deep and varied listening of a written text as a new way to engage literature. Reader's Theatre is also known as Chamber Theatre or Interpretive Theatre. Reader's Theatre became popular during and following the Second World War when resources to produce plays were scarce. There are four different types of Reader's Theatre, each an evolution of the former and each with different attributes: (1) Reader's Theatre; (2) Free Reader's Theatre; (3) Chamber Theatre; and (4) Contemporary Reader's Theatre. These styles of RT are variously performed in ethnographic and theatrical venues and purposes. In the early days, Reader's Theatre was presented using only scripts and stools or chairs. The material performed was plays, poems, narrative fiction, and non-dramatic literature. The performers' focus was offstage and limited costuming was sometimes used (often the readers wore all black to strip away character and allow for more focus on vocal interpretation of the piece). While the readers may have interpreted the scenes or poems cold, in most cases, large portions of the scripts were memorized. In these RTs, there was little to no interaction between performers or movement. Free Reader's Theatre is freer than traditional Reader's Theatre. The performers look at and interact with each other; the presence of scripts is optional. Blocking appears to suggest psychological relationships between characters and pictorial compositions (for example, if two characters hated each other, they might be at opposite ends of the stage, and as the tension rises, they might move toward each other). The performers wore additional costume pieces to help suggest character (such as a hat or shawl). Chamber Theatre focused on narrative fiction. Scripts were almost always memorized (a narrator might carry a script to make their authoritative voice). The movement became more elaborate and could be associated with more traditional theatre practices; it was used in such a way to reveal the character's role and relationships in the story. Costuming evolved into suggested or full costumes. Contemporary Reader's Theatre is far less bound by convention and uses techniques from all of the above traditions of RT. It is influenced by performance art techniques; there is an increasing emphasis on

creating a critical performance that interrogates the text instead of being faithful to it (https://en.wikipedia.org/wiki/Reader%27s_theatre).
14 The script was adapted from www.newyorker.com/news/newsdesk/the-battle-for-aleppo-syria-stalingrad-ends: The Battle for Aleppo, Syria's Stalingrad, Ends, December 13, 2016 by Robin Wright who has been a contributing writer for the magazine since 1988.
15 Inspired by my fieldwork in Ghana on the human right to water, I directed a performance entitled *Water Rites* on the campus of the University of North Carolina at Chapel Hill, Studio Six for five nights in March 2006. The posters and announcements for *Water Rites* described it as "a multi-media performance on the politics and poetics of water." *Water Rites* explored water democracy and our human relationship with water through a montage of digital imagery, comic satire, dramatic monologue, and stylized movement. *Water Rites* reflected how we all perform "water rites" in our everyday lives and how these rites variously pervade our lives and culture. *Water Rites* performed the questions: What is your first memory of water? Does anyone have the right to own water? Are water wars still taking place in the 21st century? What is the connection between local water and global profit? Included in the announcement for the show was a quote from Ismail Serageldin (former vice-president of the World Bank, 1995) when he said: "If the wars of the twentieth century were fought over oil, the wars of this century will be fought over water." In weaving performance, fieldwork data, personal reflection, and theoretical analysis, Act II becomes a multi-sited, multi-vocal, and multi-spatial account of the human right to water, water activism, and everyday water rituals.
16 This story comes Ann-Christin Sjolander Holland's (2005) *The Water Business: Corporations versus People*.
17 The script was adapted from https://theintercept.com/2016/11/21/medics-describe-how-police-sprayed-standing-rock-demonstrators-with-tear-gas-and-water-cannons. Medics Describe How Police Sprayed Standing Rock Demonstrators with Tear Gas and Water Cannons by Allen Brown, November 21, 2016.
18 Integration of Field Interview (the lost technique). This technique only appears in a review from 1971 as part of the Newspaper Theatre techniques. It relates to the concept of "hot-seating" in which you ask questions for the character to deepen political implications relevant to those in the room.
19 The script was adapted from www.democracynow.org/2016/12/7/headlines/nyc_dozens_protest_outside_wells_fargo_pipeline_symposium. NYC: Dozens Protest Outside Wells Fargo Pipeline Symposium, December 7, 2016.

Part 2

Oral history and personal narrative performance

Chapter 5

The value of oral history and life story

> I understand performance as a mode of communication, a way of speaking, the essence of which resides in the assumption of responsibility to an audience for a display of communication skill, highlighting the way in which communication is carried out, above and beyond its referential content. From the point of view of the audience, the act of expression on the part of the performer is thus laid open to evaluation for the way it is done, for the relative skill and effectiveness of the performer's display. It is also offered for the enhancement of experience, through the present appreciation for the intrinsic qualities of the act of expression itself.
>
> (Bauman 1986: 3)

> Artistic experience and practice are here best understood for their capacity to agitate at the level of sensation. And it is this force that propels a demand to know more. The communicative model of art—the focus on the impact, message or precise revelation—is countered with a notion that the stimulation of affect is what compels the participant to thought and to be engaged at every level. ... the impact of the work of participatory theatre opened us to the sustenance of sensation and the subsequent fueling of inquiry ... The effects are not foretold, but the affects stimulate—and being overcome by joy ... or dancing ... might loosen the icy grip of certain oppressive visions of how we should be in the world.
>
> (Thompson 2009)

The concern in this section is how to transform personal stories and hidden histories into public events, whether those events become the dramas witnessed by audiences on the public stage or whether they are performed in the intimacies of collectives, coalitions, or performance workshops. There is an abiding invitation that is brought into focus and set loose when narratives are made public (Denzin 1997, 2003; Hamera 2007; Johnson 2003; Pollock 2005; Rowe 2005; Spry 2011).

The public performances of oral histories "do" something (Langellier and Peterson 2004) in their life remembrances; and this doing is a performance praxis that is a pedagogical braiding of vernacular wisdoms, narrated histories, and aesthetic choices. Oral histories, as re-authored memory, exceed verifiable statements to become living testimonies of competence; socially transmitted and embodied techniques; formations of truth and belonging; how to care and not for others; the acts and consequences of language; and how to be happy and unhappy (Kurahashi 2013: 257). Oral history performances also reveal the "limits of one's own horizons and an interest in seeing alternative perspectives" (Turner in Nicholson 2014: 14). We also bear witness to how the self is constituted through narrative and how the self can also be changed through narrative. We are witness to how the other sees us, and we are, in turn, now invited to witness ourselves in and through the eyes of others (Lagones in Madison 1994: 626–637). Oral history gives us access. We learn another story. We come to realize that others live in spaces and times very much like our own. In contrast, we come to realize how others live very differently from our worlds in unimaginable ways.

Public stories abound in how systemic power operates on the level of intimacy and the body. It is a story of how ideology and value are sustained, yet changed. Because narrative performance transforms personal problems into social issues, problems are no longer "locked within the individual as some personal or unchanging characteristic or personality trait" (Sliep et al. 2013: 85). Narrative performance sets loose problems that beset our world "from the multiple relationships in which the individual is immersed" (85). Oral history performance made public enacts human consciousness as it dramatizes, clarifies, breaks open, and deconstructs taken for granted contexts. In the words of Victor Turner, oral history performance is a "contamination of contexts" as it stains the contexts of the "one dangerous story" (or hegemonic narrative) that dishonors the context of its oral history performance (Turner in Nicholson 2014: 14).

Oral history, as both singular and universal (Denzin 2003), is a blend of the profound individuality of a human life that is paradoxically inseparable from the multiple circulations across the realities and imaginings of the social life. It is here where our individuality is both made and sustained by ourselves and others. And, because "Our singular stories emerge from circulations of social beings and their productions the question becomes: Whose story is this anyway? Who owns the story in narrative performance?" (Nicholson 2014: 72)

Who owns the story?

When we perform stories and oral histories from our fieldwork and in-depth interviews, the question of "ownership" may arise. Who owns this story that we work so hard, in preparation and live event, to ultimately embody? Does the question of "ownership" belong to the performer or the interlocutor/teller/subject? This question of ownership is not an easy one. When the original narrative becomes embodied by the performer and the question of ownership or re-authoring is asked, it complicates "ownership of enunciation"[1] (Rowe 2007: 166). Are the performer and the performance simply vessels or physical transmitters to the original owner of the story? Doesn't the very nature of staging constitute what Rowe describes as "affective loading" making both the stage performer and the interlocutor owners of the narrative? (2007: 88).

For example: I was invited to participate in a post-show discussion with the scholar-performer, E. Patrick Johnson, after his solo performance, entitled, *Sweet Tea* The show has toured throughout the country for over ten years and is based upon the oral histories of Black gay men in the Southern US. The performance has evolved from its early beginnings as a staged reading, and then through various directors and staging choices, and, presently, as a meta-story through filmed documentary that narrates the making of *Sweet Tea* and the relationships between the men Johnson interviewed and performance and Johnson's own Southern roots as a Black gay man. Witnessing Johnson enact each man's story and perform empathically and viscerally inside their experiences and emotions prompts the question: After all these years and after hundreds of heart-felt repetitions in words, movement, and emotions, through all of Johnson's performances across the country—I ask: To whom do these narratives belong? Over the years, Johnson's command of the stage both as learned technique and intuitive artistry variegated in spatial arrangements, symbolic layering, movement intensity, vocalization choices, and so forth. The show has had many lives.

In memorizing the words of his interlocutors, the stories were nestled in Johnson's body each time he performed them. This is not simple imitation without embodiment of the implications, contexts, and histories embedded in each narrative. Johnson was deeply committed to these life histories from vocal matching, to embodied techniques, to historical and archival research, to interpretive renderings relative to their political, metaphorical, affective, and historical implications. This process is intellectually and emotionally invested. Understanding Johnson's investment in the stories of his interlocutor, repeated and performed over the years, while each man may have told his story, in that way and at that time, only once during the occasion of the interview reflects the commitment of the oral history performer in communicating to an audience the story of others. Interlocutors may not remember exactly, word for word, what they said in an interview, especially several years in the past. This is not to make the erroneous claim that people, who lived their lives, do not remember their own stories or value them less than those enduring performances and performers who, through time and space, enacted them. The existential distinction between lived experiences that are told from personal memory, on one hand, and the stage performances that are heard and recorded from field research, on the other, is not to be dismissed or cavalierly considered indistinguishable. It is not expected that interlocutors or interviewees tell their story hundreds of times, analytically pick it apart, memorize and embody the sequencing of every word, laugh, and weep before multiple audiences, and performatively re-live again and again the story's plot and emotions, night after night. Does Johnson know these stories, even feel the truths embedded within these histories, as much as or more than the men who told them? Performances of oral histories are inherently traveling stories and in their mobility and circulation from field to stage, the question of ownership is slippery, risky, and substantive because in performance we are often made to feel as though these stories are our own. We know, and the audience knows, that they are re-told stores, but the authority of the virtuosic performer and the mesmerizing effect of theatricality can too often overshadow our understanding of authorship; however invested and rehearsed oral history performance may be; however deeply and politically beautiful the story is re-envisioned and re-interpreted to illuminate its underlying power and consequences; however repeated, enduring, and labored in transforming the story into a framed domain of embodiment and intelligibility, the stories always and already come from beginnings that are borrowed and found through the presence of others and their memories. The interlocutors' constant imprint on the story is the fact of their being in the world at a certain time, place, and circumstance. It is both a presence and a new presence that resonates, from performance to performance, emergent in the infinite possibilities of staged artistry. At the time of the interview, the interlocutor's oral narrative may have been more improvisational and less "rehearsed" than it was planned and scripted (even though it may have been told on several occasions before). Johnson takes what was once told to him and through studied effort, research embodiment, and iterations of communicative enactment, it is no longer a question of ownership but a conscientious and studied sharing, and act of critical communication. Johnson's years of performance labor and emotional investment, in these oral histories, are no longer a question of ownership but a gift of sharing. Johnson conveys/interprets the imprint of a life and its telling to an audience of strangers and relations. This does not mean the performer and the performance are only vessels or physical transmitters, but the very nature of performance allows for "affective loading."[2] The performer carries the sense-feeling weight of the narrative in an act of delivery, from actor to audience, that is more about transference than ownership. At first glance, the tenuous demarcation of ownership becomes a *both/and* site of critical sharing. In this instance, oral history belongs to *both* the interlocutor *and* to the performer, *inside* an ever-present wavering—a back-and-forth authorship. This critical sharing where the idea of ownership vacillates can be better understood through the triad of *both/and/but*. This mean the telling belongs to *both* performer *and* interlocutor *but* will always originate as a moment in a life that may or may not be the life of the performer or the interlocutor. This means we can move away from concerns of ownership and its implications of oral history as property (and commodity) to one of communion, of the commons, of a communicative space among interlocutors, performers, and ethnographers to be passed along and transferred to generate an audience echo chamber[3] where oral histories are now shared among others near and far.

In the original oral history interview, most often the interviewee responds to questions within an improvisational moment. However, Patrick's oral history performance was not improvisational. It was a staged performance constituted by many hours of embodied labor and ethics honoring his interlocutor as owners of their storied lives now transformed through a co-presence of listener and teller, of field researcher and interlocutor, of performance ethnography and performed ethnography.

Interview with E. Patrick Johnson

DSM: *You conducted the interview, you have adapted and written the script, and now you've got to perform, what do you do?*

EPJ: *When I first decided to perform these narratives, I was not interested in fully embodying them, because I wanted the focus to be on voice, and voice working on several registers ... Voice in terms of giving them a voice in a space where they wouldn't ordinarily have one, so, using the performance to bring attention to these marginalized lives ... voice also in the sense of the storytelling. A lot of the men speak their story with a narrative arc, which I find fascinating. And I didn't understand that until I was re-listening to them. Many of them, after me asking them a question, would go into a story that had a beginning, a middle and an end. I wanted to capture that sense of narrative arc.*

DSM: *Why was this important?*

EPJ: *Because they're Southerners, I wanted to capture the musicality of language, of Southern speech.*
I really paid attention to the verbal ticks the "ums," the "ahs," um. The way that some of them would use a particular word as punctuation like one of the men uses the word "whatever."
So, I really wanted to bring that to life and performance in a way that you really can't capture on the page. Even when you're transcribing it poetically, there's still something about embodying the voice.
And it was about listening and re-listening to them over and over again. And also remembering the interview so that I could give just a sense of what the nonverbal cues were in the interview.

DSM: *You wanted to bring their original voices into the performance?*

EPJ: *Yes. I was very deliberate about wanting the audience to hear the men's original voice.*

DSM: *You play excerpts of tape recordings, during your performance, of the men where the audience is able to hear their original voices in the real time of the interview.*

EPJ: *I wanted to bring in a clip of the original interview. My intention of bringing their voices to the stage was not about me usurping their voice, but being co-present with their voice.*

DSM: *I remember your very first show. It was an experience that was poignant and beautiful, and I got a feeling of all of these stories in a poetic and remarkable way, but I didn't necessarily sit inside the stories. I sat inside a deeply ephemeral feeling.*

EPJ: *Yes, it was being inside the feelings of these experiences.*

DSM: But in the second one, I'm very interested in how that director ended up with such a great performance as a result of some of his directing failures.

EPJ: I think because it forced me, in fact, I know it forced me to show up in a way that I wasn't sure in the first show. What do I mean by that? It forced me to think more deliberately about, what is it about these stories that's most important in each one of them and how they are connected to each other? And, again, it forced me to ask the questions that I asked of those men to turn around and ask of myself. The story about my coming out experience to my mother, which in the first version, remained at the comic level. The second version was much more poignant, because I was ready to reveal some of the hurt and pain around it. I wasn't willing to do this in the first version. Honestly, I don't think the show really comes together until the third version.

DSM: Going back to the second version. Did you and the director take the script and talk about each story and certain moments in the story together and what that looked like for both of you?

EPJ: Not really. This director was really into dance, so I was dancing a lot, but in the way of contemporary culture or pop culture.

DSM: It seems like the dance was informing the script and not so much the script informing the dance.

EPJ: With the second director everything was about superimposing and not listening to the text. The first director was more interested in what the text was saying. The second director was about imposing things that might be cool or slick on stage. It was more about spectacle.

DSM: Got you, got you. Okay, so let's talk about the third director?

EPJ: The third director is when it all came together, because it was more of a collaboration. He didn't come in with any kind of predisposition about what the performance is going to be. We spent a lot of time just talking.

DSM: And what kinds of things did you talk about?

EPJ: We talked about my experience with the other productions; what things worked for me as both the performer and as the researcher and scholar; what I wanted most for the performance that was going to be the last version of the show.

DSM: And you didn't have that conversation with the other two directors?

EPJ: No, because in the first version it was a production with 14 people sitting around a table talking and then a producer. It was a producer and a producing theatre; there were a lot of hands involved and everybody had an opinion about something. And because it was my first time doing professional theatre, I'm like, yeah. The second time, same thing, it was a Tony Award-winning theatre company. There were a lot of hands involved and lots of people to please.

EPJ: The third version, that wasn't the case.

DSM: *It's just you and your director?*
EPJ: *Me and the director.*
DSM: *In a room together talking?*
EPJ: *Yes, and it freed us to imagine differently in a way that wasn't about pandering to ticket holders or to subscription holders. It freed us up to talk about what these stories wanted to be in the world. It freed us to talk about what I wanted as a performer or as a scholar. And so what ended up happening was that a lot of stuff just fell away. The set was very simple. It was interesting. We kind of went back to the Reader's Theatre version where it's not about the extra stuff. For example, in one of the oral histories, whose name was Freddie, his costume was just a scarf. After Freddie is done, that scarf is taken off and that is what moves us into the next story, which is my story. And so, I become me by taking Freddie up. It was very simple things. It allowed me to settle into these men and settle into the embodiment of these men in a way that I hadn't experienced before, because I was thinking about too many other things going on.*
DSM: *Yes, like varying dance steps, or transforming into a bird, or this symbolic gesture, or that action, or multiple cues and time zones or just too much stuff and theatricality?*
EPJ: *Yes, and what happened was just miraculous, because, I felt like I did when I performed the Reader's Theatre version. The men take-over. You no longer see E. Patrick Johnson. You're seeing this other spirit come through. To be open to that without distraction.*
DSM: *Perhaps working with the third director did not completely or necessarily make the spirits come through. What made this happen was the process—for better and worse—from the very first show up to the final version.*
EPJ: *Absolutely.*
DSM: *It's such a wonderful way to talk about how you develop oral history performance, because you encounter these different methods, contrasting and in opposition to each other, where one is more improvisational, symbolic, and abstract while still inspired by the stories, and then you have the second one that is less about the story and more about the spectacle to be found or excavated from the story. And, finally, you have this third one where you learn by contrast and comparison of the first two, by their contributions and absences. All in the service of attending to the words held within the histories of these men.*
EPJ: *Yes, absolutely, because they're elements of all the directors in that last version. The soundscape from the first version is in the third version, and the narrative structure from the second version is in the third one.*
DSM: *All this was happening through your musculature, your nervous and cellular system, your vocal cords and cerebral cortex, Yes? We so often talk about thinking as a function of the brain, but what about body intelligence and how our body holds knowledge? What*

	did you learn from your body when you look back on the various iterations of Sweet Tea?
EPJ:	*There are so many examples I can give, I'll give you this one. This is what occurred: I didn't know how we were going to stage an oral history about a person who considered themself transgender for a short time and then decided to no longer be transgender. I didn't know how to capture that or make sense of that in performance. Moreover, I didn't know how I was going to make that transformation, back and forth, physically. So, the direction was to communicate it through a skeleton. There's a moment in the narrative when this transgender person has a dream and is very shaken by the dream. Someone interprets the dream for him and tells him: "The dream means, you should stop being transgender and your embodiment of femininity must cease!" This was a challenge to bring to performance, because I myself am effeminate. I had to find a way to shed not only the effeminacy, that's natural to me, but also that I had embodied for this character. The multiple challenge was the effeminate enactment still had a resonance for me, and I naturally identified with the person's femininity, but I also understood his mimicking of what he thought masculinity should be. It was this moment of performance that caused me to think about how I do that unconsciously, myself as Patrick. I didn't discover that until I had to perform it. It was a real epiphany for me. It was working through certain performance choices with the skeleton—an object that became both the embodiment and metaphor for dream, fear, death, transition, and disassociation—when I came to a realization. Performance made me realize, in a deeper and more abiding way, how this person had to negotiate enactments of masculinity and femininity consistently in his everyday life.*
DSM:	*Something that was unconscious for you was made conscious through this call upon body intelligence that is a learning, a discovery, a realization by doing.*
EPJ:	*By doing it, by doing it. Absolutely.*

***

Oral history and narrative as permission, public pedagogy, and provocation

In summary, I offer three overarching ideas that are not meant to be exhaustive or foundational, but helpful in how the work of oral history performance critically embraces the *both/and/but*: (1) permission; (2) public pedagogy; (3) provocation.

First. *Permission.* When performing living memories that hold the lives, well-being, and futures of others in their plots and implications, we ask ourselves: What does performance do to these remembered tellings? What are the consequences for those interlocutors implicated within a history when it is represented within the theatrical frame of performance? We recognize that an oral history is told to us. We are not the tellers but the listeners on the recurring and responsive end of another's memory. The act of receptivity is more than an act of receiving like something given to us as a gift that now belongs to us. Performance of oral history is also permission to respond. Permission for a response constituted by performance that allows and honors the making and remaking of historical accounts that do not always necessitate the "true stories" of an empirical reality of past event, but the felt-sensing experiences of life remembered and lived in the imagination and hermeneutics of human memory and yearnings (within the moments of an ethnographic exchange). We are witness to how memory is partial, sometimes mistaken as fact, yet not necessarily untrue—but interpreted and contested on so many levels relative to authenticity and truth, particularly when it is embraced by entire communities. Because oral histories tease the borders between empirical truth, imaginative truth, and partial memory, the granting of permission becomes even more important because the stakes of the stories are so often both intimately imagined and communally constituted. The performance of oral narratives will take many forms, not only true and imagined, but the grand dynamics of performance considers HOW we tell stories—through style and scale of movement, sonic arrangements, visual flash points provocation of the sensory, symbolic layering, and so forth. It is narratives accompanied by the theatrics of forms that stir us and move us toward the "affective identification with a multiplicity of narratives" opening uncharted paths that "wear away fixed narratives of self and other, identity and difference, and open the spaces in-between where new insights might be generated" (Nicholson 2014: 77). This all begins with mutual trust and the interlocutor's permission to proceed with the performance. This permission is the starting point for an ethical sharing that moves from notions of narrative ownership to an act of sharing—from the narrative as commodity to the narrative as commons—for the circulation of a wider public of listeners and receivers.

Second. *Public pedagogy*. When these narratives become public, they also become public pedagogies—we learn from them. These imaginings leave an imprint, "limits of one's own horizons and an interest in seeing alternative perspectives" (Nicholson 2014: 66). James Baldwin once said that we make history and history makes us. Oral narrative performance becomes the make and remake of ourselves and history performed and learned. Moreover, that which is coded, cultural, familial, and imagined is brought forth and unveiled in the profound communion of a public performance. This is now the alchemy of particularity that pivots from discussion of belonging, human unity, and the common to what is now un-common, that is, the quintessentially different, the unshared, of the one and only story. It is this particularity—the one story—where lessons are learned and horizons extended. Tell me what I didn't know, what I never imagined and what I now come to imagine. Oral history performances are pedagogies of what we did not know or feel before, in this way.

Third. *Praxis and provocation*. We witness how social construction is constructed, how systemic power operates on the level of intimacy, and how ideology is made, sustained, and changed—true to the processes of deconstruction—things are taken apart to reveal the hidden (2014: 88). Narrative performance transforms the particularities of personal problems into the publicity of social issues (Alexander 2005; Conquergood 1997, 1998, 2000, 2002; Denzin 1997, 2003; Hamera 2007; Johnson 2008; Langellier and Peterson 2004; Pineau 2006; Pollock 1990, 1999, 2005; Spry 2016). We know that narrative performance unleashes problems from the multiple relationships in which the individual is immersed and as they move from individual discontent to interrogations of wider structures (Rowe 2007: 85). This pedagogy of oral history performance enacts personal memory and individual consciousness, influenced by matrixes of communities and belongings, to both unsettle and contextualize the hegemony as well as the agency and circulations of empowerments that ground them (Sliep et al. 2013). These provocations are now up for public consumption and more historical redistribution and re-imaginings.

Norman Denzin reminds us that oral history is both singular and universal in its political and social import (Denzin 1997). This blend of individuality and its inseparability from a history of social processes, made and sustained by others, is where our singular stories emerge, through performance possibilities, to offer up a contamination of contexts for public exposure, response, and action.

On truth[4]

> Oral historians (among others) shift the emphasis from fact to the experience of fact. They favor the messy, subjective life of the historical agent rather than his/her more "objective" accomplishments or conditions ... embracing the lives of those whose accomplishments might not be the stuff of conventional history, but whose agency thrives in the tactical politics of everyday living. The achievements of oral history suggest a postmodern history made up of small stories or what Lyotard calls "petit récits": history relieved of pretensions to a "master narrative," history as a somewhat humbler quilt of many voices and local hopes ... Critics/historians writing in their wake cast history in many roles—as reflections; as narrative and story; as a contest among truth, fact, ideology; as oral history, historical action; as the body in pain; as production; as promise; as lessons wrought in the interstices of modernity and postmodernity—all in an effort, it seems, to make the real-in-representation more meaningful than charges of mere facticity would allow.
> (Pollock 1998a: 18–19)

Much has been said and written about evidence and truth relative to oral history. It is a provocative topic, especially in these times of "alternative facts"[5] and the debates over what is a truthful statement and what is not when it can impact day-to-day lives and the policies of a nation. Truth is a time-worn and enormous topic. I value the truth beyond measure and I also know how contextual, circumstantial, subjective, and emotional the truth is, always. How do we get at the truth of oral history? Is truth telling the aim of oral history? If there really are multiple truths then shouldn't we want to know when, where, who, and how often? The insight about truth as it relates to oral history performance that Pollock offers is the notion of truth as irrefutable or as fact *conjoined with* how we experience or subjectively determine what is true. Truth can be both immutable and mutable. It can be a fact and a belief. Can truth be both unwavering, beyond space and time, existing outside human consciousness as a fact as well as a subjective, human interpretation that we know to be true? The beauty and complexity of oral history and narrative performance is that it encompasses both and teases the borders between fact and the *experience* of fact. The challenge is how we represent and perform the tensions between a fact and the experience of a fact: when to ethically decipher the difference between what is experience and what is fact; when there is no distinction between the two, when must we make the distinction. Another enumeration is needed here. This time an enumeration of reflections that help to clarify the tensions and ethical dilemmas of oral history and narrative performance relative to truth. This list of reflections now casts the telling of a human story.

Reflection one

As long as there are humans with a planet upon which to live there will always be abundant and remarkable life stories. There are more than enough stories for every human to tell and grasp. New and old life stories are never ending. We need not steal them from others or be stingy with our own. They are over-abundant and infinite. Each with its own truth.

Reflection two

The fact that all living organisms came from the stars and we are aligned with each other as a human species, our life stories lie on the borders, in the difference and sameness, of our planetary, atomic, and cellular inheritance. Stories bind us: "The shortest distance between two people is a story."[6] This short distance is where truths meet and gather.

Reflection three

Life stories take countless forms from a plot-line to a flash point, from a beginning-middle-and-end to non-sequential reversals or circulations, from an epic song to an abundance of soundscapes real and imagined, from a photograph to a living cell, and so forth. This means the infinity of life stories will always exceed any master narrative or the "danger of the one true story."

Reflection four

A life story is not only constituted by the words, feelings, and point of view of the teller, but also by the teller's political, social, and economic landscapes. Life stories are anchored and invested in specific locations, modes of belonging, identity, and social practices and contested truths.

Reflection five

A life story comprises a "telling and a told" in the act of the narrative and the narrated event there is the reciprocal power of place and time encapsulated in the "scenes" of the story and its telling where dialectics of truth rest (un)easily.

Reflection six

Both embodiment and representation conjoin in the performance of a life story. They are inseparable. As the felt-sensing body moves and transcends into the lifeworld of the story, it also signifies and communicates truths about itself and its subject, both in its embodiment and representation.

Reflection seven

In the performance of a life story, we not only experience the actions and emotions of others as we either witness or perform them (or both), but our brain and nervous system are affected by the imagined reality of the encounter: we cry, we laugh, we are afraid, and we imagine.

Reflection eight

Whose truth is it anyway? In performing life history, there is a tenuous demarcation of "ownership." The performer and the original storyteller share a *both/and* site of critical sharing that transcends ownership. The oral history belongs to *both* the interlocutor *and* to the performer, an ever-present wavering—a back-and-forth authorship. This critical sharing is actually a triad of *both/and/but*. The telling belongs to *both* performer *and* interlocutor *but* comes into being through the interlocutor from whom the performer must seek permission.

Reflection nine

When we witness the performance of a life story, our world expands into a deeper realization of truth that shapes and multiplies how our own sometimes unwavering truth is understood and lived.

Reflection ten

When witnessing the performance of a life story, we may come to realize that what we thought was true is not true. And, in telling a life story, a different truth is realized.

Notes

1. Rowe elaborates on Barthes' notion of "ownership of enunciation" (2007: 166). Meaning those stories that come from the marginalized, the "vanquished," the disempowered where their narratives, experiences, and enunciations are too often repressed, oppressed, and hidden from view. These voices claim ownership of their own enunciations because of attempts to override their freedoms and existence.
2. Rowe explains affective loading attached to events on stage (88) both as compression and expansion. A moment on stage is framed and heightened as it is both made large and expanded while simultaneously compressed within the time frame of the performance.
3. From the Alison Jeffers notion of "civil listening" in the essay on refugee performance (2013): "we have a civil responsibility to provide an echo chamber for those refugee voices that reach us from the stage, to make them reverberate and to amplify what we hear" (308).
4. From Pollock (1998: 2, 3): "At once bolstered and burdened by history, performance as both genre of practice and as analytical trope resists narrow identification with either entertainment or high art industries. It floods the chambers of insignificance, on the one hand, and preciosity, on the other, to which it is commonly dismissed. Relieved of their isolation within discourses of history, performance proves powerful; history proves affective, sensual, and generative. Together, they expand the performance field to include a broad spectrum of everyday practices and social structures and to raise endless questions about the role of spectacle in the production of social selves, about the status of generic performance events in protest efforts, about the nature and implications of representational agency, about the twin effects of bodily display and disappearance, about the imbrications of writing and acting historically."
5. "Alternative facts." On January 22, 2017, Kellyanne Conway—Counselor to Donald Trump—defended White House Press Secretary Sean Spicer's blatantly false claim about the attendance numbers of Trump's inauguration as President of the United States. When asked during a television interview (with Chuck Todd of Meet the Press) to explain why Spicer "uttered a provable falsehood," Conway stated that Spicer was giving "alternative facts." Todd responded, "Look, alternative facts are not facts. They're falsehoods." Conway's use of the phrase "alternative facts" was mocked on social media and widely criticized by journalists and media organizations. Conway's remarks were described as Orwellian. Days after the interview, the book *Nineteen Eighty-Four* increased sales by nearly 10,000 readers, which was attributed to Conway's "alternative facts" comment. The book became number one on Amazon.com.
6. This quote has been generally attributed to Patti Digh, author, activist, and master storyteller. See www.37days.com/about/.

Chapter 6

The narrative/narrated event and the anatomy of emotion

> Oral performance, like all human activity, is situated, its form, meaning, and functions rooted in culturally defined scenes or events—bounded segments of the flow of behavior and experience that constitute meaningful contexts for action, interpretation, and evaluation ... narratives are keyed both to the events in which they are told and to the events that they recount, toward *narrative events* and *narrated events*.
>
> (Bauman 1986: 3)

In this section, we will elaborate on Bauman's description of the narrated event as the account or the original story and the narrative event as the recount or scene of the telling of the story.

The narrative event

This narrative event consists of the surroundings and the "telling" of a life story. This "telling" includes dimensions that constitute narrative or life history as living gestures and vocal sounds of performance expression. This act of storytelling embodies linguistic, paralinguistic, kinesics, proxemics, artefactual, and olfactory dimensions. All these elements combine to form a "drama," which guides the meaning and power of the "telling" where documenting these dynamics comes into question. Words need not be isolated from the movement, sound, and sensory dimensions that give them substance. Words need not be placed on a page in prose and divorced from the actions of their speaker. In referring to oral narrative and life history as verbal art, Elizabeth Fine points to the ephemeral nature of these performances and to their artistry of voice and gesture. In her foundational book on the subject, *The Folklore Text*, Fine states:

> A performance of verbal art is something more than words. Each of us has, at one time or another, sat under the spell of a performer, conscious of the artistry of voice and body. Yet, critical commentary on artistic verbal performance focuses on the linguistic level. WE can read about themes, formulae, images or narrative structure, but most critics

invariably ignore or shortchange the elements which make artistic verbal performance different from written literature ... a major reason why we know so little about the poetics of verbal art performances is that they are ephemeral.

(Fine 1984: 1)

In presenting verbal art, as more than just words, Fine turns to a performance-centered text where elements of the multi-dimensions of verbal art are included. In a performance-centered text, Fine's analysis of channels helps the ethnographer capture the integrity of the original performance and pinpoint specific aspects of performance for translation. These channels include the visual, tactile, olfactory, and aural aspects of oral narratives.

The visual calls for an awareness of the performance in relationship to motion (kinesics), objects (artifact), and space (proxemics). The tactile and olfactory are concerned with the sensual dynamic of touch and smell. The aural is composed of linguistic and paralinguistic dimensions. The concern here is the mutual importance of how something is said along with what is said in a performance utterance. Performance is recorded with its linguistic layer of feeling, rhythm, tone, pitch, intonation, and volume, in combination with the other performance channels. The performance-centered text respects the dramatic and sensory dimension of this living, storytelling performer, as much as the playwright or novelist in communicating meanings and truths.

As the performance-centered text aims to capture the multi-dimensional nature of the narrative event, it embraces the personal utterance of the performer through a poetic transcription, where words are placed symbolically in relation to how they are uttered. In striving to recapture the aural experience of performance, Fine, Dennis Tedlock, and Henry Glassie have paved the way for contemporary ethnographers to translate in a more meaningful and poetic manner, with the active voice in the oral history and personal narrative interview. These thinkers broke ground in translating beyond the "good syntax" and the spelling eye of a prose writer. They embrace style and dramatic poetry with lines varying lengths, positioning words and phrases that project the rhythm, tone and personality of the human voice. Writing in the 1980s Henry Glassie states:

> For years, our perceptions were so conditioned by literary conventions that we had nothing better to call tales than prose. Recently, noting similarities between spoken narrative and modern verse (much as critics have noted similarities between folk art and modern painting), we have begun to think of them as poetry.
>
> (Glassie 1982: 39)

To illustrate Henry Glassie's point, I have taken an excerpt from an oral history interview of African American women who worked as domestic labor at the turn of the century. This interview, with the permission of the storyteller, is translated in traditional prose, and then in poetic form. The reader may see the different effects of both transcriptions:

Prose style

I think you need to talk to somebody more interesting, I'm too old. My parents died; I was an orphan. I did not get much school. I think you need to talk to someone whose life means more. I can talk about the church, but that's all. You at Northwestern? Oh, no! Those peoples, NO! I couldn't go to school, I had to work, clean people's houses. I was an orphan. I been strugglin'. My life is a struggle, didn't go to school. You find somebody else.

Poetic style

(Looking out the kitchen window with her arms folded, she turns to me in low pitched voice.)

I think you need to talk to somebody more INTERESTIN'

(Shaking her head.)

I'm too old___
My parents died
I was an orphan
I didn' get much school

(Walking toward me, to the kitchen table, she speaks in a gentler voice)

I think you need to talk to someone whose life ^^ MEANS MORE
I can talk 'bout the church
But that's all

(She takes a seat at the kitchen table and forms the outline of the napkin holder with her hands. She does not look up, but concentrates on the little plastic napkin holder.)

You at Northwestern^^^
Oh/no
THOSE PEOPLE

(She looks up now, directly into my eyes. Her hands are folded together on the table. The kitchen is filled with sunlight; A silver ring forms around her hair. She speaks in a serious and direct manner.)

I couldn' go to school
I had to work/CLEAN PEOPLE HOUSES
I was an orphan
I been strugglin'
My life is a
STRUGGLE

Didn' go to school
Fin' somebody
Else.

Tedlock compares the two styles in this quote:

> What we have done so far, if we have punctuated our visible text according to the rising and falling contours of oratorical periods and shaped its lines and stanzas according to the stops and starts of dramatic timing, is to begin to free ourselves from the inertia, from the established trajectory, of the whole dictation era, an era that stretches (in the West) all the way back to the making of the Homeric texts. We have begun to construct an *open text*—not a text whose notation closes in upon features that can be assigned certified membership in self-sufficient codes such as those of syntax and scansion, but a text that forces even the reading eye to consider whether the peculiarities of audible sentences and audible lines might be *good speaking* rather than *bad writing* ... it is a brilliant stroke of *practical poetics* that enhances the audible impact of this one particular story.
> (Tedlock 1983: 7)

Tedlocks's concept of "practical poetics" is a challenging endeavor. It requires precision, patience, and concentration. The intersemiotic translation from human voice and action, in performance, to its representation upon the printed page is a formidable process. In transcribing oral history and personal narratives, you are observing gestures and movement as well as considering what to include or exclude so as not to overburden the narrative with too many symbols and descriptions. You will want to describe in words the tone, attitude, and drama of the performance: words that capture on paper the pitch, range, volume, and timing of the performer's living voice. The recordings are then payed again to check for accuracy and to delete symbols that may distract from the flow of the narrative. The recordings are played and replayed, checked and re-checked for accuracy and meaning. It is important to note that not ALL oral histories and personal narratives are conducive for poetic transcription. The length of the interview may not allow for the amount of space required as well as the attention to every word. The purpose of poetic transcription is to emphasize what are necessarily performatively, momentous moments in an oral history for the purpose of demonstrating how a performance scene affects and becomes inseparable to what is said. Poetic transcription is for a specific purpose that deliberately aims to do more than document and analyze experience. It is a re-performance in print.

The narrated event

> The simplest vehicle of truth, the story is also said to be "a phrase of communication," "the natural form of revealing life." Its fascination

> may be explained by its power both to give a vividly felt insight into the life of other people and to revive or keep alive the forgotten, dead-ended, turned-into-stone parts of ourselves.
>
> (Trinh T. Minh-ha in Madison 1994: 466)

> When I "speak for myself" I am participating in the creation and reproduction of discourses through which my and other selves are constituted.
>
> (Alcoff 1991: 21)

The narrated event is referred to as the "story" or the "told." Although ultimately inextricable, it is more aligned with "what" is said rather than "how" it is said. History and art have demonstrated that one story can be told by an infinite number of tellers in an infinite number of ways.

> The voices of women fill most of my childhood memories: gossip, songs, testimonies, lyrical praise, and insults. I remember how these women talked, their voices rising and lowering in colorful tones and rhythms. Sometimes they would speak through cautious whispers and at other times through robust declarations. Sitting together in the kitchen, they told stories to entertain and to survive. These stories were sometimes set in laughter and sometimes in tears, but they never stopped. I remember most clearly the stories my mother told me about how to be a woman, when I should be wary of life and when I should not. Gloria Anzaldúa and Cherrie Moraga have called such stories "theories of the flesh" that "bridge the contradictions of our experience"—those root metaphors that keep us centered and sane.
>
> (Madison in Pollock 1998b: 319)

I wrote that passage almost twenty-five years ago in an essay on oral narrative performance and Black feminist thought. What still remains is the significance of "theories of flesh" as they constitute the storied lives of oral history. Theories of the flesh, in this instance, manifest the relational overlays between epistemology and experience, of felt-sensing philosophy and economies of power. When we witness theories of the flesh, inside the narrated events of oral history, we not only witness ways of knowing, but semblances of our collective humanity. We witness the ongoing making of our common web. Linda Alcoff reminds us: "We are collectively caught in an intricate, delicate web in which each action I take, discursive or otherwise, pulls on, breaks off, or maintains the tension in many strands of a web in which others find themselves moving also." She goes on to state, "When I speak for myself, I am constructing a possible self, a way to be in the world, and am offering that to others, whether I intend to or not, as one possible way to be" (1991: 21).

Case study three: holograms in a live staging of history: Triangle Shirtwaist Factory fire

Description

Using 3D computer effects, Kathleen staged the Triangle Shirtwaist Factory tragedy of March 25, 1911, in New York City, where 146 garment workers jumped from windows to their deaths to escape fire and smoke. The fire that consumed the eighth, ninth, and tenth floors of the Asch Building in Greenwich Village was projected on a large screen that covered the upstage area, which served as a backdrop, and was meant to capture the intense color, light, movement, and heat from the fire as well as the enormity and height of the building. The live actors, downstage, represented the crowds who looked on in horror and grief that day as factory workers fell to the ground, before their eyes, in front of them. Members of the crowd served as alternating narrators who told the story of the Shirtwaist fire tragedy from the perspective of six factory workers as they fell to their death. Members of the crowd later expressed feeling helpless as they witnessed the tragedy. The 3D computer effects created holographic images of slow falling bodies, at varied levels and positions of falling, as the live crowd singled out and narrated, in chorus, in alternations, and in song, individual stories of the dead and the events leading up to the fire.

Process and contents of the digital-live performance

The script

The script described the intermix of live and digital action where the projected enormity of the burning factory building became a screened backdrop against six holograms of falling factory workers, all falling in slow motion from burning windows as live actors, representing the onlooking crowd that day, stood transfixed narrating life stories of the fallen. Dancers were included to physically replicate the movement and intensity of the fire before the entrance and stage appearance of the holograms. It was during the scripting process where the digital artist designed and employed computer-generated holograms to create images of the six factory workers at varied levels of falling. Archival research of news reports, oral histories, and biographies, as well as literary fiction and non-fiction informed the structure, content, and context of the script. The script was primarily comprised of the six stories, based on the names of six recorded factory workers. The stories took the form of creative fiction where the details of the workers' lives were described through the imagination of the playwright layered and informed by non-fiction texts and various archival sources. Woven into the life stories of the fallen were recorded interviews and documented reportage from witnesses expressing the sights, sounds, and feelings that fateful day in March. For the dancers, Kathleen provided an outline of the story to guide the choreographer in sequencing the movements.

Rehearsal

The holographic video technology was described during the scripting stage and perfected during rehearsals. The holograms were photographic recordings of 3D images for each factory worker. Each actor was photographed, against a green background, in four to six falling positions. This would ultimately give the illusion of bodies moving in various figurations, each falling in slow motion, from the tall building to the ground. Each position was matched with a specific word or phrase to be in sync with the story being told. The choreography of falling motions was in accompaniment with the gesture, rhythm, and words of the narration. Unlike a camera, which captures one view through a small viewer focused by a lens, holograms capture an entire light field, which allows them to recreate the 3D image or scene. After the set-up, photographic imagery, and the holographic computer designs were complete, the next step was staging the holograms as co-performers to match the timing and cues of the live actors. Much of the rehearsal was spent setting each movement image of the falls on cue with the narratives as well as positioning the screened projections of the Asch Building, in its enormity, as an over-arching backdrop against the live actors appearing as the crowd standing below the tall building.

The show

A projection of the factory building on screen across the stage. Dancers are downstage in a line across the stage looking up at the building with their backs to the audience. Six narrators enter stage left and right, move between the dancers and, in alternating voices, tell the history of the Shirtwaist Factory fire. As the narrators begin to describe the day of the fire, when a waste bin caught on fire from a discarded cigarette, flames begin to rise as the dancers are set in motion enacting the workers as they attempt to escape. Through the words of the narrative chorus, the dancers are trapped inside locked doors, suffocating from smoke and heat, running toward the windows and jumping to their deaths. The stage floor is partially covered with the bodies of the dancers. Six projected holograms, of factory workers, fall slowly from the windows and are suspended in air as the dancers lay along the floor. The narrators stand among the fallen dancers and begin to tell alternating stories of the six factory workers. As each story is being told, the holographic worker, no longer suspended in air, slowly falls in choreographic imagery to the ground. At the end of their story, the hologram lays alongside the live, fallen body of a dancer. The narrators tell six stories. The names are from actual workers who died from the fall: Joseph, age 21, who was to be married in June; Sara, age unknown, who survived five days after she jumped from a window; Catherine Maltese, the mother of Lucia, 20 years; Rosari, 14 years, who was identified by the son of Catherine and brother of Lucia; and, Mary age 11. Kathleen took poetic license to bring a larger human story to these names by adding what they might have been thinking that day on the way to work: Mary wanting to play with friends at school; Joseph meeting his fiancée that evening for wedding plans; Catherine, Lucia, and Rosari laughing together about getting off work early for a family celebration. The scene ends with the holographic images rising from the stage floor with the dancers, as more holograms of workers appear from the window coming onto the stage to cover the factory building until it disappears into smoke. The multiple holograms of the dead workers now form a silhouette of the building as the dancers and narrators begin to rise and turn with backs to the audience, facing the holograms. The scene slowly fades to black.

Reflections

In reflection, Kathleen pondered the ethics of creative non-fiction as a means of speaking for the dead. Using poetic license for the monologues of the factory workers was intended to humanize them, but Kathleen felt it was important for her to continue to question and strive for an ethics that integrates the real and imaginary within the human story with each performance, learning from the last, what it at stake when speaking for others who can no longer speak for themselves. Another point of reflection was brought to light by an audience member who felt there needed to be a narrator who represented the present. This narrator would accompany the narrative voices represented by the factory workers and become a connective persona between the past and present. Kathleen agreed, and decided that if she were to re-stage the performance, the meta-narrator could speak more directly to the consequences of the fire in terms of the devastating loss for the families, city, and all those who suffered but also to the awareness and policy changes relative to labor laws, regulations, and organizing, as well as safety requirements and legislation. Finally, Kathleen questioned the idea of ethnography as an archival and literary endeavor. Kathleen understood her work as an ethnography of the factory fire, but the question lingered: Can an ethnography that primarily engaged history and textual forms, rather than living subjects, be a true ethnography?

Chapter 7

Anatomy of emotion

The brain, performance, and oral history

> At the core of the argument lie two related questions. The first is, Must actors really *feel* the emotions they *portray*? And the second is, Do they achieve their portrayal by controlling the *external expression* of emotion or by inducing the *internal experience*? ... Francois Delsarte "A perfect reproduction of the outer manifestation of some passion, the giving of the outer sign, will cause a reflex within." Delsarte asserted that it is the gesture that is the "direct agent of the heart ... In a word, it is the spirit of which speech is merely the letter" ... This brings us to the notion of "affective memory." It speaks to how all of our experiences hold "traces" in our nervous system, imprinted in our mind, yet not always remembered or consciously known to us ... We are not so much concerned with conjuring those identical feelings, but to recall the disposition, mood, or behavior of that experience ... What Strasberg called "emotional-memory." The body becomes the means of finding a specific feeling ... resonating with Stanislavski's statement that "In every physical action, unless purely mechanical, there is concealed some inner action, some feelings."
>
> (Wangh 2000: xvi–xli)

The brain is comprised of interconnected nerve cells. These nerve cells are primarily responsible for the function and structure of our brain. There are gaps between these interconnected neurons and these gaps are referred to as neural synapses or synaptic gaps. What occurs between or in the spaces of the millions of neurons in our brains that is relevant to performance? First, there are chemical messages that leap and flow between neurons or along the synaptic gap (the neural synapses) that are called *neural transmitters*. Second, as these neural transmitters, or chemical messages, travel through neural synapses or synaptic gaps (spaces between neurons) more and more pathways are created when we adapt a *new mental and physical task*. In other words, learning new things, taking on new tasks, acts of creation, change, and imagination all form more neural pathways in our brain. Third, our brain is continually changing as these interconnected neurons form new pathways or neural transmitters. This is referred to as brain plasticity or neuroplasticity. Meaning that our brain is a changing organism with the *ability to reorganize itself by forming new connections between brain cells,* where new pathways can be continually created and where old pathways can be reformed. Fourth, thoughts and actions that are repeated over time require "less energy to make the mental leap;" these pathways are already formed and, as a result, there is a "lower synaptic threshold," where new neural transmitters are lessened (Stanislavski 1967: 47).

Proprioception

> Proprioception is the neural feedback system that gives us information about bodily position and well-being, and contributes to the sense of self.
>
> (Kemp 2012: 128)

The interdependence between the brain and the body forms a continuing relationship of cause and effect between the two. The brain responds to what the body does, and the body responds to what the neural transmitters or the pathways in our brain do. As we train our body to do something different or to learn new techniques, we are also restructuring and expanding neural pathways in the brain (Norman Doidge). In turn, the neural transmitters in our brain send signals to our body and musculature that can re-structure and change the way our bodies move and feel. This bi-directional flow—body to brain and brain to body—creates a feedback loop that also governs and directs our emotions, for example, empathy, anger, desire, joy, sorrow, and so forth. This means that certain physical actions and muscles movement can affect the emotional centers in our brain, just as certain emotional centers in our brain can affect our body or physicality. This neural feedback system is called proprioception.

Imagination and feelings are invoked through movement and ideas are provoked when we consciously or intentionally choose certain gestural activity (2012: 61). It follows that our movement patterns or how and where we experience our body moving in the physical world shapes how we think and how we conceptualize our world. Kemp states: "Altered postures and gestures work proprioceptively to create a different sense of self." He adds that "Using postures and gestures that are different from those that we employ in everyday life is likely to create an altered sense of self" (2012: 155).

> Consciously chosen muscular actions affect emotional states. While researching the configuration of facial muscles used in expression of emotion, Ekman and his assistant discovered that they began to experience the conscious effect of the emotion as they controlled the arrangements of their facial muscles to denote primary emotions such as fear, anger, and surprise. The experiments showed that the subjects did indeed experience the emotion associated with the facial expression as a result of simply organizing the muscles of the face in certain ways.
>
> (Kemp 2012: 167–168)

Mirror neurons and simulation theory

"Images create neural patterns in the brain (just like if it were really happening and as if the body had done this activity) ... Imaginative responses to fiction are to some extent the actual experience of what fictional characters do" (Kemp 2012: 155). We are reminded that making a technical, physical choice produces emotional truth. In a physically challenging Grotowski workshop, of such precise challenging and focused movements, Wangh reflected: "exhilaration of the bodily exertion itself seemed to spur my emotional courage" (Wangh 2000: xxii).

My granddaughter once asked me what causes people to cry at sad movies, or become frightened at horror films, or laugh when someone is laughing, or smile when someone is smiling. We then had the *mirror neuron* conversation. I explained that as human beings, we are wired for compassion and to feel what others feel. This makes sense as we acknowledge the work of our mirror neurons. Mirror neurons are special brain cells that permit and enhance our ability to learn from and empathize with others by listening to them and paying attention to their actions. When we simply listen and watch someone else, these particular brain cells fire. For example, in a solo performance, an old man remembers how, as a child, he was mercilessly bullied and beaten both by his schoolmates and his father because he looked and acted like a "girl." The actor embodied the pain and humiliation of a child living through insufferable fear and torture at the hand of those who were supposed to serve as father and friends. He re-lived those memories as the audience witnessed this staged reality. There was not a dry eye in the theatre when just moments before we were robustly laughing at the actor's comic antics in a prior scene. We all knew we were watching a performance, but our brain signals the information (or representation) as though it were actually happening. Our nervous system does not make a distinction between performance and reality. As children and adults observe an action, our mirror neurons fire and form new neuro-pathways in the same way we would perform the action ourselves. It follows that when an emotion is stimulated by the imagination, it also follows the same neural pathways as one that is stimulated by an event in lived experience (Kemp 2012: 174).

Understanding how mirror neurons work in our brain is a testament to the power and influence of performance, both as audience members and as actors. As audiences empathize (and mirror) the thoughts, feelings, and experiences of characters, it is mirror neurons that allow actors to empathize with (and mirror) the characters they portray. For the audience it is witnessing the character (or the actor's representation) that fires the mirror neurons, but for the actor it is the actual embodiment. As observers or audience members, we can mirror or empathize through *witnessing*. As performers or actors, we can mirror or empathize through enactment. If we believe that mirror neurons are important for understanding the actions and intentions of other people, both as representation (witnessing) AND embodiment (enactment), it would follow that mirror neuron activity generates higher emotional connections in the ability to empathize with others. All this is in line with simulation theory, where we simulate the mental states of others in order to understand their behavior (2012: 155).

> [O]ne of the perennial dualities in acting theory—does the actor have to feel an emotion in order to express it, or does he or she simply reproduce the physical signs of the emotion? ... Since *physiological indicators are the stimulators of Feeling in many emotions, the conscious reproduction of those symptoms can provoke the affective experience of emotion.*
> (Kemp 2012: 166)

When more parts of the brain are engaged, we are more stimulated. This is the gift of creative engagement. The film *Gifted* is about a young girl who is a genius at math. She far excels any of her classmates as well as the other adults in the film. She is gifted for her math skills; there is no mention of any other subject at which she excels. There is a revealing moment in the film when a male classmate, smaller in size than the rest, is bullied on the bus and tripped while carrying his art project. The art project falls to the ground breaks into small pieces and is ruined. In a later scene, our gifted protagonist stands up before the class and proclaims the beauty and creativity of the boy's artistry. This is an example where we see that creativity and the creative mind have a tensive relationship with what is determined as intellect—the left brain is favored over the right brain. As Kandel says, "some highly creative people are slow readers or poor at arithmetic ... [a] creative mind-set derives ... from a variety of features ... including wonderment, independence, nonconformity, flexibility" (Kandel 2012: 457).

In summary: key points for performance

- The fulfillment of gestures and physical actions can invoke inner feelings and psychological dispositions, even *supersede* them.
- Imagination is aligned with movement and the felt-sensing body and can therefore creatively influence *experiences of perception*.
- The proprioceptive system is a *neural feedback system* that responds to body movement, posture, and position, which contribute to self-awareness and the control and awareness of our actions.
- The power and clarity of an *imaginative representation* is greater if motor systems are in action.
- The body does not have memory, *it IS memory*. What you must do is unblock the body-memory (Wangh 2000).
- Embodied impulses *invoke* language, utterances, and sound.
- There are *limitations* to linguistic analysis.

Chapter 8

Performing oral history and life stories

> In my teaching, I have always given priority to the external world over inner experience. It is more important to observe how beings and objects move, and how they find a reflection in us ... I do not search for deep sources of creativity in psychological memories.
>
> (Lecoq in Kemp 2012: 91)

A common method is to begin with the rehearsal and workshop process and make notes of the raw materials and discoveries that emerge during games, exercises, improvisations, and so forth. This means paying close attention to images, movements, feelings, stories, and moments of insight from embodied work and in discussions. Conversations ranging from field notes to rehearsal work unleash ideas that also form a repertoire of material that can be scripted for the final performance. It is helpful to record the rehearsals. Think of the rehearsal as another ethnographic site where there are a range of occurrences—both deliberate, planned, and conscious, as well as arbitrary, spontaneous, and unconscious—that can make their way into the final performance. Recording rehearsals is most helpful to remember and playback what in the moment might have felt inconsequential, but seeing it again in recordings, you might find something useable and profound to be carried forward to audiences. The recordings may vary from written notes, tape recordings, and video or to whatever is available, from phones to notepads.

Solo performance

The beginning questions for performance

Why perform oral history? Sometimes we know and sometimes there are many reason that change over a period of time. Sometimes, we discover more complex and unconscious reasons during the process: rhetorical, advocacy, the desire to create, to make something beautiful from something beautiful. Is there a story you want to make known to the world? As a solo performer, one of the first things I suggest is to try and visualize the performance from beginning to end: Do you enter the stage or are you on stage already? What images do you imagine? How do you see yourself moving in the space? What are the sounds of your performance? What do you want your voice to do? What do you see as the rhythm and variation of your performance? What does the ending look and sound like? What kind of audience do you hope for? What do you see your performance doing?

How are you positioned in this oral history?

In the book, *Body, Paper, Stage,* Tami Spry states that "autoethnography is ... a critical reflection upon one's experiences within specific social/cultural/political locations" (2011: 130, 131). This can be applied to oral history performance whether you are performing your life or the oral history of another. As we perform the oral histories of others, we may employ Spry's question relative to our own positionality within the home places and histories of the individuals we enact. Spry offers two sets of questions that I have borrowed and re-envisioned for oral history performance: (1) critical self-reflection and (2) the questioning body.

Critical self-reflection questions include the following: Is it necessary for me to take up the question of motivation? When and where do I, or, do I not, hold privileges as the performer of another's life? When and where do I encounter agency? Am I a cultural outsider to this world that I enter? What forms of social hierarchies does this performance reveal? The questioning body includes: How will my body respond to transformations across this performance? How should my body intentionally work against or fulfill expectations? How will my body move and map the story space? How does my body, in movement and gesture, represent the context of this experience in ways that are not dependent on language? Added considerations to ponder as you step into rehearsal and final performance will inspire more and lingering questions, for example:

- *The magic if:* What if I create this movement as a metaphor instead of speaking the line? What if I stand still when the story says run? What if this history entails a life moment that I can't imagine?
- *Enemy of truth:* Am I indicating when I should be actualizing? Am I exaggerating when the small gesture is more truthful? Am I playing on clichés and stereotypes lost in a false notion of this history?
- *Prana, flow, energy:* How does radiating power or energy influence performance? How does mutual influence affect flow in solo performance? How do I perform prana through rhythm, space, and force?
- *Universal poetic awareness:* Can I play "nature as the first language"[1] in performance of oral history? Can I perform poetry as a "source of nourishment" beyond the words? How do I perform the idea that "the observation of animals is essential" to the poetics of oral history?

Your oral history performance is a story that has been told before

Sometimes we worry that the theme or topic is a repeated narrative that has been told many times. Before you become discouraged imagine someone saying to you: "No, this life is unique." The plotline might be familiar, most every plotline is and has already been played. The difference is in the lives of the characters: the matrix of desire, love, power, joy, belongings, and conflict across the geography of their lives. Every life history is uniquely different from another. It is our creative work that illuminates this fact. Learn from similar performance work—what is missing, what to add, what to change—or do not see them. Some are concerned they might be inadvertently influenced. But do ask yourself: What is my inspiration? List the large and small moments or gestures of inspiration in the oral history—small moments might include a mother welcoming her child home from school; the first butterfly to land in a newly growing garden that was once a site of violence and conflict—small unique moments as well as the epochal one. It is also important to remember the significance of endowment and that you will "endow the space, people, and objects around the personal life and meaning derived from the given circumstance" of this particular history (Stanislavski 1967: 143).

Set time to work and deadlines for drafted elements

Whether you are working from a completed oral history monologue or adapting the performance from composite interviews, it is vital to set goals that measure and organize your time. These timeline goals should be measured into step-by-step deadlines of *drafts*. One goal of a final draft is often less effective and usually more frustrating than a series of incomplete drafts! Think in terms of small steps. Completing each small step is a success. You will polish each unit in rehearsal and throughout your process. Do not polish and strive for perfection in the writing or the blocking plan. This is the purpose of the rehearsal. Yet, it is still important to make deadlines for each drafted element of the performance. If you don't set deadlines, even at the drafting stages, it only causes delays and makes you more nervous and tense. Don't try to make a perfect performance in the beginning and blind yourself to the spontaneity of what you discover on your feet in rehearsal. Setting time to work—blocking your time—on a regular and consistent basis so that your work time evolves in a ritual or habit will get it done with more energy, intelligence, and joy. Without work habits and ritual, you can fall prey to procrastination and squandering your time, and this is a nervous feeling.

Talking about your work and explaining it to others

Capecci and Cage offer a clear and compelling way of talking about creative and advocacy work in a way that conveys one's commitment and passion with reason and persuasion. They assert that a "key message and clear intent" are necessary and that they be comprised of full sentences that are "concise" and "specific," making sure what you say is *limited to three to five points that people can remember*. You are not giving a "mission statement" or a "treatise," but a concise and specific statement that will hopefully leave a lasting impression of your performance work. They also suggest that as you "connect the message to specific moments in your story ... What are the powerful and illustrative moments of connection?" Talking about our work—making all that we feel about and do for oral history performance intelligible to others—is nearly impossible. But, what we can articulate is the essence or overriding beauty of the work (and what it does) that will give them reason to see it or the interest to learn more about it. This means it is important that you take time to seriously think about how you will explain your work to others, keeping in mind the suggestions above. Having an honest, thoughtful, and heartfelt "script," of sorts, explaining what the performance is for and about is not only of great significance in communicating your work, but with every explanation you will feel more secure. You will come to know the work itself better, even if you receive suggestions, criticisms, or challenging questions. In contrast, some of your encounters will cause you to worry, waver, or be more circumspect about your work and how you are explaining it. You might feel the need to re-think your oral history performance. Your explanation may invoke self-reflection and change or, instead, more security and confidence. Whatever your responses or encounters might be, as you talk about your work, what you say will never be exactly the same in each instance. But hopefully you will learn or experience more and more each time (Figures 8.1 and 8.2).

Figure 8.1 Labor Rites. Two moments in time: Occupy Wall Street and the narrative event reflected in the journal. Photograph by Rafi Letzter.

Figure 8.2 Labor Rites. Two moments in time: Occupy Wall Street and the narrative event reflected in the journal. Photograph by Rafi Letzter.

Exercises

Warming up to start: beginning questions and considerations to get started

1. Six-word story

> Inspired by Hemingway's famous six-word tale, "For sale: baby shoes, never worn," the "six word story" has served as a prompt for decades, testing writers' ability to create their own succinct masterpieces with all sorts of clever results, including the popular 2006 Six Word Memoirs project. Now, the well-worn idea has gotten new life on Tumblr and Reddit, where users are posting their own hyper-short creations online to show off their creativity and pithiness.
>
> (Roncero-Menendez 2014)

A six-word story gives the impression of a complete story. This exercise is meant to encapsulate, in six words, what you believe to be the essence or substance of the oral history narrative. A six-word story includes a moment of conflict, action, and resolution. This exercise will give a sense of the full oral narrative. Here are more examples from the Tumbler contest of six-word stories:

> *"Can I scratch out my existence?"*
> *"Why are you in my selfie?"*

"You're my certain kind of sadness"
"Artist Bane: Fresh Ideas, Empty Pen"
"Dinner for two, widower and memories"

1. *Warm-up and reflection.* Lie on the floor or rest in a chair and close your eyes. Relax every part of your body. Breathe deeply. Give your attention to the narrative, or a section from the narrative, you wish to transform into a six-word story. Focus on the story calmly and quietly. Restfully focus from one minute to twenty, depending on your time and needs.
2. *Gibberish and the vocal gesture.* Now slowly rise. Take a deep breath and gently stretch out and open with arms up to the sky and feet comfortably apart. Take a few more deep breaths. Playing with pitch, volume, tempo, and duration, encapsulate the overriding sense of the oral history narrative in gibberish. Instead of crafting six words to represent the story, in a few seconds, speak the essence of the story in gibberish. You are not relying on words for expression, but the pitch, volume, tempo, texture, and duration of your voice carried forward in the nonsensical sounds of gibberish. Practice the gibberish story once or twice. If this is a group exercise, you may go twice around the circle.
3. *Now add movement and gesture to the gibberish.* Practice the movement phrases with the gestures once or twice. If this is a group, you may feel free to go twice around the circle.
4. *Composing the six-word story.* Now compose the story. Do not take more than ten minutes to write it or think it through. Keep to six words. It cannot be any more or less than six words.
5. *Adding movement to the six-word story.* Keeping in mind your movement repertoire from Viewpoints, Laban, and Roth, you will add a movement phrase to your six-word story.

This exercise serves to assist in embodiment, vocalization, and interpretation of the narrative. It also helps in strengthening your attention and focus as well as attending to what elements you feel of the narrative are most significant.

II. Opening line and trailer

1. *Opening line.* Think about the opening line for your oral history performance. Will you begin with the beginning verbatim line from the narrative or choose a different line within the narrative that you feel may present a more powerful opening? Will you decide to open with a line that is not in the narrative, but serves as a prologue or frame for the narrative—something from a poem, novel, or your own writing? In this exercise you will experiment with various opening lines and a range of movements, gestures, and vocalizations to enact the line.

This is a useful warm-up and a means, early on, to work with characterization, tone, and mood.

2   *Trailer.* If you are adapting an oral history from composite interviews and/or archival and literary sources as well as your own writing, a "trailer" can serve as a first rough draft and starting point. Examples may resemble trailers from movies or television, radio shows, or blurbs from books.

The trailer prompts you to focus on the "essentials of your performance, distils the essence of what you are doing, and is suited to the style and content of our work" (Bruno and Dixon 2014: 33).

III. Moving through the performance space

1   *The space of the narrative and the narrated event.* Where is the space of your performance? Are you performing the space of the narrated event (the surroundings and location where and when it was told to you)? Are you performing the space of the narrative event (the actual location inside the content of the narrative)? Are you performing a created or newly imagined space? Are you performing directly to the audience, from the stage, without a fourth wall? Or, will you create a multidimensional spatial world that will encompass juxtapositions of all the above? Once you have made your decision, walk through the space as a tour guide directing us through the space and describing what is inside the space and its purpose, for example, a chair by a window to contemplate a life well lived? A kitchen table where you sat with your mother and learned the secret she told no one but you? The door frame where you left and never returned?

This is not only a beginning point in thinking about how to design your performance space, but it also is a starting point for movement and composition.

2   Bruno and Dixon suggest a short prologue for the performance that begins with "This is a show for …" Such examples include: This is a show for those who don't like bullies. This is a show for those who've had an unforgettable journey. This is a show for those who hate being misunderstood. This is a show for those with a bossy friend. This is a show for those who've broken a promise. This is a show for those who know love and loss.

If you choose a prologue for the oral history performance this will help you determine a theme and set in motion the content.

IV. Building your character

1   *Body meditation and awareness.* Sit in a chair and "listen" to your body with your eyes closed—pay attention to how your body feels from head to feet. First, stand as your character and assume the posture or your

character. Pause. Relax and now assume your natural posture. Pause. Relax now assume your character's posture. Repeat three or four times going back and forth becoming more and more familiar with the difference between your everyday and natural posture and that of your narrator. Now continue the same exercise with repeatedly sitting as yourself and the narrator, with walking at different speeds, at moving through the space with different gestures and tasks, for example, bending down to pick up a heavy bag, gently placing a glass on the table, swatting a fly, reaching the top shelf for a book. Try pulling, pushing, slashing. Now sit still with no movement as yourself and as the narrator. What is the difference between you and your narrator? Are you taller or smaller? More slouched or straighter, more energy or less energy, more turned and twisted or more direct and open? Are you more confident or less confident? How would you describe the difference? This helps with character embodiment and intention.

In this exercise you must note the differences between what your body does and your interlocutor or the character you interlocutor conveys. You can make deliberate choices regarding posture, body rhythm and speed, and so forth (Bruno and Dixon 2014).

2 *Endowing objects.* Make a list of objects that can be used in your oral history performance. Then improvise actions associated with these objects or actions that the objects require. Next, improvise actions that are more symbolic, that are unexpected, and creatively different from the objects' intended usage. Examples: make a hat into your heart beating against your chest; speaking through an empty picture frame, held up to your face, to indicate a different character or speaker; a chair turned upside down to become the steering wheel of a car; a scarf that becomes a baby in your arms; an overcoat that become the American flag being folded in memoriam.

You are reminded that you can endow an object to become most anything and sometimes endowing objects makes the scene far more interesting and symbolic than the literal or "real object."

3 *Clothing meditation.* Choose a piece of clothing that matches or relates to the oral narrative or a character within it. Create improvisations around the use of a clothing item pertaining to meaning or metaphors in the narrative, for example, wearing a shawl wrapped as a belt, then as a hijab to represent a different location or character; a coat hung over the arm to represent class status and transformed into a hood or head covering to signal rain or an ominous mythical figure.

Clothing items are wonderful sources of focus points and stage business, giving you interesting things to do with your hands or those pensive moments as you gaze into the crease in your shirt during a confessional, or ringing and twisting your hat when you must deliver a shameful admission or reveal a difficult truth.

4   *Objects of history*. Enter the stage with a box containing five to six items that represent or relate to the oral history or composite histories. The objects may also represent abstract or conceptual elements of the histories. You will enter the performance space, holding the box, as your interlocutor or character. You will open the box and, one at a time, you show each item to the audience while describing the value of the item to you. You may us a combination of prompts: describe how the item is used; remember how you came upon the item; share what the item makes you think about or what memories the item invokes; what you love or hate about the item. After all the items are unpacked, they must be placed somewhere. Where do you place them? Do you handle all the items in the same way or do you handle some objects differently from others? Do you place them about the stage in a particular design? In the corner of the stage? To the audience? On your body? All of the above?[2]

The context and history of the narrative is physicalized as well as visualized. You are reaching into the larger social worlds and imaginings of the narrative.

V. Mapping the performance space

In the rehearsal space, try out and experiment with these positions. It will be useful to improvise or ad-lib words or moments from the performance to get a better idea of how it feels and the communicative effectiveness of each. After you try out the five points of focus, you need not feel restricted to only these configurations. You may imagine other possibilities for your performance. Ask yourself: What might be other designs or spatial arrangements? Draw your own diagram that suits your unique performance.

The labyrinth. Find an open rehearsal space where you create a maze or labyrinth. You can make your labyrinth anywhere: the beach, park, backyard, living room, school hallway, and so on. Sean Bruno and Luke Dixon state: "You can do this in many ways. By drawing in the sand. Laying yarn around the room. Making a trail of crumbs or stones" (2014: 134). They then suggest that you make Post-it notes with texts or significant moments from the performance. Color coding the Post-its according to themes, time, place, and so on, from the oral history might assist in organizing and mapping where these moments might be placed or fit within the labyrinth. If you feel the Post-its might be too restrictive and you would rather it be more spontaneous then you may skip the notes or only use them sparingly.

"Walk the labyrinth of your performance. Talk through your journey as you go, making notes that you can use in performance. Explore different possible routes" and keep in mind the "most direct is not necessarily the most interesting" (2015: 134).

Figure 8.3 Labor Rites. Life story of Lucy Parsons recounting the execution of Albert Parsons and passing down the story, in her shawl, as a symbolic gesture to the Girl/Recorder. Photograph by Rafi Letzter.

Figure 8.4 Labor Rites. Mother Jones recounts giving her shoes to those striking workers in need as she passes down the stories, symbolized in her shoes, to the Girl/Recorder. Photograph by Rafi Letzter.

Figure 8.5 Labor Rites. Labor Rites. Rose Schneiderman recounts the New York Shirtwaist Factory fire where workers jumped from windows and fell to their death. Photograph by Rafi Letzter.

Notes

1 Jacques Lecoq 2001: "It may be many years later, when an actor finds himself with a text to interpret. The text will set up resonances in his body, meeting rich deposits awaiting expressive formulation. The actor can then speak from full physical awareness. For in truth nature is our first language" (2001: 44).
2 This is a revision of an exercise from Sean Bruno and Luke Dixon (2014: 82). See bibliography.

Chapter 9

Viewpoints in rehearsal

> The rise of Viewpoints and the emergence of the contemporary global justice movement are connected by a set of aesthetic and organizational principles that constitute a shared poetics of materialist action ... For Viewpoints inventor Mary Overlie, Viewpoints produces a radical new subject by training democratic citizens ... Rather, the material stuff of theater—time and space as matter and energies—are of equal importance to the actor and their body on stage. In what could be called an "anti-discipline" in its refusal to "tame" the body, Viewpoints is founded in the notion of what Overlie calls, "working on the Horizontal," the commitment to de-hierarchizing the artistic elements of theatrical practice.
>
> (Perucci 2015: 109)

In the 1970s, Mary Overlie[1] developed the original Six Viewpoints as a method of movement improvisation. SYSTEMS is a mnemonic device for Overlie's six elements—the actual acronym is spelled SSTEMS: Space, Shape, Time, Emotion, Movement, and Story. Over the years, those "recognizing the genius of her [Overlie's] innovations and their immediate relevance to the theater, have extrapolated and expanded her Viewpoints for their own uses" (Bogart and Landau 2005: 5). For Anne Bogart and Tina Landau,[2] Overlie's method of generating movement (primarily focused on dance) was "applicable to creating viscerally dynamic moments" for actors, performance workshops, and a range of embodied collaborations (2005: 5). Spanning over two decades of collaboration and experimentation, Bogart and Landau extended Overlie's Six Viewpoints to nine physical viewpoints, as well as five vocal viewpoints. The outline below represents a synthesis of Viewpoints from Overlie and Bogart and Landau.

Examples

Space

Architecture. The physical environment and all the solid mass, textures, light, color, and sound the space contains.

Spatial Relationship. Distances between elements: objects on stage; one body in relation to another, to a group, and to the architecture.

Topography. The movement within and across the performance space: the floor pattern, design and colors. "To understand floor pattern, imagine that the bottoms of our feet are painted red; as you move through the space, the picture that evolves on the floor is the floor pattern that emerges over time" (2005: 11).

Shape

Shape. The contour or outline of bodies in space; the shape of a single body in relation to other bodies and in relation to the architecture. Shapes are comprised of lines, curves, angles, and their combinations. Shapes are both moving and non-moving in space.

Gesture. (a) Behavioral gesture: everyday, realistic gestures such as waving, pointing, clapping, shaking hands, and so on. (b) Expressive gesture: abstract, metaphoric, or symbolic gesture expressing a concept, inner state, story element, or emotion. "Gesture is Shape with a beginning, middle, and end" (2005: 9).

Time

Tempo. How fast or slow an action or movement on stage.

Duration. How long something occurs over time; how long a person or a group sustains or "stays inside a certain section of movement before it changes" (2005: 8).

Kinesthetic Response. A spontaneous response to an occurrence outside of yourself. An instinctive reaction to an external stimulus. "Someone claps in front of your eyes and you blink in response; or someone slams a door and you impulsively stand up from your chair" (2005: 8).

Repetition. (a) Internal: repeating a movement done with your own body. (b) External: repeating a movement occurring outside of your body

Emotion

Psychological, narrative, or affective reading of a movement.

Movement

Motion of your body and the range of physical changes, positions, and actions different parts your body creates.

Story

How we perceive perceptual ability to see and understand logic systems as an arrangement of collected information.

Vocal

Pitch. The high to low tone of your voice.
Volume. The level of sound.
Accentuation. Sound of emphasis.
Vocal Gesture. The sound of a non-word while speaking.
Repetition. To repeat a word of group of words.
Tempo. The changing speed of your voice; the speed of words and sounds.
Silences/Pauses. Moments of quietness for emphases.
Timbre. Color, texture, and quality of the sound. "Opera singers are often renowned for their particular sound and their timbre. The particular physical resonators, the shape and substance of her bodies and lungs determine a singer's distinctive sound" (2005: 114).

Notes: Bogart and Landau place under the category of Space: shape, gesture, architecture, spatial relations, topography. Shape is substituted under the category of Space in Bogart and Landau's Viewpoints. Bogart and Landau add Volume as a category under Viewpoints

Anne Bogart and Tina Landau from *The Viewpoints Book: A Practical Guide to Viewpoints and Composition*, pp. 19–21.

Surrender

Viewpoints relieves the pressure to have to invent by yourself, to generate all alone, to be interesting and force creativity. Viewpoints allows us to surrender, fall back into empty creative space and trust that there is something there, other than our own ego or imagination, to catch us. Viewpoints helps us trust in letting something occur onstage, rather than making it occur.

Possibility

Viewpoints helps us recognize the limitations we impose on ourselves and our art by habitually submitting to a presumed absolutely authority, be it the text, the director, the teacher. It frees us from the statement: "My character would never do that." In Viewpoints, there is no good or bad, right or wrong—there is only possibility and, later in the process, choice.

Choice and freedom

Viewpoints leads to greater awareness, which leads to greater choice, which leads to greater freedom. Once you are aware of a full spectrum, you do not need to

choose all of it all the time, but you are free to, and you are no longer bound by unconsciousness. Range increases. You can begin to paint with greater variety and mastery.

Growth

Viewpoints becomes a personal litmus test, a gauge for your own strengths and weaknesses, for discovering how you are free and how you are inhibited, what your own patterns and habits are. Again it is awareness that offers us this gift—the option to change and grow.

Wholeness

Viewpoints awakens all our senses, making it clear how much and how often we live only in our heads and see only through our eyes. Through Viewpoints we learn to listen with our entire bodies and see with a sixth sense. We receive information from levels we were not even aware existed, and begin to communicate back with equal depth.

On Overlie's Anarchist

For Overlie, the central figure of Viewpoints is whom she calls, "The Original Anarchist," the artist who is able to function as an "observer/participant" and who can function amidst the radical elements of the stage without the need to dominate them ... Arising in the context of the NYC downtown scene, Viewpoints was highly politicized for Overlie from its inception. For her, the project of developing the Viewpoints was characterized by the impulse of feminism that was so fundamental to the work of that community, such as her "hero" Yvonne Rainer. Overlie states that the political intervention in developing the Viewpoints in that context was not primarily driven by issues of representation, but rather was learning to develop your strength and find power where you have been stripped of it. That power is constituted especially through the development of capacity to perceive, respond to and manipulate the material aspects of the theatrical event. Viewpoints responds by empowering the marginalized subject by encouraging the actor to see themselves as "equal to the task of reading space" such that in the performance moment, "you are Archimedes" (Overlie in Perucci 2015: 107) (Figures 9.1 and 9.2).

Figure 9.1 Labor Rites. Viewpoints. Spatial relationship, gesture, duration, and shape. Window factory workers contemplating a strike for living wages. Photograph by Rafi Letzter.

Figure 9.2 Labor Rites. Viewpoints. Spatial relations, topography, rhythm, kinesthetic response. The anarchist Lucy Parsons recounts the four labor activists sentenced with her husband, Albert. Each makes an abrupt turn to look up at Lucy when their sentence is called, against the stillness of Albert, looking out to the audience. Photograph by Rafi Letzter.

Selected viewpoints for oral history performance

Imagine the grid

Part 1. A series of straight lines, crisscrossing each other at 90 degree angles on the ground. Imagine a giant piece of graph paper on the floor. The angles correspond to the walls of the room—no curves or diagonals—the group moves anywhere along the lines of this imagined grid on the floor. You are free to move throughout the room within the grid.

Part 2. Moving through the grid, experiment with Tempo, Duration, Kinesthetic Response, Repetition, Topography.

Making body shapes

(Choose a short excerpt from the oral narrative of script.)
(a) Make shapes that only include angles, lines, and hard edges (use more than arms, use your whole body).
(b) Now translate the angular shapes into curves.
(c) Combine lines and curves (isolate different body parts and having one in a straight line and another in a gentle curve). Create contrast, juxtaposition, and tension in your various shapes.
(d) Pay attention to how you are making a shape, stopping, then starting a new one. Try to keep the movement fluid, so one shape leads to the next, and the process is of one shape evolving into another.
(e) Add changes to the tempo and pay attention to how tempo leads to different shapes.

Open Viewpoints

(Begin by moving by focusing on specific elements: distance, lines, and clusters.) Express the teller or figure in the narrative through topography. *What is the typography of teller or figure, that is, the floor plan? Are your steps directed, moving in straight lines? Are your steps unidirectional? Are you moving "all over the place" ... or who takes up space ... hides in the corner ... passive aggressive?*
Life story ... life begins in big small steps, big circles, tired movement ...
Text: speak while moving; tell the story after seeing the movement, and then join movement with text.
Grid work. Unlike the horizontal, you are standing in a grid at different points and directions on stage. Move in any direction that conforms to a grid—no diagonal lines and no circles. Move kinesthetically with others.
Open Viewpoints. Free movement where grid and lane are not predetermined. Begin with stillness and move through the space keeping in mind all the Viewpoints. Time: tempo, duration, repetition, kinesthetic response. Space: shape, gesture, architecture, spatial relations, topography (this is best from 10 to 15 minutes).

Mirror: Tempo, duration, kinesthetic response, repetition

1. Make an image based on a theme or phrase from a story.
2. Add a rhythmic movement to the image.
3. The rhythmic movement, within the image, now utters a phrase or theme.
4. The image repeats its rhythmic gesture, saying its phrase, and then starts doing something, some movement or action.
5. Make a second image.
6. Add a second rhythmic movement to the second image.
7. Utter a different phrase or theme.
8. The image repeats its rhythmic gesture, saying its phrase, and then starts doing something, some movement or action.
9. And a third image, phrase, movement.
10. Repeat the sequence, let it evolve, until you are asked to stop.

Case study four: the storyteller's magnified embodiments in real-time telling

Description

In staging a solo performance of her grandmother's oral history, Lee decided to emphasize her grandmother's philosophy and desire for "Home." Lee's performance included projected, magnified images of smaller, more detailed, elements—hardly visible to the audience—of her live performance on a large upstage screen. Each magnified image was variously projected in fast or slow motion, in still images, or larger than life augmentations. The videographer moved about downstage filming Lee (in real time), while simultaneously casting angles and remnants of the performance on two large screens upstage.

Process and contents of the digital-live performance

The script

Lee transcribed the interview of her grandmother's oral history, highlighting specific sections where the grandmother focused on her life-long search, battles, and hope for a home of safety and belonging. Lee decided to stage a public performance of the oral history and consulted with a friend, Kara, whose directing she admired to guide her through rehearsals, providing insights on blocking and characterization, as well as finalizing the script adaptations. As Kara and Lee worked together, Kara suggested that Lee include digital imagery, as points of emphases, to bring the liveness of her staged enactments into larger view through screen projections to better serve the emotional force of the story and the poignancy of her grandmother's relationship to home.

The rehearsal

John was experienced at integrating digital imagery into live performance where screened projections were deeply interactive and integral to the actor's intentions, the integrity of the narrative, and the relevance of the performance. Lee, Kara, and John wanted to do more than project slides throughout the narrative. They intended for the "eye" of the camera to work as a subtext, metaphor, and scene for home. As Lee, Kara, and John brought movement blocking and narrative together during the rehearsal process, they each individually marked points of emphases where elements of home appeared—obviously and discreetly—in the performance. Kara noted and listed their collective points of emphasis and then outlined a design and cue sheet for the projection effects. John began with Kara's organized input, based on their three suggestions, but was encouraged to use his own expertise to experiment and improvise projection choices and design. John's creativity as a videographer also included being conscious of his presence on stage relative to movement, blocking, and discreetly shadowing Lee as the on-stage focus. The rehearsals were primarily concerned with four overriding dimensions: (1) Lee's solo enactment of the narrative and all that a solo performance must consider; (2) designating which elements of Lee's performance would be projected as resonances and embellishments of home; (3) how these visual magnifications should be projected ranging from fast, slow, still, zoom-in, zoom-out, focus, out of or in focus, and all the ranges and combinations in between; (4) choreographing and blocking John's varying angles and positions on stage to avoid distraction, yet to discreetly note the significance of the videographer's creative choices and skilled design of visual, collaborative storytelling.

The show

Lee's solo performance, staged under the backdrop of two large screens circling the stage was further framed by John, as videographer, moving along the downstage stage borders filming her actions. Lee moved throughout center stage with only a chair, a clothes rack, and a small table that held a book, a lamp, and a glass bottle. Performing in epic mode, Lee enacted her grandmother as the storyteller as well as various characters depicted within the time and space of the oral history. The camera focus, cast upon the screens, transformed what could not be seen by the naked eye into writ large cinematic projection. The still images were projected, as stops and starts, throughout Lee's ongoing enactment of memories, for example, Lee picking up and quickly setting down assorted photographs, on the table, of the front steps of the childhood home, the broken window, great-grandmother's garden, the day of the fire, and Lee holding up the lamp shade above her head like a hat—with its tiny burnt tear along the edges—and then placing it on the lamp rescued that day, long ago, now sitting it on the stage table. The still images served as punctuation points against the ongoing movements of memory enacted on stage. The slow-motion images captured those moments of conflict and violence, for example, when Lee frantically circled the stage enacting fire and flames as her voice rose in volume and intensity embodying the cries of her grandmother as a small child watching her home burn and hearing her little sister calling for her through the smoke-filled rooms. The slow-motion images became mirrors of contrast against Lee's physical speed and rhythms. The zoom-in images became dramatic portraits embellishing the details of Lee's facial and gestural expressions, for example, the veins in her left hand as she held her grandmother's diary, the hunch of her shoulders under the old torn coat of her grandfather, her eyes tightening, then widening under the furrowed brow of her great-grandmother's admonishments. John's screen projections of Lee's performance exceeded these three examples; he combined and juxtaposed various effects into a visual montage that enlarged the stage action and underscored the liveness of performance.

Reflections

During the rehearsals and performance, the collaborators were always questioning if the camera was ever a distraction for the audience or when and at what points was the camera becoming one. Upon reflection, Lee wondered if those magnified moments were best served as pre-recorded projections on the screen rather than a live feed that was deliberately being filmed before the audience. The majority of the feedback was favorable toward the onstage camera as very effective in underscoring the "present-ness" or "liveness" of the narrative, while simultaneously marking the camera as real-time action of a recording process. The camera became a double-sightline of camera operator and the screened, camera projection. Most felt this enhanced the focus, like watching an animated magnifying glass moving to the meaning of the story thereby resulting in a heightened intensity of watching. After considering the various responses, the collaborators decided to add sound to the screened imagery that would include rhythms of breathing and human heartbeats. Lee felt the challenge would be to align and synchronize the added sound effects with the solo performer's narrative voice where the sounds of breathing and heartbeats would underscore both the screened imagery and the live performer.

Notes

1 Mary Overlie (born January 15, 1946) is an American choreographer, dancer, theatre artist, professor, author, and the originator of the Six Viewpoints technique for theatre and dance. The Six Viewpoints technique is both a philosophical articulation of postmodern performance and a teaching system addressing directing, choreographing, dancing, acting, improvisation, and performance analysis. Overlie is the co-founder of several long-lasting art institutions such as Danspace Project, the Studies Project, Movement Research, and the Experimental Theater Wing at New York University. Her choreography, both solo and for Mary Overlie Dance Company (1978–1986), has toured extensively through Europe and has been performed in New York at the Holly Solomon Gallery, The Kitchen Center for Music, Video and Dance, St. Mark's Danspace, Dance Theater Workshop, The Museum of Modern Art, and numerous lofts in New York. Overlie has been granted two Bessie Achievement Awards, the first for creating the Studies Project, shared with Wendell Beavers, and the latter for her lifetime contribution to dance. Overlie founded the Six Viewpoints Studio at Tisch School for the Arts in 2006 and continued teaching at The Experimental Theater Wing until 2015 when she retired and moved to Bozeman, Montana. After 20 years of working on the manuscript for the Six Viewpoints, Overlie completed and self-published *Standing in Space: Six Viewpoints Theory and Practice* in 2016. She currently resides in Bozeman, Montana, teaches workshops in America and Europe and is organizing an advanced Six Viewpoints School. The Six Viewpoints is a philosophical and practical approach to articulate a postmodern perspective on performance. The practice involves deconstructing the physical stage and physical performance into its six materials of composition: Space, Shape, Time, Emotion, Movement, and Story. These six elements have existed historically within a rigid hierarchy, which gives prevalence to story and emotion in theatre, and shape and movement in dance. The Six Viewpoints releases the materials from this fixed construct into a fluid non-hierarchical environment for re-examination. The act of deconstructing performance into its six materials invites the performer, director, and artist to engage with the individual materials "allowing these elements to take the lead in a creative dialogue." For Overlie, this shift in attention re-defines art and the role of the artist from a "creator/originator" mindset to what she calls the "observer/participant," which centers on "witnessing, and interacting ... working under the supposition that structure could be discerned rather than imposed." Overlie observes this redefinition of the artist's endeavor to correspond with the artistic shift from modernism to post-modernism. The theory and practice of the six viewpoints is organized in two parts: The Materials and The Bridge. When working with the materials, the artist is instructed to turn off the impulse to control or own the material, and is challenged to work very specifically with each material as an independent entity. Overlie recommends the artist to gather as much "useless" data as they can and to take time to explore. Overlie states: "The seed of the entire work of The Six Viewpoints is found in the simple act of standing in space. From this perspective the artist is invited to read and be educated by the lexicon of daily experience. The information of space, the experience of time, the familiarity of shapes, the qualities and rules of kinetics in movement, the ways of logic, how stories are formed, the states of being and emotional exchanges that constitute the process of communication between living creatures ... Working directly with these materials the artist begins to learn of performance through the essential languages as an independent intelligence" (https://update.revolvy.com/topic/MaryOverlie).

2 In their book, *The Viewpoints Book: A Practical Guide to Viewpoints and Composition*, Anne Bogart and Tina Landau identify the primary Viewpoints as those relating to Time—which are Tempo, Duration, Kinesthetic Response,

and Repetition—and those relating to Space—which are Shape, Gesture, Architecture, Spatial Relationship, and Topography. In addition, Bogart and Landau have added the Vocal Viewpoints, which include Pitch, Volume, and Timbre. In the book, the authors outline the basics of the Viewpoints training they both espouse as well as specific methods for applying the Viewpoints to both rehearsals and production. For Bogart and Landau, the Viewpoints represent not only a physical technique but also a philosophical, spiritual, and aesthetic approach to many aspects of their work. Bogart references her work with the SITI company, and Landau with the Steppenwolf Theater Company (https://en.wikipedia.org/wiki/Viewpoints).

Chapter 10

Jerzy Grotowski's[1] plastiques and Viola Spolin's[2] speech and sound

The brain of the body and the body of the brain

> [T]he plastiques can serve as muscular reminders, provocations, goads that stimulate submerged feelings to surface once again. By observing the images and emotions that pour through us as we work with our bodies, we begin to "know" ourselves, and we can begin to catalogue the particular physical keys that open our personal emotional doorways.
>
> (Wangh 2000: 125)

> We do not possess memory, our entire body is memory, and it is by means of the "body-memory" that the impulses are released.
>
> (Kumiega 2011: 120)

> My job is not to make political declarations but to make holes in the wall. Things that have been forbidden to me must be permitted after me; doors which have been locked must be opened; I must solve the problem of liberty and tyranny in practical ways—that means that my activity must leave traces, *examples*, of liberty. It's not the same as leaving complaints about the subject of freedom ... All that deserves to be chucked away with the garbage. You must actually get things done ... This is the problem of social activity through culture.
>
> (Grotowski in Wangh 2000: 31)

Grotowski did not emphasize acting as technique, what he called "positive techniques" in his work with actors. He stated, "No tricks or systems to use, only *negative training* [emphasis mine] to remove personal blocks." At the center of acting training was to let go and release the constraints and inhibitions that inhibited individual freedom and creativity. Stephen Wangh states: "almost all of us learned to hide at least a few of our emotions—just as surely as we learned to cover our bodies with clothes." Wangh adds that "to clothe our emotional lives, we constricted our voices and armored our bodies with muscular tensions" (2000: xi). The method of "freeing these imprisoned abilities" is what Grotowski called the *via negativa* or the "road backward" (2000: xi). The emphasis here is less focused on new techniques but more on the socially transmitted, embodied techniques we hold and carry with us as well as our intuitive abilities and the will to be creatively free. Grotowski's signature acting process, *via negativa*, or the pathway back to our uninhibited, free selves was realized through what he called "plastiques." In describing *les exercices plastiques*, it is important to note that plastiques may appear simply as each part of the body moving in isolation, as though completing isometric exercises, they are also about energy, space, and imagination. Although plastiques concern the physical isolation of movement with distinct parts of the body, these isometric movements are also interpretive and creative explorations of one body part at a time moving and discovering the many directions of movement in space and its multiple implications (2000: 75).

Interview with Stephen Wangh[3]

DSM: *Is there an experience from your years of teaching plastiques and Grotowski methods where something did not work in the performance space, a particular challenge where you had to change something in your method or approach?*

SW: *I tell a story in my recent book,* The Heart of Teaching, *about a black woman who was a wonderful actress and very talented, but if I didn't pay any attention to her she was angry with me for not paying attention. If I did pay attention, she'd push back against anything I said. I dared to say, "Hey, is there another teacher you feel comfortable with?" She mentioned a woman who taught in the department, and the three of us sat down together. And again, it was a situation of me just needing to listen to her. I just needed to hear her out about how she wasn't safe with me. I was a white man who was trying to teach her, and there was no way she was really going to be comfortable with me, but after I heard her out and simply said "I understand what you're saying," in the presence of this other teacher, in a subtle way, things changed. It was always important with her that I say something really positive first after her scene presentation. Which wasn't bad because she was really very good. It wasn't hard at all to do. If I let that space open up then it was possible for me to point to one thing or another thing that she could actually work on.*

DSM: *Using embodied pedagogy or psychophysical approaches, the challenge is that not all bodies are the same. Not all bodies move in the same way or can do what other bodies can do in the same way or to the same capacity. As teachers and guides how do we accept this?*

SW: *A few years ago I worked with a group of acting students, one of whom had real physical incapacities, things that prevented her from moving or sitting as others could, and she had enormous issues with herself about it. She had a lot of judgment against herself: what she couldn't do, what she would never be able to do, and so on.*

> It was true there were things that other people could do in the class that she couldn't do, but what was getting in her way as an improvisor, were her judgments. She was actually quite good. She was the best singer in the group and when she allowed herself to really take the stage, she invented absolutely terrific things. But when I began working with them, she could never allow herself to know that. My sense is that very often when working with different bodies, that the central problem is that people think there's a central problem. A lot of what I find myself teaching has to do with the idea that there are problems, rather than that whatever is going on is what is going on, then labeling something a problem is always extra, is on top of that; little by little she began to discover that when she would dare to take whatever risk she took, she could see that the group and I were appreciating it a lot. And, little by little she took larger and larger risks until she became one of the central improvisors. She was able to improvise long monologues; she was able to suddenly go into song; she was able to do group work and it was really a wonderful transformation. It was like watching somebody little by little taking off layers of armor. My sense is a lot that Grotowski works that way, that it's about people discovering their own armor and finding step by step how to let go of the armors that they've been holding on to. My job as a teacher is not actually to teach anything, but to help them understand it doesn't even ... I think I say this in the new book, it isn't really that I'm making a safe space, it's giving the illusion of making a safe space, which actually the students are learning how to make for themselves. They're learning that they can make their own risks. My job isn't to push people constantly into the unknown. A thing that I've learned to say over and over is, habits are habits. Habits aren't bad habits, habits are habits. There are reasons why all of us have the habits that we have. There are reasons that we've learned to protect ourselves in one way or another. Whether it is because of particular traumas or simply the trauma of living in our society, people have learned to protect themselves one way or another. The work is about noticing that at least under certain conditions, inside an acting class, it's possible to go beyond those self-imposed restrictions.

DSM: What have you experienced as one of the recurrent challenges or problems as a teacher who honors embodied knowledge?

SW: *The little things that you thought of as problems, the way your eyes suddenly look away from the audience, or you're feeling "I hate this, I want to sit down," or whatever, are all sources. Sources to be used. Like a long-distance runner that talks about going through the wall and then they have energy on the other side, I think that when I have taught this improvisation work, we* do a lot of working with boredom. An actor goes on stage and there's nothing there but the actor and maybe a box, and at first people will try to do clever things with the box. And then people will give up, and then they will want to exit. And if they hang out long enough interesting things start to happen. You know in the first book after I finished it, I gave it to André Gregory and he said "oh, Steve, you forgot entirely about time." I think I've been trying to understand more about time. How long things take, and that one does need to hang out ... I would connect this problem with the problems of the American relationship to entertainment in general. We somehow have a low opinion of what we can bear. Actors in the Grotowski work learn that they can bear enormous emotion. Just emotions that they thought were terrible. But the same is true with whatever's going on behind the boredom. The same is true with American politics nowadays I think, my sense is that theatre can help people understand that we can bear things, hard things, enormous emotions. Pain beyond what we thought we could bear. Sorrow, especially sorrow beyond what we thought we could bear. Americans are so full of busyness and dizziness that they don't allow themselves to feel the sorrow beneath it. That's been my feeling when I've gone to Israel, that it's a country full of people who don't allow themselves to feel fear and sorrow, they go to anger instead. I think that happens at the extremes of American politics also, there's this need to grasp something strong like anger rather than allowing oneself to feel what's happened.

DSM: How do you teach through mistakes and help students discover alternatives?

SW: In my teaching, I think I mentioned this also in the new book, I think teachers are always waiting for what they call a teachable moment. Sometimes it's a long wait. There are many times when you see a student having a problem and it's very clear to me what this problem is, I've seen that problem hundreds of times, I know exactly what they need to do. But this is not a moment in which I can point to that.

If I see someone who I feel, viscerally, 'this person needs to scream at their scene partner right on this next line' but I can see clearly that's not what they want to do, it's often very helpful for me to say, "Let's try a number of things. Try running away from your scene partner, try hiding, try screaming at your scene partner." It's much more useful for somebody to explore alternatives and figure out for themselves what's going to work than for me to say, "this is the alternative." Sometimes that doesn't work, but when it does it's something that the person has found for themselves. That's better than anything I could possibly teach.

The plastique isolations from Stephen Wangh

An acrobat of the heart: a physical approach to acting inspired by the work of Jerzy Grotowski, pp. 76–8

Each plastique is itself an emotive gesture. When you shrug your shoulders, for instance, you become aware of the feeling that goes with that shrug: "I don't know," or "I don't care." The feeling inhabits the shrug itself.

The eyelids can open and close. They can open partway. One eye can open. One eye can wink. Both eyes can blink. The eyelids can flutter. They can be heavy and keep trying to close. They can snap open.

The eyes can move left or right or up or down. They can move quickly or slowly. They can circle. They can scan the horizon or focus close to the body. They can move below half-shut lids. They can race around, looking for something. They can stare blankly. They can be wide awake or tired. (Through all of the rest of the **plastiques**, the eyes stay engaged. When and how they focus can change the quality of every other isolation.)

The muscles of **the face and the mouth** can move in every direction possible. Groups of muscles can work together opposite one another.

The head and neck. The head can slide forward or back or left or right while remaining upright. It can tilt left or right or forward or back. And it can roll around. It can also turn left and right. It can move quickly or slowly. It can shake or wobble or nod or twist.

The shoulders. One shoulder can move up, down, forward, or back. Then it can move in any combination of these directions. It can move in circles, connecting each direction, and the circles can be in either direction and in different rhythms. The movements can be smooth or broken, sudden or gradual. Then there is the other shoulder. And there are the two shoulders together: both forward, both backward, one forward while the other goes back, one suddenly up while the other slowly down, circles in the same direction, circles in opposite direction, and so forth.

Each elbow can move out from the body or in toward it. It can move left or right. It can pull backward or reach forward. Each elbow can circle clockwise or counterclockwise. It can rock left and right. The elbows can move together; they can press toward each other or stretch away from each other. They can fly, or swing or pound or dig or caress.

The wrists can lift or circle. They can move left or right, in staccato or in gentle movement. They can pull away from each other with tension or with ease. They can move up and down in constant rhythm. They can push away from the body or slide in toward it.

The hand and fingers can claw, punch, twist, or caress. They can close as if to grab suddenly, or grasp finger by finger. They can undulate: wrist, palm first knuckle, second, third. They can push, pull, lift, tickle, or poke.

The shoulders, arms, hands, and fingers can undulate from the shoulder outward. The shoulders, arms, hands, and fingers can stretch up for something out of reach. They can push through the air, or punch, or claw. They can pull against one another. One hand can pull while the other pushes. The fingers can type, play the piano, tickle, or scratch. They can fly. And the arms, hands, and fingers can receive. They can open to the sunlight; they can accept the rain. They can reach out for help. They can hang in despair.

The chest can slide forward and back while remaining upright (be sure it is the chest that is working now, not the shoulders). It can slide right or left (try reaching with the arm and hand, pulling the chest to the side.) The chest can circle by moving progressively in all four directions. And it can tilt forward and backward, left and right. Then the chest and arms can work together, or opposite one another. The arms, hands, and the chest can all reach upward, yearning for something beyond reach. The chest can shake, shimmy, or twist. It can inflate and deflate. It can collapse.

The back can push, lift, twist, or wriggle. The arms and back together can lift.

The pelvis can lift forward or backward, or left or right. It can slide back and forth quickly or slowly, I can circle. It can move on its own or in relation to the arms. The pelvis can push suddenly or move smoothly. It can ride or bump or twist.

The whole upper body can undulate from the pelvis upward. It can lift a heavy weight from the floor to the sky. It can undulate from the head downward. It can shimmy, shake, tremble, whip, flail, undress, hug, enclose, or fly.

(To expend the plastiques down through the legs, you can continue to stand, but it can be helpful to sit or lie on the floor so that the legs are completely free to move.)

The knees can lift in each direction. They can circle clockwise and counterclockwise. They can push toward each other or pull away.

The ankles and feet can circle, rub, and kick. They can push forward or back. And they can shake, scratch, and caress.

Stand back up again.

The legs can walk, run, jump, and kick. (Try running in place.) And working with the eyes, the legs can run away from something behind you, or run toward something in front of you, jump up for something above you, or leap away from something below you.

Examples

The plastique river

You imagine your body as a river, flowing freely, where one part flows to another part or the next plastique. This is a continuous movement. It is important that areas of the body move in an ongoing and fluid sequence. Do not over-think, because you are moving on impulse and intuition. The movement flow does not always need to be smooth or even; it can be uneven. If you do not have an impulse to move pause and begin with a new area. You will open to the intuition of your body to begin making large movements that guide you through space and small ones that express one small body part. Allow your body's impulses to discover interesting contrasts of large and small movements and then add fast and slow movements. Each movement is a plastique that is part of a moving conversation. As the variations of the sequential continues, plastiques take form, the conversation will take on varying forms and intensities, various volumes and responses. Begin to stay in one plastique for about 30 seconds and experiment with the variation and details that emerge. Allow your body's impulse and intuition to guide you, in other words, allow the plastiques to lead. Wangh reminds us that what makes something a plastique is that the movement is specific, filled with imagery and energy, unveiling a movement dialogue. Wangh goes on to state: "the movement of one finger; or of an eye, even a completely internal movement could be a plastique if it is imbued with emotion and connected to an image" (Wangh 2000: 84).

Extended sound

> This game shows that sound occupies space.
>
> (Spolin 2001: 67)

Stand in the center of the space and send a sound (not a word) to a particular object in the room and let it meet or land on the object. Focus on the sound as you set it forth into space. Make another contact by sending a different sound to another object in the space. Extend a different sound to various objects. Each sound will be sent forth and extended from the body of the player to the body of the object. The sound travels through space with clarity and intent. Each object is given its own special and focused sound that is set forth. If there are other players, stand at a distance from one another. One person will send a sound through the space to another player where it will land; that person will then send a different sound to another player. Continue until everyone has set forth a sound. In the next round, with the same focus and intent, send a word to an object or person and, again, allow the sound to land. In the third round, focus on setting forth a sentence. Keep in mind that with focus and a deep breath, the sound will travel in space and meet or (in Spolin's words) "land" on the object or person. Your body will move intuitively or naturally with the sound and words you create. Just as in the river exercise, allow the body to move on impulse, but this time with the force, intent, and variation of sound and voice. You will stop or pause the movement when your voice is silent

The sounds of your own voice

Drawing from your fieldwork experiences or an oral history interview, you will choose a memorable image. You will then vocalize a response to the image. Search for a sound that graphically interprets the image, even if it verges on melodrama and spectacle. The vocalization takes the form of sounds, words, or phrases, but not sentence groups or short monologues. After you have identified your image, experiment with the sound and allow your body to respond to the sound, similar to the "extended sound" game. This time, the body response begins to lead and takes over the sound expression. The body response becomes more intense and "larger" than the original sound. Now the sound is responding to the body instead of the body responding to the sound. Experiment and become mindful of how movement of the body responds to sound, becomes heightened, and can change where sound responds to movements of the body. You are experimenting with the reciprocity and intensity of body movement and vocality in the slippery nature of their cause and effect. For example, if the image encompasses crying, vocalize crying (in whatever that sounds like or means for you). You will then use the plastiques to experiment with what the body can do with crying. What movement imagery can be made from this human crying? The plastiques, with the power of their images, now begin to supersede what the voice does with crying. The voice is now responding to the crying body. Now the voice becomes more energized by the body—the body invokes the voice—and the body now leads the voice. This is an exercise of voice invoking movement and movement invoking voice in a back and forth dance of cause and effect. This can be done with images that vocalize anger, laugher, servitude, authority, labor, playfulness, and so forth. The river, extended sound, and sound of your own voice all come together in this exercise.

Object plastiques

Arrange several objects along the center of the floor that represent your field research or moments in an oral history. The objects are large soft objects such as scarves, sweaters, bags, and so forth (Wangh warns that smaller, hard things object such as boxes, shoes, and books usually lead to more reliance on your hands instead of the whole body). Before engaging the objects begin with the plastique river work, playing with your whole body as you experiment with movement. You are moving on feeling, intuition, and impulse, bringing the top of your head to the bottom of your feet. When your river is flowing "hard and fast," pick one object from the floor and allow it to guide your river. The object is leading you and transforming you. Feel free to "let it touch you in different places, and let it keep surprising you. Let it attack you, let it make love to you. And let it abandon you" (2000: 218). Keep in mind the object is leading you through the plastique river as you discover different movement images and tableaus, including actions from the abstract to the quotidian.

> Singing dialogue
> Sing out the words! Heighten it!
> Elongate the word! Repeat the word!
> Sing with your whole body!
> (Viola Spolin)

You can now add singing dialogue to object plastiques. After the object has led you through plastique river, you may now improvise or take up excerpts from your fieldwork text or oral history and "create a flow of sound" (Spolin 2001: 70). Focus on extending the sound (as you did in extended sound). Sing with the same impulse and intuition of your moving body. Do not worry about being a good singer, because everyone can sing, and this is not the point of the exercise. What is needed here is the extension and flow of sound. Your object is guiding you through the plastique river and your song is the accompaniment and commentary along the way. Your song is also in conversation with your object and movements. The singing invites repetition, tone, volume, duration, and utterance. Let the song fill the space as it intensifies the object and movement.

Circus walks

Walk, normally, around the space for about one minute or so, and let go of any tension as you calm your mind. First, as you walk, change the way your feet meet the ground, for example, walk on your tiptoes, edges of your feet, rolling out your foot slowly from heel to toe, slide your feet, and so forth. Second, allow your new feet to change the way your legs move. You are not concerned with changing your legs, but observing how your feet change how your legs move. Third, add a movement change for your pelvis to coincide with the new legs. Fourth, add the lower back and stomach to coincide with your feet, legs, and pelvis. Fifth, now add the upper back and chest, the shoulders, the arms, hands and fingers, the neck, the head, and the face. Sixth, as you add each new body part, pay attention to how the changes have affected each muscle group, no matter how slight a change. Seventh, the next steps attend to paying attention to the changed body relative to building character or making a scene. Your body now has a new shape; try to sit, lie down, stand, run, and walk with this new shape. Wangh states, "allow the new body to find its breath and voice. Try out the voice alone for a minute, and then let yourself talk with other people. Play with listening and speaking, examining the rhythms and gestures of the character." He adds, "After a few minutes, let these adjustments go. Shake out your body and return to your neutral walk." Eighth, after completing one cycle of the circus walk repeat it by beginning with a new walk. Again, paying attention to how each part of your body changes and accumulates to transform into a new and different body.

> Seeing the Word
> Were you able to leave the word and go into the experience?
> (Viola Spolin)

After one or two cycles of the circus walks, you will choose an excerpt from your fieldnotes or oral history to be read aloud as you begin a new walk cycle. This time you will focus on the sensory elements of the text as you form plastiques to create sensory images suggested in the text. You are reading with emphases and heightened awareness of sight, sound, taste, touch, and smell. The reading need not reflect the meaning of the text, but must focus on the senses aligned with sensory shapes and images formed by the body. How do colors, sounds, and other sensory elements form your body in this new circus walk cycle?

Character word jam

Select phrases or excerpts from the oral history or fieldnotes that are more challenging and difficult to say. First, select a phrase and begin to "jam" or play with the words. Second, be imaginative with the words and improvise a range of choices relating to sensibilities, moods, dispositions, or characterizations. Change pitch, word order, intonation, rhythm, volume, and so forth, keeping in mind vocal Viewpoints, while allowing your body to change with your voice. Wangh states: "Move as you work, play with gestures and images. Purposefully try choices you know won't feel right, and then return to ones you like better." Be mindful of which physical and vocal choices that you are "jamming" are most effective and preferred. Choose the vocalization and remain with that voice and body for a few moments. Third, move on to another phrase and "jam" through plastiques until you find the right image and fit of body and sound. Fourth, continue through the text keeping the choices you've made. As you think about a final choice, "If you find a voice that somehow seems right, do not worry at this point if it feels 'stereotyped' or 'too obvious.' You will work on refining it later." He continues, "For now just keep playing with the choice you've made, allowing variation for different emotions that the character exhibits" (2000: 271) (Figures 10.1 and 10.2).

Figure 10.1 Labor Rites. High jump and body in motion with arms up high to reflect the digital image of multiple arms held high in joy and command for economic justice. Choreography by Joel Valentine-Martinez. Photograph by Rafi Letzter.

Figure 10.2 Labor Rites. The full body reach and stretch of factory work and collective labor. Choreography by Joel Valentine-Martinez. Photograph by Rafi Letzter.

Notes

1 Jerzy Grotowski. "Polish theatre practitioner Jerzy Grotowski (1933–1999) is best known for his intense actor training processes in the 1960s and 1970s. At the Laboratory Theatre in Opole, Grotowski and his small groups of actors experimented with the physical, spiritual, and ritualistic aspects of theatre, the nature of role, and the relationship between actor and spectator. Grotowski was a key figure of avant-garde theatre. His comprehensive acting system is probably the most complete approach to role since the work of Stanislavski. Today, Grotowski is recognized as one of the great directors of the modern theatre and a significant innovator of the experimental theatre movement. His techniques are easily grasped by school students. Poor Theatre can be performed in any bare space, so school drama departments with few resources often find this style of theatre attractive. Grotowski coined the term 'poor theatre', defining a performance style that rid itself of the excesses of theatre, such as lavish costumes and detailed sets (hence 'poor'). Poor Theatre pieces centre on the skill of the actor and are often performed with only a handful of props. As a director, Grotowski preferred to perform works in non-traditional spaces such as buildings and rooms, instead of mainstream theatre houses with traditional stages. Typically, the audience was placed on many sides of the action or in and amongst the action, itself. Acting in the style of Poor Theatre places emphasis on the physical skill of the performer and uses props for transformation into other objects, sometimes of great significance … The concept of Poor Theatre strips away all of theatre's excesses; Poor Theatre is non-commercial theatre; the antithesis of modern-day blockbusters; Grotowski argued theatre could never compete with film and television, so it should never attempt to; the term 'paratheatre' is often associated with Grotowski ('para' meaning 'beyond'); paratheatre saw Grotowski

experiment with actors in training programs and other non-performed works; Grotowski's 'poor theatre' phase was between 1959 and 1970; 1975 marked the end of all public performances connected to Grotowski; Grotowski's collected writings on theatre are published in 'Towards a Poor Theatre' (1968)" (www.thedramateacher.com/poor-theatre-conventions/).

2 Viola Spolin. "November 7, 1906 to November 22, 1994. Viola Spolin was an actress, educator, director, author, and the creator of Theater Games, a system of actor training that uses games she devised to organically teach the formal rules of the theatre. Her groundbreaking book *Improvisation for the Theater* transformed American theatre and revolutionized the way acting is taught. Originally published in 1963 by Northwestern University Press, it remains an essential theatre text. She developed her methods while working as a drama supervisor in Chicago for the WPA, at her Young Actors Company in Hollywood, and as Director of Workshops at The Second City. Her son, director Paul Sills, who is credited with popularizing her work, used her Theater Games when he co-founded Compass, Playwrights Theatre Club, The Second City, and created Story Theater. The modern improvisational theatre movement is a direct outgrowth of Spolin's methods, discoveries, and writings … Viola Spolin's improvisational Theater Games are a complete system of actor training. Each game or exercise has a focus, a problem to be solved by the players as a group, so that lessons are learned through play (experience). She wrote: 'Everyone can act. Everyone can improvise. Anyone who wishes to can play in the theater and learn to become stageworthy. We learn through experience and experiencing, and no one teaches anyone anything … 'Talent' or 'lack of talent' has little to do with it.' Through focused attention, a player can be in the present time, their intuition activated and their whole body alert and ready to play—physical states that benefit theatrical communication and liberate the individual to explore their environment and make new discoveries. In moments of pure spontaneity, cultural and psychological conditioning fall away, allowing for the player to explore the unknown. In Theater Games, space objects replace props and sets, which opens the possibility for theatrical transformation. Spolin called transformation the heart of improvisation. She believed cultural and familial authorities often use approval and disapproval to control others, limiting the individual's capacity for experience. Her evaluation methods instead involve the whole group in a non-judgmental process that lets students learn for themselves. Spolin called her teaching methods non-authoritarian, non-verbal, and non-psychological" (www.violaspolin.org/bio).

3 Stephen Wangh is a renowned acting teacher, playwright, and director. He has taught at Emerson College, New York University, and Naropa University. He is author of *An Acrobat of the Heart: A Physical Approach to Acting* inspired by the work of Jerzy Grotowski and his most recent book, *The Heart of Teaching: Empowering Students in the Performing Arts*. This interview was conducted October 29, 2017.

Epilogue
The intermix of performance, ethnography, and communication

Dear reader

I would like to end with a story of sorts. In July 2017, the Center for Global Culture and Communication with the Department of Performance Studies at Northwestern University invited graduate students and recent graduates for a five-day Summer Institute on *improvisation, narrative, and beauty*. I served as convener of the Institute for 2017, and the focus was on embodied techniques of improvisation, the rhetorical power of narrative, and the ethics of beauty. The ongoing question was: In the workshop space, how can improvisation, narrative, and beauty merge to embody moments of freedom and justice? Each day seminar participants worked with renowned artist-scholars in a practice-based workshop format.[1]

On the first day of the workshop, I began by expressing to the over 20 selected participants that I hoped we would emerge into a community of relations, an array of connections, and journeyers through insights and emotions centered on justice, beauty, and fairness. I said that we would emerge into a *community* of embodied practitioners. Drawing from ecology, by community I mean *a group of interdependent organisms of different individuals growing together, being together, and experiencing transformations together in a specified space*. I believed this would materialize through the alchemy of embodied work conjoined by concepts and principles: the inseparability of mind and body; the interplay of theory and practice; the codependence of reason and feeling.

This alchemy—constituted by the dynamics of improvisation, narrative, and beauty conjoined with a community of embodied practitioners—would cause some things to change us and would cause us to change some things. I expressed that I was most interested in witnessing this emergence. For five days—from seven to eight hours a day—a few examples of embodied work that emerged from the Institute included the following: site specific solo performances as disruptive action of misremembered stories; humming between sounds of rhythmic breathing and human sonic effects from the collective of voices, feelings, and mood; physical endurance, force, and propelled movements from both the counter and dual energies of performance partnering; and group improvisation inspired by our own colors, fabrics, words, objects, and drawing installations of terrible beauty.

On the last day, I sat in the back of the theatre as everyone began to return from their improvisations in outside locations across the campus. Honey Pot Performance led the final workshop in an extraordinary experience of ritual theatre. I watched in the back as everyone sat in a circle on the floor. Everyone seemed especially animated and energized by their work this July afternoon. All week, they had done the labor of embodied practice that did, in fact, emerge into a community of relations.

It is now October and last week I received an email from one of the participants, Kelsey Klotz, who is presently a Postdoctoral Fellow at Emory University. Kelsey informed me she had published an article about her experience in the workshop. The article is a sincere reflection on embodied knowledge as transformational. Describing her thoughts on the first day of the workshop, she writes:

> Standing at the edge of the space, I considered the research time lost that day to struggles against imaginary constraints, or running around the room while guiding a partner whose eyes were closed, or slowly lifting myself from the fetal position to standing without using my hands.
> (Klotz 2017: 4)

> "I'm an academic!" My mind would silently rage. "Don't you know that I need to think, that my body doesn't move like this?" But even as my mind chafed at what was being asked of my body, I complied, moving further into the discomfort of relying on my body over my mind.
> (Klotz 2017: 16)

When I first read this, I also remembered back on those first days of the Summer Institute and how disheartened I was in turning down so many deserving applicants. Too many applications for too few openings. I remembered their names, wished I had been able to garner more funds to accept them. I remembered Kelsey those first days. I thought: "She does not seem to want to be here." Then, I thought about all the applicants who really did want to be here and were denied. But, over the five days, I witnessed Kelsey begin to open to an enlivenedness, an authenticity of connection, and to an unfolding and articulate engagement with the space in the prompts and embodiments of improvisation, narrative, and beauty. I remember on that last day thinking, yes, this is why Kelsey and all of us are here. I am so grateful that she is in the room. After describing her group improvisation, during those last days of the Institute, she writes: "in those moments, my academic knowledge of [Judith] Butler's recognition became informed by embodied experience" (2017: 16). She continues:

> But even more, my understanding of Ellison's concept of responsibility and invisibility intensified as I connected with women of different racial, disciplinary, and performance backgrounds from myself. ... Ellison

Figure E.1 The Summer Institute, 2017.
Standing (L–R): Taylor Scott, Keisha Bennett, D. Soyini Madison, Austin Jackson, Kelsey Klotz, Joe Martinez, Geneva Gluck, John Paul (JP) Staszel, Elizabeth Painter (Ellie), Eleanor Russell, Angelina Moles, Nathan Logan, Larry Cox, Jr., Mohamadreza Babaee, Chaunesti Webb, Laronika Thomas, Adam Wayne Nixon.
Sitting (R–L): Patrica Nguyen, Jennifer Ligaya, Kristen Wright, Brittney Harris, Ryan Brownlow, Gabriel Randle (not shown).

writes, "Irresponsibility is part of my invisibility ... Responsibility rests upon recognition, and recognition is a form of agreement."

(Klotz 2017: 14)

As I write this months after the fact, I cannot help but think about the politics of recognition and racial power dynamics at play in those moments—about how I, as a white woman, may or may not have felt recognition differently from ... women whose race has historically determined the amount of recognition and visibility they receive, I found myself responsible to them in ways that I would not have been able to feel without those moments of connection.

(Klotz 2017)

It is these "moments of connection" this book hopes to provide with methodologies, techniques, and tools. From ethnographers and fieldworkers, to classroom teachers and graduate students, and finally for directors and workshop performers, I hope that what has been offered here, in this mix of embodied thinking and doing, more than anything else, will be *useful* to you in imagining and materializing brave and lasting performances. For the sake of connection (Figure E.1).

Sincerely
D. Soyini Madison
Evanston, Illinois

Note

1 The scholar-artists included Honey Pot Performance, Virginie Magnat, Tony Perucci, Elyse Pineau, and Chloe Johnston.

Appendix
Illustration of creativity and the brain

The **brain stem** is comprised of the midbrain and hindbrain. The brain stem connects with all areas of our nervous system from heart rate, breathing, and blood pressure to digestion, alertness, and sleeping ability. The **cerebellum** is responsible for co-ordination, posture, muscle tone, and balance. The **cerebrum**, primarily made up of the forebrain, contains our brain lobes: *frontal* (concentration, memory, decision making, judgement, emotional response, impulse control, language, voluntary movement); *parietal* (pain perception, touch and sensation, temperature, awareness of body in space and time); *occipital* (vision); *temporal* (behavior, memory, language and interpretation, hearing ability, elements of visual perceptions). In sum, the cerebrum is responsible for memory, intellect, language, and sensory information, as well as body and movement awareness. The cerebrum comprises four domains: (1) the limbic system or emotional brain; (2) amygdala—learning/memory storage/motivation/controlling emotions; (3) the thalamus transmits sensory information to the cortex; (4) the cortex is responsible for perception (attributed to the arts), abstract reasoning, memory, and high cognitive functioning; (4) the hypothalamus regulates displays of emotion as well as sleeping, temperature, and reproductive function.

Left and right hemispheres of the brain. There is a popular notion that individuals who are right brain thinkers are more creative, intuitive, emotion centered, and inclined toward metaphor and movement, while left brain thinkers are more logical, analytical, categorical, and inclined toward science and math. Daniel H. Pink from *A Whole New Mind* states:

> The two hemispheres of our brains don't operate as on-off switches—one powering down as soon as the other starts lighting up. Both halves play a role in nearly everything we do ... both sides work together [note 24]—but they have different specialties: The left handles logic, sequence, literalness and analysis. The right takes care of synthesis, emotional expression, context, and the big picture. NOTE: Synthesis, here means "finding connections between different ideas, styles, disciplines" ... "this is considered a higher-order cognitive function and also is essential to invention and other forms of creativity and yet is handled by the right hemisphere" ... this "disputes left hemisphere superiority."

> To oversimplify just a bit, the left hemisphere handles WHAT is said: the right hemisphere focuses on HOW it is said [note 27].
>
> (Pink 2008: 50–51)

We can surmise from this discussion that the basic grammatical sequencing of words is inclined toward left brain thinking, while interpreting contextual meaning, abstract concepts: metaphor, interplay between tone and word meaning, sarcasm and irony are the territory primarily, but not exclusively, of the right brain.

Bibliography

Ackroyd, J. and J. O'Toole. (2010). *Performing Research: Tensions, Triumphs and Trade-offs of Ethnodrama*. Stoke-on-Trent: Trentham.
Alcoff, L. (1991). "The Problem of Speaking for Others." *Cultural Critique* 20: 5–32.
Alexander, B. (2005). "Performance Ethnography: The Re-enacting and Inciting of Culture." In *The Sage Handbook of Qualitative Research*. Eds. N. K. Denzin and Y. S. Lincoln. London: Sage Publications, 411–441.
Alexander, B. (2006). *Performing Black Masculinity: Race, Culture, and Queer Identity*. New York, NY: AltaMira Press.
Anderson, B. (1991). *Imagined Communities*. London: Verso.
Anderson, M. (2007). "Making Theatre from Data: Lessons for Performative Ethnography from Verbatim Theatre." *Journal of Drama Australia* 31.1: 79–91.
Angrosino, M. V. (1994). "On the Bus with Vonnie Lee: Explorations in Life History and Metaphor." In *Qualitative Inquiry and Research Design: Choosing among Five Approaches*. Ed. J. Creswell. Thousand Oaks, CA: Sage, 251–263.
Auslandar, P. (1999). *Liveness: Performance in a Mediatized Culture*. New York, NY: Routledge.
Bacon, J. (2006). "The Feeling of the Experience: A Methodology for Performance Ethnography." In *Research Methodologies for Drama Education*. Ed. J. Ackroyd. Stoke on Trent: Trentham Books, 135–158.
Bagley, C. and M. B. Cancienne. (2001). "Educational Research and Intertextual Forms of (Re)Presentation: The Case for Dancing the Data." *Qualitative Inquiry* 7.2: 221–237.
Bailey, M. M. (2013). *Butch Queens Up in Pumps: Gender, Performance, and Ballroom Culture in Detroit*. Ann Arbor, MI: University of Michigan Press.
———. (2014). "Engendering Space: Ballroom Culture and the Spatial Practice of Possibility in Detroit." *Gender, Place & Culture: A Journal of Feminist Geography* 21.4: 489–507.
Bailey, S. (2010). *Barrier-free Theatre*. Enumclaw, WA: Idyll Arbor.
Bakhtin, M. (1981). *The Dialogic Imagination*. Ed. M. Holquist. Trans. C. Emerson and M. Holquist. Austin, TX: University of Texas Press.
———. (1990). *Art and Answerability: Early Philosophical Essays*. Eds. M. Holquist and V. Liapunov. Trans. V. Liapunov. Austin, TX: University of Texas Press.
———. (1993). *Toward a Philosophy of the Act*. Eds. V. Liapunov and M. Holquist. Trans. V. Liapunov. Austin, TX: University of Texas Press.
Balfour, M. (2013). "Preface." In *Refugee Performance: Political Encounters*. Ed. M. Balfour. Bristol, UK: Intellect, xxi–xxv.

Barker, C. (1978). *Theatre Games*. New York, NY: Drama Book Specialists.

———. (2010). *Theatre Games: A New Approach to Drama Training*. London: Bloomsbury Publishing.

Barone, T. (2002). "From Genre Blurring to Audience Blending: Reflections on the Field Emanating from an Ethnodrama." *Anthropology and Education Quarterly* 33.2: 255–267.

Barone, T. and E. W. Eisner. (2012). *Arts Based Research*. Thousand Oaks, CA: Sage.

Barthes, R. (1985a). "The Grain of the Voice." In *The Responsibility of Forms*. Trans. R. Howard. New York, NY: Hill & Wang, 267–277.

Bauman, R. (1986). *Story, Performance, and Event: Contextual Studies of Oral Narrative*. Cambridge: Cambridge University Press.

Bennett, P. G. and S. French. (2015). *Experiencing Stanislavsky Today: Training and Rehearsal for the Psychophysical Actor*. New York, NY: Routledge.

Berlant, L. and M. Warner. (1998). "Sex in Public." *Critical Inquiry* 24.2: 547–566.

Bhabha, H. (1996). "Aura and Agora: On Negotiating Rapture and Speaking Between." In *Negotiating Rapture: The Power of Art to Transform Lives*. Ed. R. Francis. Chicago, IL: Museum of Contemporary Art, 8–17.

Boal, A. (1992). *Games for Actors and Non-actors*. London: Routledge.

———. (1998). *Legislative Theatre*. New York: Routledge.

Bogart, A. and T. Landau. (2005). *The Viewpoints Book: A Practical Guide to Viewpoints and Composition*. New York: NY: Theatre Communications Group.

Booth, W. (1999). *For the Love of It: Amateuring and Its Rivals*. Chicago, IL: University of Chicago Press.

Bourdieu, P. (1984). *Distinction*. Trans. R. Nice. Cambridge, MA: Harvard University Press.

Brecht, B. (1964). "The Street Scene." In *Brecht on Theatre: The Development of an Aesthetic*. Ed. and Trans. J. Willett. London: Methuen, 121–129.

Brook, P. (1968). *The Empty Space*. New York, NY: Macmillan Publishing.

Bruno, S. and L. Dixon. (2014). *Creating Solo Performance*. New York, NY: Routledge.

Butler, J. (1988). "Performative Acts and Gender Constitution: An Essay in Phenomenology and Feminist Theory." *Theatre Journal* 40.4: 519–531.

———. (1993). *Bodies That Matter: On the Discursive Limits of "Sex."* New York, NY: Routledge.

Callery, D. (2002). *Through the Body: A Practical Guide to Physical Theatre*. London: Routledge.

Capecci, J. and T. Cage. (2012). *Living Proof: Telling Your Story to Make a Difference: Essential Skills for Advocates and Spokespersons*. Minneapolis, MN: Granville Circle.

Chang, H. (2008). *Autoethnography as Method*. Walnut Creek, CA: Left Coast Press.

Cheeseman, P. (2005). "On Documentary Theatre." In *Talking to Terrorists*. Ed. R. Soans. London: Oberon, 104–107.

Chekhov, M. (2015). "Improvisation and Ensemble." In *The Improvisation Studies Reader: Spontaneous Acts*. Eds. R. Caines and A. Heble. London: Routledge, 169–174.

Clandinin, J. and M. Connelly. (2010). *Narrative Inquiry, Experience and Story in Qualitative Research*. San Francisco, CA: Jossey-Bass.

Connerton, P. (1989). *How Societies Remember*. Cambridge: Cambridge University Press.

Conquergood, D. (1991). "Rethinking Ethnography: Towards a Critical Cultural Politics." *Communication Monographs* 59: 179–94.

———. (1997). "Street Literacy." In *Handbook of Research on Teaching Literacy Through the Communicative and Visual Arts*. Eds. J. Flood, S. B. Heath, and D. Lapp. New York, NY: Macmillan, 334–375.

———. (1998). "Beyond the Text: Toward a Reformative Cultural Politics." In *The Future of Performance Studies: Visions and Revisions*. Ed. S. J. Dailey. Washington, DC: National Communication Association, 25–36.

———. (2000). "Rethinking Elocution: The Trope of the Talking Book and Other Figures of Speech." *Text and Performance Quarterly* 20: 325–341.

———. (2002). "Lethal Theatre: Performance, Punishment, and the Death Penalty." *Theatre Journal* 54: 339–367.

———. (2003). "Performing as a Moral Act: Ethical Dimensions of the Ethnography of Performance." In *Turning Points in Qualitative Research: Tying Knots in a Handkerchief*. Eds. N. K. Denzin and Y. S. Lincoln. Walnut Creek, CA: AltaMira Press, 240–310.

Crossley, M. (2007). "Narrative Analysis." In *Analysing Qualitative Data in Psychology*. Eds. E. Lyons and A. Coyle. London: Sage, 131–144.

Csikszentmihalyi, M. (2008). *Flow: The Psychology of Optimal Experience*. New York, NY: Harper Perennial Classics.

———. (2015) "Theoretical Model of Enjoyment." In *The Improvisation Studies Reader: Spontaneous Acts*. Eds. R. Caines and A. Heble. London: Routledge, 150–161.

Cunningham, M. (2015). "The Impermanent." In *The Improvisation Studies Reader: Spontaneous Acts*. Eds. R. Caines and A. Heble. London: Routledge, 165–168.

Damasio, A. (1994). *Descartes' Error: Emotion, Reason, and the Human Brain*. New York, NY: Penguin Putnam.

Davies, C. A. (1999). *Reflexive Ethnography: A Guide to Researching Selves and Others*. London: Routledge.

Davis, C. S. and C. Ellis. (2008). "Emergent Methods in Autoethnographic Research: Autoethnographic Narrative and the Multiethnographic Turn." In *Handbook of Emergent Methods*. Eds. S. N. Hesse-Biber and P. Leavy. New York, NY: Guilford Press, 283–302.

de Certeau, M. (1984). *The Practice of Everyday Life*. Vol. 1. Trans. S. Rendall. Berkeley, CA: University of California Press.

———. (1986). *Heterologies: Discourse on the Other*. Trans. B. Massumi. Minneapolis, MN: University of Minnesota Press.

DeFrantz, T. F. (2004). *Dancing Revelations: Alvin Ailey's Embodiment of African American Culture*. Oxford: Oxford University Press.

Deleuze, G. (1990). *Expressionism in Philosophy: Spinoza*. New York, NY: Zone Books.

Deleuze, G. and F. Guattari. (1987). *A Thousand Plateaus*. Minneapolis, MN: University of Minnesota Press.

Denzin, N. (1997). *Interpretive Ethnography: Ethnographic Practices for the 21st Century*. Thousand Oaks, CA: Sage.

———. (2003). *Performance Ethnography: Critical Pedagogy and the Politics of Culture*. Thousand Oaks, CA: Sage.

———. (2004). Lecture: Arizona State University, Tempe. Reported in J. Saldaña, ed. (2006). *Ethnodrama: An Anthology of Reality Theatre*. Walnut Creek, CA: AltaMira.

Denzin, N. and Y. Lincoln. (2006). "Foreword." In *Ethnodrama: An Anthology of Reality Theatre*. Ed. J. Saldaña. Walnut Creek, CA: AltaMira, xi–xiii.

Derrida, J. (1995). *Archive Fever: A Freudian Impression*. Trans. E. Prenowitz. Chicago, IL: University of Chicago Press.

Diamond, E. (1996). "Introduction." In *Performance and Cultural Politics*. Ed. E. Diamond. New York: Routledge, 1–12.

———. (1997). *Unmaking Mimesis*. London: Routledge.

Dilley, B. (2015). *This Very Moment: Teaching Thinking Dancing*. Boulder, CO: Naropa University Press.

Dolan, J. (2001). *Geographies of Learning: Theory and Practice, Activism and Performance*. Middletown, CT: Wesleyan University Press.

———. (2005). *Utopia in Performance: Finding Hope at the Theater*. Ann Arbor, MI: University of Michigan Press.

Doxtader, E. (2001). "Loving History's Fate, Perverting the Beautiful Soul: Scenes of Felicity's Potential." *Cultural Studies* 15.2: 206–221.

Ellis, C. (2008). *Revision: Autoethnographic Reflections on Life and Work*. Walnut Creek, CA: Left Coast Press.

Filewood, A. (2009). "The Documentary Body: Theatre Workshop to Banner Theatre." In *Get Real: Documentary Theatre Past and Present*. Eds. A. Forsyth and C. Megson. New York, NY: Palgrave Macmillan, 55–73.

Fine, E. C. (1984). *The Folklore Text: From Performance to Print*. Thousand Oaks, CA: Sage.

Fischlin, D. (2015). "Improvised Responsibility: Opening Statements (Call and) Responsibility: Improvisation, Ethics, Co-Creation." In *The Improvisation Studies Reader: Spontaneous Acts*. Eds. R. Caines and A. Heble. London: Routledge, 289–295.

Fischlin, D. and Heble, A. (2004). *The Other Side of Nowhere: Jazz, Improvisation, Rights and the Ethics of Cocreation*. Durham, NC: Duke University Press.

Fischlin, D., Heble, A., and Lipsitz, G. (2013). *The Fierce Urgency of Now: Improvisation, Rights, and the Ethics of Cocreation*. Durham, NC: Duke University Press.

Fleishman, M. (2012). "The Difference of Performance as Research." *Theatre Research International* 37.1: 28–37.

Foster, S. L. (1986). *Reading Dancing: Bodies and Subjects in Contemporary American Dance*. Berkeley, CA: University of California Press.

———. (1995). "Choreographing History." In *Choreographing History*. Ed. S. L. Foster. Bloomington, IN: Indiana University Press, 2–21.

———. (2015). "Improvisation in Dance and Mind." In *The Improvisation Studies Reader: Spontaneous Acts*. Eds. R. Caines and A. Heble. London: Routledge, 398–403.

Foucault, M. (1988). "Technologies of the Self." In *Technologies of the Self: A Seminar with Michel Foucault*. Eds. L. Martin et al. Amherst, MA: University of Massachusetts Press, 16–49.

Fox, H. (2010). *Zoomy Zoomy: Improv Games and Exercises for Groups*. New Paltz, NY: Tusitala Publishing.

Freeman, J. (2010). *Blood, Sweat & Theory: Research through Practice in Performance*. Faringdon: Libri Publishing.

Gates, H. L. Jr. (2014). *Monkey: A Theory of African American Literary Fiction*. New York, NY: Oxford University Press.
Giddens, P. (1984). *When and Where I Enter: The Impact of Black Women on Race and Sex in America*. New York, NY: HarperCollins.
Gingrich-Philbrook, C. (2001). "Love's Excluded Objects: Staging Irigaray's Heteronormative Essentialism." *Cultural Studies* 15.2: 222–228.
Glassie, H. (1982). *Passing the Time in Ballymenone: Culture and History of an Ulster Community*. Philadelphia, PA: University of Pennsylvania.
Goodall, H. L. (2000). *Writing the New Ethnography*. Boston Way, MD: AltaMira.
Goodall, J. (2008). *Stage Presence*. London and New York, NY: Routledge.
Gordon, A. (1997). *Ghostly Matters: Haunting and the Sociological Imagination*. Minneapolis, MN: University of Minnesota Press.
Gray, R. E. and C. Sinding, eds. (2002). *Standing Ovation: Performing Social Science Research about Cancer*. Walnut Creek, CA: AltaMira Press.
Grossberg, L. (1994). "Bringing it All Back Home: Pedagogy and Cultural Studies." In *Between Borders: Pedagogy and the Politics of Cultural Studies*. Eds. G. Giroux and P. McLaren. New York, NY: Routledge, 1–25.
Grotowski Institute. (2012). Grotowski Institute website. Retrieved from www.grotowski-institute.art.pl, accessed October 27, 2017.
Grotowski, J. (1968). *Towards a Poor Theatre*. Holstebro: Odin Teatret.
———. (2002). *Towards a Poor Theatre*. Ed. E. Barba. New York, NY: Routledge.
Halberstam, J. (1995). *Skin Shows*. Durham, NC: Duke University Press.
Hall, S. (1997). *Representation: Cultural Representation and Signifying Practices*. London. Sage
Hamera, J. (1990). "Silence that Reflects: Butoh, *Ma*, and the Crosscultural Gaze." *Text and Performance Quarterly* 10.1: 53–60.
———. (1994). "The Ambivalent, Knowing Male Body in the Pasadena Dance Theatre." *Text and Performance Quarterly* 14.3: 197–209.
———. (2007). *Dancing Communities: Performance, Difference and Connection in the Global City*. New York, NY: Palgrave Macmillan.
Hammond, W. and D. Steward, eds. (2008). *Verbatim Verbatim: Contemporary Documentary Theatre*. London: Oberon Books.
Harvey, D. (2000). *Spaces of Hope*. Edinburgh: Edinburgh University Press.
Hawes, L. C. (1998). "Becoming-Other-Wise: Conversational Performance and the Politics of Experience." *Text and Performance Quarterly* 18.4: 273–299.
Hochschild, A. R. (2003). *The Managed Heart: Commercialization of Human Feeling* (2nd ed.). Berkeley, CA: University of California Press.
Holland, A.-C. S. (2005). *The Water Business: Corporations versus People*. London: Zed Books.
hooks, b. (1990). *Yearnings*. Boston, MA: South End.
———. (1994). "Homeplace (a Site of Resistance)." In *The Woman That I Am: The Literature and Culture of Contemporary Women of Color*. Ed. D. S. Madison. New York: St. Martin's, 448–454.
Hughes, J. and H. Nicholson. (2016). *Critical Perspectives on Applied Theatre*. New York, NY: Cambridge University Press.
Jagodowski, T. J., D. Pasquesi, P. Victor, and A. Sedaris. (2015). *Improvisation at the Speed of Life: The TJ and Dave Book*. New York, NY: Solo Roma.
Jeffers. A. (2013). "Hospitable Stages and Civil Listenings: Being an Audience for Participatory Refugee Theatre." In *Refugee Performance: Political Encounters*. Ed. M. Balfour. Bristol: Intellect, 297–310.

Johnson, E. P. (2003). *Appropriating Blackness*. Durham, NC: Duke University Press.

———. (2008). *Sweet Tea: Black Gay Men of the South*. Chapel Hill, NC: University of North Carolina Press

Jones, J. L. (2002). "Performance Ethnography: The Role of Embodiment in Cultural Authenticity." *Theatre Topics* 12.1: 1–14.

Jones, O. O. J. L. (2015). *Theatrical Jazz: Performance, Àṣẹ, and the Power of the Present Moment*. Columbus, OH: Ohio State University Press.

Kandel, E. R. (2012). *The Age of Insight: The Quest to Understand the Unconscious in Art, Mind, and Brain, from Vienna 1900 to the Present*. New York, NY: Random House.

Kemp, R. (2012). *Embodied Acting: What Neuroscience Tells Us about Performance*. London: Routledge.

Klotz, K. (2017). "Body and Soul: An Academic Discovers the Body's Knowledge of the World." Retrieved from https://commonreader.wustl.edu/c/body-and-soul/, accessed October 23, 2017.

Knowles, J. G. and A. L. Cole, eds. (2008). *Handbook of the Arts in Qualitative Research: Perspectives, Methodologies, Examples, and Issues*. Thousand Oaks, CA: Sage.

Kumiega, J. (2011). *The Theatre of Grotowski*. New York, NY. Methuen Drama.

Kurahashi, Y. (2013). "Theatre as a Healing Space: Ping Chong's Children of War." In *Refugee Performance: Practical Encounters*. Ed. M. Balfour. Chicago, IL: Intellect, University of Chicago Press, 247–260.

Langellier, K. (1999). "Personal Narrative, Performance, Performativity: Two or Three Things I Know For Sure." *Text and Performance Quarterly* 19.2: 125–144.

Langellier, K. M. and Peterson, E. E. (2004). *Storytelling in Daily Life: Performing Narrative*. Philadelphia, PA: Temple University Press.

Lecoq, J. (1987). *Le théâtre du geste: mimes et acteurs*. Paris, France: Bordas.

———. (2001). *The Moving Body (Le Corps Poétique): Teaching Creative Theatre*. New York, NY: Routledge.

Lefebvre, H. (1980). *La Présence et l'absence*. Paris: Casterman.

———. (1996). *Writings on Cities*. Trans. and Ed. E. Kofman and E. Lebas. London: Blackwell.

Levinas, E. (1996). *Emmanuel Levinas: Basic Writings*. Eds. R. Bernasconi, S. Critchley, and A. Peperzak. Bloomington, IN: Indiana University Press.

Liamputtong, P. (2009). *Qualitative Research Methods* (3rd ed.). Victoria: Oxford University Press.

Lionnet, F. (1995). *Postcolonial Representations*. Ithaca, NY: Cornell University Press.

Lomax, A. (1968). *Folk Song Style and Culture*. Washington, DC: American Association for the Advancement of Science.

Madison, D. S., ed. (1994). *The Woman That I Am: The Literature and Culture of Contemporary Women of Color*. New York: St. Martin's.

———. (1999). "Performing Theory/Embodied Writing." *Text and Performance Quarterly* 19.2: 107–124.

———. (2000). "Oedipus Rex at *Eve's Bayou* or the Little Black Girl Who Left Sigmund Freud in the Swamp." *Cultural Studies* 14.2: 311–340.

———. (2012). *Critical Ethnography: Method, Ethics, and Performance* (2nd ed.). Thousand Oaks, CA: Sage.

Magnat, V. (2015). *Grotowski, Women, and Contemporary Performance: Meetings with Remarkable Women*. New York, NY: Routledge.

Mahmoud, J. (2014). "'What a Body Can Do': A Praxis Session by Ben Spatz, Zihan Loo, Christine Germain, Donia Mounsef, Ira Murfin, Justin Zullo and Krista DeNio." *Performance Research* 19.3: 150–151.

Martin, R. (1998). *Critical Moves: Dance Studies in Theory and Politics*. Durham, NC: Duke University Press.

Mauss, M. (1973). "Techniques of the Body." Trans. B. Brewster. *Economy and Society* 2.1: 70–88.

———. (2006). *Techniques, Technology and Civilisation*. Ed. N. Schlanger. New York, NY: Durkheim Press.

McRobbie, A. (1997). "Dance Narratives and Fantasies of Achievement." In *Meaning in Motion: New Cultural Studies of Dance*. Ed. J. C. Desmond. Durham, NC: Duke University Press, 207–231.

Mienczakowski, J. (1995). "The Theater of Ethnography: The Reconstruction of Ethnography into Theater with Emancipatory Potential." *Qualitative Inquiry* 1.3: 360–375.

———. (2001a). "Ethnodrama: Constructing Participatory, Experiential and Compelling Action Research through Performance." In *Handbook of Action Research, Participative Inquiry and Practice*. Eds. P. Reason and H. Bradbury. London: Sage Publications, 219–227.

———. (2001b). "Ethnodrama: Performed Research—Limitations and Potential." In *Handbook of Ethnography*. Ed. P. Atkinson. Thousand Oaks, CA: Sage, 468–476.

———. (2003). "The Theatre of Ethnography: The Reconstruction of Ethnography into Theater with Emancipatory Potential." In *Turning Points in Qualitative Research: Tying Knots in a Handkerchief*. Eds. N. K. Denzin and Y. S. Lincoln. Walnut Creek, CA: AltaMira Press, 415–432.

Mienczakowski, J. and T. Moore. (2008). "Performing Data with Notions of Responsibility." In *Handbook of the Arts in Qualitative Inquiry: Perspectives, Methodologies, Examples and Issues*. Eds. J. G. Knowles and A. L. Cole. Thousand Oaks, CA: Sage Publications, 451–458.

Miller, S. (2006). *My Left Breast*. New York, NY: Playscripts.

Moran, D. (2000). *Introduction to Phenomenology*. London: Routledge.

Muñoz, J. E. (1999). *Disidentifications: Queers of Color and the Performance of Politics*. Minneapolis, MN: University of Minnesota Press.

Musher, S. A. (2015). *Democratic Art: The New Deal's Influence on American Culture*. Chicago, IL: University of Chicago Press.

Myerhoff, B. (1979). *Number Our Days*. New York, NY: Touchstone.

Nicholson, H. (2003). "The Performance of Memory: Drama, Reminiscence and Autobiography." *Journal of Drama Australia* 27.2: 71–92.

———. (2014). *Applied Drama: The Gift of Theatre*. New York, NY: Palgrave Macmillan

Norris, J. (2010). *Playbuilding as Qualitative Research: A Participatory Arts-based Approach*. Walnut Creek, CA: Left Coast Press.

Oddey, A. (1994). *Devising Theatre: A Practical and Theoretical Handbook*. London: Routledge.

Oliver, K. (2001). *Witnessing*. Minneapolis, MN: University of Minnesota Press.

Oida, Y. (1992) "An Actor Adrift." Quoted in Wangh, S. (2000). *An Acrobat of the Heart*. New York: Vintage.

Orti, P. (2014). *Your Handy Companion to Devising and Physical Theatre: Including Five Plays to Play With*. Lexington, KY: Paperplay.
O'Toole, J. (2006). *Doing Drama Research: Stepping into Enquiry in Drama, Theatre and Education*. Brisbane: Drama Australia.
Paget, D. (1987). "Verbatim Theatre: Oral History and Documentary Techniques." *New Theatre Quarterly* 3.12: 317–336.
Park-Fuller, L. (2003). "A Clean Breast of It." In *Voices Made Flesh: Performing Women's Autobiography*. Eds. L. C. Miller, J. Taylor, and M. H. Carver. Madison, WI: University of Wisconsin Press, 215–236.
Patterson, W. (2008). "Narratives of Events: Labovian Narrative Analysis and Its Limitations." In *Doing Narrative Research*. Eds. M. Andrews, C. Squire, and M. Tamboukou. London: Sage, 22–40.
Pelias, R. (2008). "Performative Inquiry: Embodiment and Its Challenges." In *Handbook of the Arts in Qualitative Research: Perspectives, Methodologies, Examples, and Issues*. Eds. J. G. Knowles and A. L. Cole. California: Sage Publications, 184–194.
Perucci, T. (2015). "Dog Sniff Dog: Materialist Poetics and the Politics of the Viewpoints." *Performance Research: A Journal of the Performing Arts* 20.1: 105–112.
Phelan, P. (1995). "Thirteen Ways of Looking at *Choreographing Writing*." In *Choreographing History*. Ed. S. L. Foster. Bloomington: Indiana University Press, 200–210.
Pineau, E. L. (2006). "Mercury: An Untimely Story." *Liminalities: A Journal of Performance Studies* 2.3.
Pink, D. H. (2008). *A Whole New Mind: Why Right-Brainers Will Rule the Future*. Singapore: Marshall Cavendish.
Pollock, D. (1990). "Telling the Told: Performing 'Like a Family.'" *Oral History Review* 18.2: 1–36.
———. (1998a). "Introduction: Making History Go." In *Exceptional Spaces: Essays in Performance and History*. Ed. D. Pollock. Chapel Hill, NC: University of North Carolina Press, 1–45.
———, ed. (1998b). *Exceptional Spaces: Essays in Performance and History*. Chapel Hill, NC: University of North Carolina Press.
———. (1999). *Telling Bodies Performing Birth*. New York, NY: Columbia University Press.
———. (2005). *Remembering: Oral History Performance*. New York, NY: Palgrave.
Poulos, C. N. (2008). *Accidental Ethnography: An Inquiry into Family Secrecy*. Walnut Creek, CA: Left Coast Press.
———. (2010). "Transgressions." *International Review of Qualitative Research* 3.1: 67–88.
Read, A. (1993). *Theatre and Everyday Life: An Ethics of Performance*. New York, NY: Routledge.
Rohd, M. (1998). *Theatre for Community, Conflict, and Dialogue: The Hope Is Vital Training Manual*. Portsmouth, NH: Heinemann.
Richards, T. (1995). *At Work with Grotowski on Physical Actions*. New York, NY: Routledge.
———. (2008). *Heart of Practice*. New York, NY: Routledge.
Richardson, L. (1990). *Writing Strategies: Reaching Diverse Audiences*. London: Sage.

———. (2000). "Writing: A Method of Inquiry." In *Handbook of Qualitative Research* (2nd ed.). Eds. N. K. Denzin and Y. S. Lincoln. Thousand Oaks, CA: Sage Publications, 923–948.

Rickman, A. and K. Viner, eds. (2006). *My Name Is Rachel Corrie*. New York, NY: Theatre Communications Group.

Riley, S. R. and L. Hunter, eds. (2009). *Mapping Landscapes for Performance as Research: Scholarly Acts and Creative Cartographies*. New York, NY: Palgrave Macmillan.

Roach, J. (1993). *The Player's Passion: Studies in the Science of Acting*. Ann Arbor, MI: University of Michigan Press.

Roncero-Menendez, S. (2014). "In Six Words, These Writers Tell You an Entire Story." www.huffingtonpost.com/2014/05/16/six-word-story_n_5332833.html, accessed May 16, 2014.

Rowe, C. A. (2005). "Be Longing: Toward a Feminist Politics of Relation." *NWSA Journal*, 17.2: 15–46.

Rowe, N. (2007). *Playing the Other: Dramatizing Personal Narratives in Playback Theatre*. London: Jessica Kingsley Publishers.

Rudakoff, J. (2015). *Dramaturging Personal Narratives: Who Am I and Where Is Here?* Wilmington, NC: Intellect.

Salas, J. (1991). *Improvising Real Life: Personal Story in Playback Theatre*. Dubuque, IA: Kendall Hunt.

Saldaña, J. (1998). "Ethical Issues in an Ethnographic Performance Text: The 'Dramatic Impact' of 'Juicy Stuff.'" *Research in Drama Education* 3.2: 181–196.

———. (2010a). "Reflections on an Ethnotheatre Aesthetic." *Arts Praxis 2*. Retrieved from http://steinhardt.nyu.edu/music/artspraxis/2/reflections_on_an_ethnotheatre_aesthetic, accessed May 5, 2017.

———. (2010b). "Writing Ethnodrama: A Sampler from Educational Research." In *New Approaches to Qualitative Research: Wisdom and Uncertainty*. Eds. M. Savin-Baden and C. H. Major. London: Routledge, 61–69.

———. (2011). *Ethnotheatre: Research from Page to Stage*. Walnut Creek, CA: Left Coast.

Scarry, E. (1985). *The Body in Pain: The Making and Unmaking of the World*. New York, NY: Oxford University Press.

———. (1999). *On Beauty and Being Just*. Princeton, NJ: Princeton University Press.

Schechner, R. (1985). *Between Theatre and Anthropology*. Philadelphia, PA: University of Pennsylvania Press.

———. (2015) "Playing." In *The Improvisation Studies Reader: Spontaneous Acts*. Eds. R. Caines and A. Heble. London: Routledge, 386–397.

Schechner, R. and L. Wolford. (1997). *The Grotowski Sourcebook*. New York, NY: Routledge.

Schneider, R. (1997). *The Explicit Body in Performance*. New York, NY: Routledge.

Scholes, R. (1989). *Protocols of Reading*. New Haven, CT: Yale University Press.

———. (1992). "Response to 'Reading Robert Scholes: A Symposium.'" *Text and Performance Quarterly* 12.1: 75–78.

Sliep, Y., K. Weingarten and A. Gilbert. (2013). "Narrative Theatre as an Interactive Community Approach to Mobilizing Collective Action in Northern Uganda." In *Refugee Performance: Practical Encounters*. Ed. M. Balfour. Chicago, IL: Intellect, University of Chicago Press, 77–98.

Smith, A. D. (1993). *Fires in the Mirror: Crown Heights, Brooklyn and Other Identitites*. New York, NY: Anchor Books.

———. (2000). *Talk to Me: Listening between the Lines*. New York, NY: Random House.
Snyder-Young, D. (2010). "Beyond an 'Aesthetic of Objectivity': Performance Ethnography, Performance Texts, and Theatricality." *Qualitative Inquiry* 16.10: 883–893.
Soans, R. (2004). *The Arab-Israeli Cookbook*. Twickenham: Aurora Metro Press.
———. (2007). *Life after Scandal*. London: Oberon Books.
Soja, E. W. (1996). *Thirdspace*. London: Blackwell.
Spatz, B. (2015). *What a Body Can Do: Technique as Knowledge, Practice as Research*. New York, NY: Routledge.
Spolin, V. (2001). *Theater Games for the Lone Actor: A Handbook*. Evanston, IL: Northwestern University Press.
Spry, T. (2011). *Body, Paper, Stage: Writing and Performing Autoethnography*. Walnut Creek, CA: Left Coast.
———. (2016). *Autoethnography and the Other: Unsettling Power through Utopian Performatives*. London: Routledge.
Stallybrass, P. (1999) "Clothes, Mourning, and the Life of Things." *Yale Review* 81.2: 35–51.
Stanislavski, K. (1967). *My Life in Art*. Trans. J. J. Robbins. Harmondsworth: Penguin Books.
Stone-Mediatore, S. (2003). *Reading across Borders: Storytelling and Postcolonial Struggles*. Basingstoke: Palgrave Macmillan.
Suzuki, T. (1993). *The Way of Acting: The Theatre Writings of Tadashi Suzuki*. Trans. J. R. Thomas. New York, NY: Theatre Communications Group.
Taylor, D. (2003). *The Archive and the Repertoire*. Durham, NC: Duke University Press.
Tedlock, D. (1983). *The Spoken Word and the Works of Interpretation*. Philadelphia, PA: University of Pennsylvania Press.
Thompson, J. (2009). *Performance Affects: Applied Theatre and the End of Effect*. Basingstoke: Palgrave Macmillan.
Tolle, E. (2004). *The Power of Now: A Guide to Spiritual Enlightenment*. Vancouver: Namaste Press.
Tsing, A. L. (2005). *Friction: An Ethnography of Global Connection*. Princeton, NJ: Princeton University Press.
Tuan, Y.-F. (1977). *Space and Place: The Perspective of Experience*. Minneapolis, MN: University of Minnesota Press.
Turner, V. (1982). *From Ritual to Theatre: The Human Seriousness of Play*. New York, NY: PAJ Publications.
———. (1986). *The Anthropology of Performance*. New York, NY: Performing Arts Journal Publications.
Turner, V. and E. Bruner, eds. (1986). *The Anthropology of Experience*. Urbana, IL: University of Illinois Press.
Ukaegbu, V. and Ewu, J. (2010). "Performing Histories: Voices of Black Ritual Community." In *Performing Research: Tensions, Triumphs and Trade-offs of Ethnodrama*. Eds. J. Ackroyd and J. O'Toole. Stoke on Trent: Trentham Books, 169–185.
Veblen, T. (1899) *The Theory of the Leisure Class*. New York, NY: Macmillan.
Wallace, R. (2015). "Writing Improvisation into Modernism." In *The Improvisation Studies Reader: Spontaneous Acts*. Eds. R. Caines and A. Heble. London: Routledge, 187–200.

Wangh, S. (2000). *An Acrobat of the Heart: A Physical Approach to Acting Inspired by the Work of Jerzy Grotowski*. New York, NY: Vintage Books.

Waterman, E. (2015) "Improvised Trust: Opening Statements." In *The Improvisation Studies Reader: Spontaneous Acts*. Eds. R. Caines and A. Heble. London: Routledge, 59–62.

Weigler, W. (2001). *Strategies for Playbuilding: Helping Groups Translate Issues into Theatre*. Portsmouth, NH: Heinemann.

"What Dance Has to Say about Beauty." (2000). *New York Times*, 23 July: AR26+.

White, H. (1995). "Bodies and Their Plots." In *Choreographing History*. Ed. S. L. Foster. Bloomington, IN: Indiana University Press, 230–234.

Wolford, L. (1996). *Grotowski's Objective Drama Research*. Jackson, MS: University Press of Mississippi.

Wright, M. (2009). *Playwriting in Process: Thinking and Working Theatrically* (2nd ed.). Newburyport, MA: Focus Publishing.

Wylam, L. W. (2008). "Living Tradition: Continuity of Research at the Workcenter of Jerzy Grotowski and Thomas Richards." *Drama Review* 52.2: 126–149.

Young, H. (2010). *Embodying Black Experience: Stillness, Critical Memory, and the Black Body*. Ann Arbor, MI: University of Michigan Press.

Zarrilli, P. B. (1995). *Acting (Re)Considered*. New York, NY: Routledge.

———. (2002). "The Metaphysical Studio." *Drama Review* 46.2: 157–70.

———. (2009). *Psychophysical Acting: An Intercultural Approach after Stanislavski*. With DVD-ROM by P. Hulton, Arts Archives. New York, NY: Routledge.

Zarrilli, P. B., J. Daboo, and R. Loukes. (2013). *Acting: Psychophysical Phenomenon and Process*. New York, NY: Palgrave Macmillan.

Index

References in *italics* refer to figures, those followed by 'n' refer to notes.

5Rhythms 89–92, *109*, 112–113n

A Whole New Mind 183–184
Ackroyd, J. 51, 56, 58
Acting: Psychophysical Phenomenon and Process 111n
activism xxviii, xxix, 7, *15*, 30–31, 113–114n, *159*
"aesthetic shape" 44
affective energy 35, 36
"affective loading" 120–121, 122, 131n
affordances 24n
African Waltz 31
Afrofuturism 77n
Alcoff, Linda xxiv, 136
Aleppo 94–96
"alternative facts" 128–129, 131n
amygdala 183
An Acrobat of the Heart 178n
anarchism xxiii–xxiv, 158, *159*
anatomy of emotion 140–143
ankles (plastique) 171
Anzaldúa, Gloria 72, 136
architecture (Viewpoint example) 155, 160, 165n
arms (plastique) 171
articulation/framing of embodied techniques 40
"artistic journey" 43–44
autoethnography 145

back (plastique) 171
Badu, Erykah 64
Bag Ladies 64
Bakhtin, Mikhail xxii, 34
Baldwin, James 127
Barad, Karen 7
Barker, Clive 84, 111n

Bartenieff, Irmgard 86, 87, 88, 111–112n
Bauman, R. 119, 132
beauty 179
Beavers, Wendell 164n
belonging xx–xxiii, xxvi, xxvii, xxxin, 14–15, 26, 61, 120, 127–128, 130, 161
BESS (Body, Effort, Shape, and Space) 86–89
better to hear you with! exercise 55–56
Black Feminist Futures workshops 69–70
Blandon, Ari ("Mamá Ari") 20, 21
blocking your time 146
Boal, Augusto 92–93, 96, 108, 113–114n
Body (BESS framework) 86, 87–89
body meditation 150–151
Body, Paper, Stage 145
Bogart, Anne 155, 157–158, 164–165n
both/and/but site of critical sharing 122, 126, 130
both/and site of critical sharing 122, 130
brain stem 183
Brecht, B. xv, 114n
"British School of Cultural Studies" xxviii
Brook, Peter xxix
Bruno, Sean 150, 152
"burden of liveness" xx
Burke, Kenneth 4
Burvill, Tom xxiii
Butler, Judith 180

Cage, T. 146–147
Callery, D. 35

Capecci, J. 146–147
cerebellum 183
Chaos (5Rhythms) 90–91, *109*
character word jam 175
Chekhov, M. 30
chest (plastique) 171
Chicago bop 14–15
Choice and Freedom (Viewpoint) 157–158
Chong, Ping 53–54, 76n
choral exchange 57
Choreutics 81
Circle story exercise 55
circle, clump, line exercise 88
circus walks exercise 174–175
citizenship xx, xxiv
"civil listening" 131n
Class improvisations *8, 38–39, 62–63*
"cliff-hanger paragraph" 55
clothing meditation 151–152
code-switching 12
collective action *16*
collective reading and listening *15*
Commedia dell'arte 110n
communal idea boards 46–48
communal participation 44–45
Complementary Reading (Newspaper Theatre) 105
composite body 25–26, 40, 78
Conway, Kellyanne 131n
cooking 12–13
Cooper, Anna Julia 26
"corporeal encounter" xxiii
cortex 183
Craft, Renée Alexander 17–23
creating/re-creating movement phrases 40
critical self-reflection 145
cross-cutting dialogue 57
Crossed Reading (Newspaper Theatre) 99
Csikszentmihalyi, M. 45
CTO (Center for the Theatre of the Oppressed) 114n
Cunningham, M. 30
"cuts" 7–8

Dabbing (effort) 81, 82, 84
Dakota pipeline 100–102
dancing narratives 73, 74–75
"dark play" 32
Daste, Jean 110n
data xvii, xviii–xix, xx, xxiv, xv, 108, 115n; and devised theatre 44–45, 51–53, 55, 57–61, 82; and improvisation 25, 29, 31

Davies, Charlotte Aull xx
De Loney, Margarita 20, 21
deadlines 61, 146
Delsarte, Francois 140
demographics information 52–53
Denzin, Norman 128
descriptive and expressive scene 60
devised theatre 43–44; digital dialogic performance 73–75; ethnographic data 44–45, 51–53, 55, 57–61, 82; Honey Pot Performance interview 61, 63–72, 66–67, 76n; and identities 43, 44, 61, 64, 66, 72, 76n; improvisation 48, 49–51, 53–56, 57–58, 60–61, 62–63, 64–65, 69–70; stage one 45–51; stage two 51–56; stage three 56–60; suggested stages 45–61
dialogue xx–xxiii; cross-cutting dialogue 57; and devised theatre 57–58; "dialogue-in-action" 34; digital dialogic performance 73–75; singing dialogue 174
digital media/performance 8, 17–18, 19, 73–75, 137–139, 161–162
Digital Portobelo 17–23
Direction (factor) 81, 82
Dixon, Luke 150, 152
documentary materials 53
"Dog Sniff Dog" xxviii–xxix
double Dutch 5–6, 23n
drafts 61, 146, 150
duration (Viewpoint example) 156, *159*, 160–161, 164–165n

"echo chamber" xxiii–xxvi, 122, 131n
Ecole Internationale de Mime et de Théâtre 110n
"economic form" 44
Effort (BESS framework) 86, 87–89
efforts and factors (EF) 80–85, 88, *109*
ego 30, 33, 112–113n, 157
Eight Basic Efforts of Action 81–85, 88
élan 36
elbows (plastique) 170
embodied practice 3–4, 5–6, 9–10, 179–180; devised theatre *see* devised theatre; Digital Portobelo initiative 20–21; examples 12–14; improvisation *see* improvisation
embodied research 6–9, 23n, 45–46
embodied technique 3–5, 9–10; devised theatre *see* devised theatre; Digital Portobelo initiative 20–21; examples 11–15; improvisation

see improvisation; and life stories 120–121; and movement 78, 86, 89; *via negativa* 166–167
Emotion (Viewpoint) 155, 156
"emotional-memory" 140
"emotion-manufacturing" xxix
endowing objects 151
enemy of truth 145
energy 35–37, 89–91, 113n, 145
"equipment for living" 4
Esquina, Gustavo 21
exchanging audiences/stories 73, 75
Experimental Theater Wing (New York University) 164n
extended sound exercise 172–173
external expression 140
eyelids (plastique) 170
eyes (plastique) 170

face muscles (plastique) 170
familial and community vocal techniques 11–12
feet (plastique) 171
Fine, Elizabeth 132–133
fingers (plastique) 171
first snow and play time exercise 79
Fischlin, D. 31, 37
Flickering (effort) 81, 82, 84
Floating (effort) 81, 82–83
flow 30–31, 81, 82
Flowing (5Rhythms) 89–90
flowing phrase 60
fluid sculptures 41–42
Folk Song, Style and Culture 112n
Forum Theater 93, 114n
Foster, Susan 32
Four Movement Factors 81, 82–85, 88
Fox, Hannah 55–56, 76n
Free Reader's Theatre 114n
frontal lobes 183
fufu 12–13

Gallese, Vittorio xxx
Gates, Henry Louis 88
Gatt, Caroline 8, 10
gesture (Viewpoint example) 156, *159*, 160, 165n
gibberish 28, 149
Gifted 143
Glassie, Henry 133
Gliding (effort) 81, 82, 85
"golden moments" 53, 75–76n
Golden, Manuel "Tatu" 21
Goldman, Alvin xxx
Gregory, André 169

grey area of third space xv–xvi
grid exercise 41
Grossberg, Lawrence xxvii
Grotowski, Jerzy 36, 142, 166–167, 168, 169, 177–178n
Growth (Viewpoint) 158

habits 168
Hall, Stuart xxviii
Hamera, Judith 4, 5
hands (plastique) 171
happy sandwich exercise 80
head (plastique) 170
Hemingway, Ernest 148
hemispheres of our brains 183–184
historic figures 44
Historical Reading (Newspaper Theatre) 102
Holman, Felicia 64, 65–66, 68, 69, 70, 71–72
holograms 137–139
Honey Pot Performance 61, 63–72, 66–67, 76n, 180
hooks, bell (Gloria Jean Watkins) xxi
hope 37, 40
House music/culture 64–66, 68–69, 76–77n
"How to Tame a Wild Tongue" 72
hypothalamus 183

identities xx, xxi, xxiv–xxv, xxvii–xxviii, xxx; and devised theatre 43, 44, 61, 64, 66, 72, 76n; and improvisation 25–27; and movement 78, 86, 89, 108; and oral history 127, 130; "rebellious identities" 108; speaking techniques 12
Image Theater 93, 114n
image, sound, text exercise 49–50, 75n
imaginative representation 143
imagine the grid exercise 160
imitation xxix–xxx, 11
improvisation: BESS exercises 87–89; *better to hear you with!* exercise 55–56; Circle story exercise 55; Class improvisations 8, 38–39, 62–63; and data 25, 29, 31; and devised theatre 48, 49–51, 53–56, 57–58, 60–61, 62–63, 64–65, 69–70; efforts and factors 82–85; energy 35–37; examples 40–42; *first snow and play time* exercise 79; flow 30–31; *happy sandwich* exercise 80; hope 37, 40; and identities 25–27; *image, sound, text* exercise 49–50, 75n; inherited bodies

25–28; key concepts 28–40; listening 32–35; and movement 79–80, 82–85, 87–89, 91, 92, 102–103, 105–108; *museum, thief, and sleeping guard* exercise 79; *next step sculptures* exercise 51; *object, topic, and story* exercise 50–51; and oral history 25, 29, 122, 125, 151–152; and plastiques 168–169; response(ability) 31–34; Summer Institute workshop 179–180; *taking shape* exercise 50; *talking hands* exercise 79–80; and Theater Games 178n; Viewpoints framework *see* Viewpoints; Walking and Waiting exercises 27, 54–55, 87, 174–175; Yes–No exercise 28; *you and the bee* exercise 80
Improvisation (Newspaper Theatre) 105–108
Improvisation for the Theater 178n
Insertion into Actual Context (Newspaper Theatre) 105
institutionality 7, 8–10
internal experience 140
intersubjectivity xxv, 51
interviews 17–22, 52–3, 59, 120–123, 133–135; Ben Spatz 6–11; E. Patrick Johnson 123–126; Honey Pot Performance 61, 63–72, 66–67; Stephen Wangh 167–169
Invisible Theater 93
"Is It a Human Being or a Girl" 30–31

Jagodowski, T. J. 31
jazz acting 28–29
Jeffers, Alison xxiii, xxiv, 131n
John (digital in dialogic performance) 73–75
John (solo performance, digital imagery) 162–163
Johnson, Abra M. 64–65, 66, 68–69, 70, 71, 72
Johnson, E. Patrick xxix–xxx, 121–126
Jones, O. 28–29, 43, 60, 92, 108
Juke Cry Hand Clap 64–65, 69
justice 10

Kara 161–162
Kathleen 137–139
Kemp, R. xxx, 141, 143
kinesthetic response (Viewpoint example) 156, *159*, 160–161, 164–165n
Klotz, Kelsey 180–181
knees (plastique) 171

Kofi 73–75
Kumiega, J. 166

Laban, Rudolf 80–81, 86, 88, 111n, 149
Labor Rites 6, 7, *15–16, 109–110, 147–148, 153–154, 159, 176–177*
labyrinth mapping exercise 152
Lach, Pam 19
Ladies Ring Shout 71, 72
Landau, Tina 155, 157–158, 164–165n
Latour, Bruno 7
Le Théâtre du Geste 111n
Lecoq, Jacques 36, 78, 110–111n, 144, 154n
Lee 161–163
Lefebvre, H. xv–xvi
legs (plastique) 171
leisure 13–14, 24n
Levinas, E. xxiii–xxiv
life stories 132, 137, 160; and oral history xxvi, 129–131, 144–152, *153*
limbic system 183
Lindy Hop 14, 24n
listening xxiv, 19–20, 54, 123–124, 142; and improvisation 28–29, 32–35
logos 9, 10–11
Lomax, Alan 112n
Lugones, Maria xv
Lyrical (5Rhythms) 91

Madison, D. Soyini 6, 9–10, 17–22, 64–65, 68–72, 123–126, 136, 167–169
magic if 145
magnified embodiments 161–163
Mahmoud, Jasmine 40, 42n
making body shapes exercise 160
"Mamá Ari" (Ari Blandon) 20, 21
mapping sessions 66–67, 68
mapping the performance space 152
Martin, Randy 25
Mary Overlie Dance Company 164n
mask work 40, 78–80, 110n
Masking Her 69–71, 72
Materializing the Abstract (Newspaper Theatre) 96, 99
McNeal, Meida T. 64, 65, 66, 68, 69, 70, 71, 72
Me and my shadow 96–99
Medusa's 69
Megel, Joseph 18
Meyerhold, Vsevolod 36, 41, 78
mindfulness 30, 54, 89, 90, 91–92, 173, 175

Minh-ha, Trinh T. 136
"minoritarian subject" xx
Mirror exercise 161
mirror neurons (MNs) xxx, 142–143
"mirroring" xxix–xxx
"moments of connection" 181
Moraga, Cherrie 136
mouth muscles (plastique) 170
movement: 5Rhythms 89–92, *109*, 112–113n; BESS framework 86–89; efforts and factors 80–85, 88, *109;* and identities 78, 86, 89, 108; improvisation 79–80, 82–85, 87–89, 91, 92, 102–103, 105–108; mask work 78–80, 110n; neutral position 78; Newspaper Theatre 92–108, *110*, 115n
Movement (Viewpoint) 155, 156
Munoz, Jose Estaban xx
museum, thief, and sleeping guard exercise 79
Musher, S. A. 92, 93

Nancy, Jean-Luc 32–33
narrated events 130, 132, 135–136, 150
narrative events 130, 132–135, *147–148*, 150
neck (plastique) 170
negative training 166
neural feedback system 141, 143
neural transmitters 140–141
neuroplasticity 140–141
neutral mask 40, 78–80
neutral position 40, 78
Newspaper Theatre 92–108, *110*, 115n
next step sculptures exercise 51
Nineteen Eighty-Four 131n
Noh theatre 110n

O'Toole, J. 51, 56, 58
object plastiques exercise 173–174
object, topic, and story exercise 50–51
objects of history 152
occipital lobes 183
Occupy Wall Street *147–148*
Oddey, Alison 43
Oida, Yoshi xxix
Oliver, Kelly 31, 35
Open Viewpoints 160
opening line 149
oral history xxvi–xxxi, 119–120; anatomy of emotion 140–143; Digital Portobelo initiative 18, 19–21; E. Patrick Johnson 121–126; embodied technique and practice 9; and identities 127, 130; and improvisation 25, 29, 122, 125, 151–152; and life stories xxvi, 129–131, 144–152, *153;* narrated events 130, 132, 135–136, 150; narrative events 130, 132–135, *147–148*, 150; ownership of 120–123, 130, 131n; and permission 126–127; plastiques 173–175; and provocation 128; and public pedagogy 127; and representation xxviii–xxxi; and selfhood xxvii–xxviii, 120, 136; solo performance 121–123, 142, 144–152, *147–148*, 161–163; and truth 128–131; Viewpoints 160–163
Otherness xx, xxi, xxii–xxiv, xxvi, xxxin
Overlie, Mary xxviii, 155, 158, 164n

Parallel Reading (Newspaper Theatre) 99
parietal lobes 183
pelvis (plastique) 171
Performance Style and Culture Research Project 112n
performed ethnography, terminology of xvii–xix, xxxin
Perls, Fritz 113n
permission 126–127
Perucci, Tony xxviii–xxix, 155
picture maps 59
Pink, Daniel H. 183–184
plastique river 172
plastiques 167–175
Playback Theatre 41, 76n
playfulness 30
poetic form and style 133–135
poetic license 139
poetic transcription 133, 135
Pollock, D. 128, 129, 131n
Poor Theatre 177–178n
"Portobelo Panama Intergenerational Oral History Project" 20–22
"positive techniques" 166
Possibility (Viewpoint) 157
"practical poetics" 135
prana, flow, energy 145
preliminary research 46
"presence work" xxviii–xxix
Pressing (effort) 81, 82, 84
proprioception 141, 143
provocation 128
public pedagogy 127
Punching/Thrusting (effort) 81, 82, 83
punctuation and marking 41
purposeful banter 57

Index   201

questioning body 145

Rainer, Yvonne 158
Reader's Theatre 114–115n, 125
"rebellious identities" 108
Reinforcement Reading (Newspaper Theatre) 99–102
"relational infrastructure" 5
relational labor 32, 43
repetition (Viewpoint example) 156, 157, 160–161, 165n
Repetition of BESS exercise 87–88
representation xxviii–xxxi, 99, 130, 142–143, 158
response(ability) 31–34
responsibility xxiii–xxiv, xxviii, 71–72, 180–181; and improvisation 31–32, 34
rhythm 13–14, 50, 86, 133, 145, 170, 175; 5Rhythms 89–92, *109*, 112–113n; and improvisation 31, 36–37
Rhythmical Reading (Newspaper Theatre) 102–105
ritual theatre 180
"road backward" 166
Roncero-Menendez, S. 148
Rose, Barbara xxix
Roth, Gabrielle 36, 89, 91, 112–113n, 149
Rowe, Aimee Carrillo xxii
Rowe, N. 120–12, 131n

Saldaña, Johnny 56, 57, 75–76n
scene with objects 60
Schechner, Richard 32
Sedaris, Amy 29
selfhood xxvii–xxviii, 120, 136, 141
Shape (BESS framework) 86, 87–89
Shape (Viewpoint) 155, 156, *159*, 165n
shoulders (plastique) 170, 171
Sills, Paul 178n
Simple Reading (Newspaper Theatre) 93–96
simulation theory 143
singing dialogue 174
Six Viewpoints School 164n
six-word stories 73, 74, 148–149
Skype 73, 74
Slashing (effort) 81, 82, 83
"slice-of-life" performances 56–57
Smith, Anna Devere xxix–xxx
Smith, Linda Tuhiwai 7
social dancing 14–15
social transmission 5–6, 25, 40–42, 166–167

solo performance 121–123, 142, 144–52, *147–148*, 161–163
soul work 10
SoundCloud 19
sounds of your own voice exercise 173
Space (BESS framework) 86, 87–89
Space (Viewpoint) 155–156, 157, 160
spatial relationship (Viewpoint example) 156, *159*, 160, 165n
"spatial territorialization" xxvii–xxviii
Spatz, Ben 3, 4–5, 6–11, 23–24n, 25, 78
speaking techniques 11–12, 24n
speculative fiction 70–71
Speed (factor) 81, 82
Spicer, Sean 131n
Spolin, Viola 172–173, 174, 175, 178n
Spry, Tami 145
Staccato (5Rhythms) 90
Stallybrass, Peter 4
Standing in Space 164n
Stanislavski, Konstantin 140, 177n
stillness 36–37, 91–92
Stolte, Dr. Laurel Cadwallader 20, 21, 23
Story (Viewpoint) 155, 156
story in a box exercise 88
Strasberg, Lee 140
Studies Project 164n
subjectivity xx–xxiii, xviii, xxx, xxxi, 52, 61, 63, 128–129; intersubjectivity xxv, 51
Summer Institute workshop 179–182, *181*
Surrender (Viewpoint) 157
Sweat Your Prayers 113n
Sweet Tea 121–122, 123–126
synaptic gaps 140
SYSTEMS framework 155–156, 157

Tableau with objects exercise 87
taking shape exercise 50
talking about/explaining your work 146–147
talking hands exercise 79–80
teachable moments 169
Tedlock, Dennis 133, 135
tempo 36, 156, 157, 160–161, 164–165n
temporal lobes 183
Text out of Context (Newspaper Theatre) 96–99
thalamus 183
The Folklore Text 132–133
The Heart of Teaching 167, 178n

The Moving Body 111n
The Viewpoints Book 157, 164n
Theater Games 178n
Theater of the oppressed 93, 108, 114n
Theatre Games 111n
"theatrical text" 58–59
"theories of the flesh" 136
third space xv–xvi
Thompson, J. 119
timbre (vocal viewpoint) 157
Time (Viewpoint) 155, 156, 160–161, 164–165n
Todd, Chuck 131n
Together across borders 106–108
Tolle, E. 36
topography (Viewpoint example) 156, 159, 160, 165n
trailer 150
"transmitted knowledge" 5–6, 11–15, 25, 78
traveling stories 103–105, 121–122
Triangle Shirtwaist Factory tragedy 137–139
"true stories" 104, 105, 127, 128–131
Trump, Donald 131n
trust 26, 31–32, 33–34, 37, 40, 46, 127, 157
Tubman, Harriet 72
Turner, Victor 120

universal poetic awareness 145
upper body (plastique) 171

Veblen, Thorstein 24n
via negativa 166–167
Viet Nam War 14–15
Viewpoints xxviii, 88, 149, 155, 164–165n; case study 161–163; examples 155–158, *159;* and oral history 160–163; SYSTEMS framework 155–156, 157; vocal viewpoints 155, 157, 165n
vocal collages 57–58, 100
vocal viewpoints 155, 157, 165n

Waiting exercise 27
Walker, Alice 10
Walking exercises 27, 54–55, 87, 174–175
Walking through BESS exercise 87
Wallace, Rob 29
Wangh, Stephen 28, 140, 142, 166, 167–172, 173, 175, 178n
Washington, Harold Lee 68, 69, 77n
Water Rites 115n
Waterman, Ellen 33
Watkins, Gloria Jean (bell hooks) xxi
Weight (factor) 81, 82
When the Devil Knocks 17
White, Allon 4
Whiting Public Engagement Fellowship 20, 21–22
Wholeness (Viewpoint) 158
word clouds 48, 49
WordPress 19
"Worn Worlds: Clothing and Mourning" 4
Wringing (effort) 81, 82, 85
wrists (plastique) 170

Yes–No exercise 28
you and the bee exercise 80
YouTube 19